THE COOK'S ENCYCLOPEDIA OF
FISH & SHELLFISH

THE COOK'S ENCYCLOPEDIA OF
FISH & SHELLFISH

KATE WHITEMAN

LORENZ BOOKS

This edition published in 2000 by Lorenz Books
27 West 20th Street, New York, NY 10011

LORENZ BOOKS are available for bulk purchase for sales promotion
and for premium use. For details, write or call the sales director,
Lorenz Books, 27 West 20th Street, New York, NY 10011;
(800) 354-9657

© Anness Publishing Limited 2000

Lorenz Books is an imprint of Anness Publishing Inc.

Publisher: Joanna Lorenz
Executive Editor: Linda Fraser
Copy Editor: Jenni Fleetwood
Indexer: Hilary Bird
Designer: Nigel Partridge
Photography: William Lingwood, assisted by Vanessa Davies
Food for Photography: Sunil Vijayakar, assisted by Tonia Hedley (recipes) and
Annabel Ford (reference section)

Also published as *The World Encyclopedia of Fish and Shellfish*

1 3 5 7 9 10 8 6 4 2

CONTENTS

INTRODUCTION

Since man evolved as a hunter-gatherer, the world's rivers, lakes and seas have served as a limitless pantry, providing a bountiful supply of fish and shellfish almost infinite in its variety. From tiny streams to backyard ponds to great oceans, all waters yield some kind of fish and shellfish, almost all of them edible, although in many cases you might not guess this from their outward appearance.

Although for many years fish was undervalued in the western world, particularly in areas far from the coast, its importance as a highly nutritious and delicious food is now universally recognized. As controversial farming methods make many important foods such as meat, dairy products and cereals less attractive than they once were, fish has really come into its own as a healthy alternative.

There is no doubt that fish is good for you. All fish and shellfish is low in fat and high in proteins, minerals and vitamins; oily fish can actually improve your health by lowering cholesterol levels and unclogging arteries. The Japanese, whose diet consists largely of fresh raw fish, have the lowest incidence of heart disease in the world.

Good health is only one of many reasons to eat fish, however. When properly prepared and cooked, it can be among the most delicious foods imaginable. Unfortunately, too many of us were brought up on institutional offerings of heavily-breaded deep-fried shrimp, or unpalatable, overcooked or watery fish, whose delicate flavor was

Below: In many areas, good fish stalls, like this one in Venice, Italy, are becoming increasingly hard to find.

Right: Octopus and baby squid on sale at the Tsukiji fish market in Tokyo.

often rendered tasteless, or masked with floury sauces. Well-cooked fish is quite another matter, however. Really fresh fish needs little cooking or embellishment, and most takes very little time to prepare, a huge bonus for the modern cook whose time is often very limited. It is easy to rustle up the most elegant fish dish in under half an hour.

Every fish and shellfish has its own unique flavor, offering something for all tastes. It is unlikely that there is a recipe for a piscatorial dessert, but fish and shellfish can be featured in every other part of a meal, including appetizers, main courses, salads and savories.

It is hard to understand why fish has been undervalued for so long. Perhaps it has something to do with the fact

that it was traditionally eaten on fast days, as a substitute for meat, so is associated with self-denial and penance. In times of plenty, easily-obtainable seafoods, such as salmon and oysters, were regarded as foods fit only for the poor. Medieval apprentices complained bitterly and refused to eat oysters more than three times a week. Bland, easily-digested white fish was perceived as invalid food and rejected by those with more robust constitutions.

Probably the main reason for eschewing fish, however, was lack of understanding of how to prepare it. Skinning, filleting, scaling and shelling all seemed like really hard work. Nowadays, despite the demise of many fishmongers, there is no need to do all the hard work yourself. Just visit your local supermarket and choose ready-prepared fish or, better still, follow the instructions given in this book, which will guide you through the complexities of handling and preparing all kinds of fish and shellfish.

Fish and shellfish are rewarding to cook and extremely versatile. Although some types have become scarce through over-fishing, and therefore very expensive, the price of others has plummeted, thanks to advances in fish farming. Salmon, for example, has come full circle. Once despised as being too common, its subsequent rarity made it one of the most expensive and sought-after fish. Now, once again, it has become one of the cheapest types of fish available. Be wary, however, of buying very cheap farmed fish. Careless farming results in poor quality specimens. Poor fish farming can also promote diseases, which may spread to other sea creatures in their natural habitat. Consumers must not repeat the mistakes of the past, when demand for ever-cheaper meat and other foods had disastrous consequences in terms of health and ecology. Fish and shellfish are superb natural foods and should remain so. That said, well-managed fish and shellfish farms produce healthy specimens and help counteract the disastrous effects of over-fishing of wild stocks.

The variety of edible underwater creatures is staggering. I often wonder which intrepid (or desperately hungry) soul was the first to imagine that a hideous lumpfish, malevolent eel or multi-limbed octopus might serve as a snack, or spot the potential in a spider crab, sea urchin or slimy sea cucumber for providing a palatable meal. Imagine what pleasures we might have missed had our ancestors been repelled by the appearance of such strange creatures. With a few poisonous exceptions, almost everything that swims, crawls, scuttles or merely lurks in the water can supply us with food.

One of the greatest pleasures when traveling is to visit the local fish market and see the dazzling array of brightly colored fresh fish and shellfish set out on the stalls. However strange their shapes and forms, all have a unique beauty and character. Modern methods of fishing and transportation have made sea creatures from all over the world accessible to adventurous cooks, so allow yourself the pleasure of experimenting and enjoy the infinite variety of textures, flavors and colors of the fruits of the sea.

KATE WHITEMAN

Right: There are fish and shellfish from all over the world on sale on this stall at an indoor market in the Champagne region of France.

EQUIPMENT

Although it is perfectly possible to prepare and cook fish without special equipment, there are a few items that make the process much easier. Some, such as the fish kettle, take up quite a lot of storage space, other gadgets, such as the fish scaler, are quite tiny, but all will prove invaluable for fish and shellfish cooking.

KNIVES, SCISSORS AND SCALERS

Chef's knife

A large heavy knife with a 8–10-inch blade is essential for cutting fish steaks and splitting open crustaceans such as crayfish and lobster.

Filleting knife

For filleting and skinning fish, you will need a sharp knife with a flexible blade, which is at least 6 inches long. This type of knife can also be used for opening some kinds of shellfish. It is essential to keep a filleting knife razor sharp.

Oyster knife

This short, stubby knife—sometimes called a shucker—has a wide, two-edged blade to help prise open the shells of oysters and other bivalves. Make sure that it has a safety guard above the handle to protect your hands.

Kitchen scissors

A sturdy, sharp pair of scissors with a serrated edge is needed for cutting off fins and trimming tails.

Fish scaler

Resembling a small, rough grater, a fish scaler makes short work of a task that few relish.

Below: Fish scalers

Below: Chef's knife

Below: Filleting knife

Below: Scissors

PANS

Fish kettle

Long and deep, with rounded edges, this attractive utensil has a handle at either end, and a tightly-fitting lid. Inside is a perforated rack or grid on which to lay the fish. This, too, has handles, and enables the cook to lift out the fish without breaking it. Most modern fish kettles are made of stainless steel, but they also come in aluminum, enameled steel and copper with a tin-plated interior. Fish kettles are used on the stove and are invaluable for cooking whole large fish, such as salmon and sea trout. Fish kettles can also be used for steaming other foods.

Left: Oyster knives

Above: A fish kettle takes up a lot of storage space in the kitchen, but if you want to cook whole fish, such as salmon, it is well worth buying.

Right: Oval frying pan

Right: Grill pan

Right: Chinese bamboo steamers

Above: Stainless steel steamers

Oval frying pan

Such a simple idea, but intensely practical, this large pan enables you to cook whole fish flat instead of bending them to fit a round pan and spoiling their shape.

Grill/Griddle pans

A ridged cast-iron grill pan is ideal for searing and cooking fish. Griddle pans can be round, oval or rectangular. Some of the large griddles need to be used over two electric rings or gas burners on top of a stove.

Steamer

If you steam food frequently, a stainless steel steamer set is a good investment. This has a lidded, deep outer pan and a perforated inner basket. Choose the widest type that you can find. Chinese bamboo steaming baskets are an economical alternative. They come in a variety of sizes, from very small dim sum baskets to very wide baskets that are about 14 inches across. Chinese steaming baskets can be stacked one on top of each other so that several layers of food can be cooked at one time. Cheapest of all is a small, collapsible, perforated steamer, which unfolds like a flower to fit any pan.

Wok

A 14 inches wok with a lid will be large enough to cope with most types of fish and will prove invaluable in the kitchen. There's no need to reserve this piece of equipment for stir-frying; a wok also makes an effective steamer and can also be used for deep-frying.

SPECIALIST ITEMS

Barbecue grilling rack

A hinged rack in the shape of a fish makes cooking—and turning—a single large fish relatively easy. Also available are shaped racks designed to hold 6–12 sardines. These can be rectangular or round. More useful for general purposes is a double-sided hinged grill rack. These can be square or rectangular and have long handles so that several steaks or small fish can be barbecued and turned over simultaneously. However, the flat sides do tend to squash the delicate flesh of some fish. Always oil grilling racks before use to prevent the fish from sticking to them.

Smoker

The cheapest home-smoker is a lidded metal box with a rack to hold the fish. Smoke produced by placing dampened aromatic wood chippings or herbs on the coals gives extra flavor. More convenient (and much more expensive) are electric smokers. Stove-top models can be used indoors.

Above: A single-handled wok can be used for steaming and deep-frying as well as stir-frying.

Below: Double-sided hinged rack

Above: Barbecue grilling rack for whole large fish

Below: Sardine rack

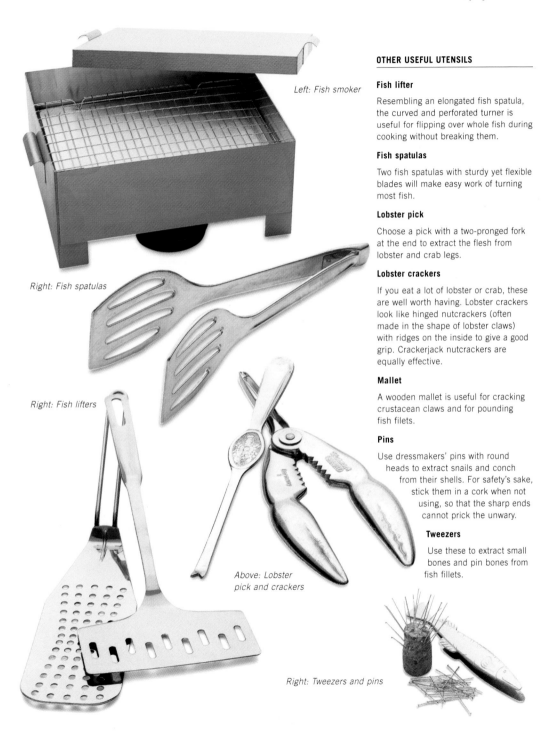

Left: Fish smoker

Right: Fish spatulas

Right: Fish lifters

Above: Lobster pick and crackers

Right: Tweezers and pins

OTHER USEFUL UTENSILS

Fish lifter

Resembling an elongated fish spatula, the curved and perforated turner is useful for flipping over whole fish during cooking without breaking them.

Fish spatulas

Two fish spatulas with sturdy yet flexible blades will make easy work of turning most fish.

Lobster pick

Choose a pick with a two-pronged fork at the end to extract the flesh from lobster and crab legs.

Lobster crackers

If you eat a lot of lobster or crab, these are well worth having. Lobster crackers look like hinged nutcrackers (often made in the shape of lobster claws) with ridges on the inside to give a good grip. Crackerjack nutcrackers are equally effective.

Mallet

A wooden mallet is useful for cracking crustacean claws and for pounding fish filets.

Pins

Use dressmakers' pins with round heads to extract snails and conch from their shells. For safety's sake, stick them in a cork when not using, so that the sharp ends cannot prick the unwary.

Tweezers

Use these to extract small bones and pin bones from fish fillets.

BUYING AND PREPARING FISH

Fish is only worth buying if it is absolutely fresh, and it is best if you eat it on the day you buy it. Fresh fish have shiny skin with a metallic glint and they are covered with a transparent mucus that becomes opaque when the fish is old and stale. The eyes should be clear, bright and slightly bulging. The flesh should feel firm and springy when you press it lightly with your finger; if it feels limp and your finger leaves an indentation, the fish is past its prime. Stale fish has an unpleasant "fishy" smell, the skin looks dull, dryish and unattractive and the eyes are sunken.

The best test of freshness for whole fish is to open up the gills; they should be a clear red or rosy color, not a dull brown. Look for a firm tail and plentiful, shiny close-fitting scales. A fish that has been dead for an unacceptable length of time, or that has not been properly kept, will shed its scales all over the counter. Saltwater fish should have a pleasant odor, redolent of seaweed; freshwater fish should smell of waterweeds. There should never be more than a hint of a "fishy" smell.

Ready-prepared white fish fillets, steaks and cutlets should be neatly trimmed, with moist, firm, translucent flesh. If you must buy frozen fish, make sure that it is frozen solid, with no sign of thawing, and that the packaging is not damaged.

When buying fish, shop with an open mind and be prepared to purchase whatever looks freshest and best on the day. If you want a specific type of fish, it is best to ask the fishmonger in advance so that it can be bought fresh from the market for you. It pays to develop a relationship with one particular fishmonger—if you show that you are really interested in what you are buying, you are sure to get a much better standard of service.

An accommodating fishmonger will gut and clean your fish for you and even scale, skin and fillet it. It is not unreasonable to expect this service, but it does take time. At busy periods, therefore, be prepared to place an order and come back later to collect it. However, if you do have to prepare fish

yourself, don't despair; it is really not difficult, given a sharp, flexible knife and a little dexterity.

Quantities

Allow about 6 ounces fish fillet, or steak per serving for a main course. There is a lot of wastage in whole fish, so allow at least 11 ounces per person if buying fish this way.

Storing fish

Fresh fish should be eaten as soon as possible after purchase, but most types can be kept in the refrigerator for a day or overnight if necessary. Remove the wrapping or packaging and rinse the fish in very cold water. Pat dry with paper towels and place on a plate. Cover with plastic wrap and store in the refrigerator.

Frozen fish

Although fresh fish is much better than frozen, for practical reasons it is not always possible to buy it, and on some occasions frozen fish may be your only option. Of course, you cannot apply the usual tests for freshness—prodding, smelling and judging the color—so it is important to buy frozen fish from a reputable store with a quick turnover. Transport it in a freezer bag if possible and get it home and into your own freezer without delay. White fish can be kept in the freezer for three months and oily fish for two months.

Commercially frozen fish is frozen extremely rapidly and at a lower temperature than can be attained by the average domestic freezer. This preserves the delicate texture of the flesh. It is not advisable to freeze fish at home, but if you must, it should be kept at 0°F or below.

Thawing fish

If possible, thaw frozen fish overnight in the refrigerator. If you need in a hurry, microwave the fish on the defrost setting. Separate the pieces as soon as they are thawed enough and spread out in an even layer. Remove from the microwave while still slightly icy; if fish is over-thawed it will become dry.

ROUND FISH

Scaling

Smooth-skinned round fish such as trout and mackerel do not need scaling. For others, such as sea bass and snapper, it is vital.

First, trim off all the fins with a strong pair of scissors. Take care with the dorsal fins on the back, as they can have sharp spines. Work in the sink, preferably under running water, or the scales will fly all over your kitchen. Otherwise you can cover the fish with a damp cloth to catch the scales. Ideally, you should use a proper fish scaler to do the job, but the back of a round-bladed knife will do almost as well. Always scale fish before filleting if you are going to cook it with the skin on.

1 Wash the fish under cold water. Cut off the three fins that run along the stomach, and the dorsal fins on the back, using strong, sharp scissors.

2 Hold the fish firmly by the tail (a cloth will give a better grip). Using a fish scaler or the back of a knife, and working from tail to head, scrape against the grain of the scales to remove them. Wash the fish again to detach any clinging scales.

Gutting/cleaning

This is a messy job, so always work on several layers of newspaper topped with waxed paper. There are two ways of gutting a whole round fish: through the belly or through the gills. The former is the more usual method for round fish, but gutting through the gills is preferred if splitting the fish open would spoil its appearance. In either case, the gills should be removed before the fish is cooked because they taste bitter. Do this by holding the fish on its back and opening the gill flaps. Push out the frilly gills and cut them off at the back of the head and under the jawbone with a sharp knife.

Cleaning through the belly

1 Starting at the site of the anal fin, slit open the belly from tail to head, using a short sharp knife.

2 Gently pull out the innards, severing them at the throat and tail if necessary. Keep any roes and red mullet livers, which are a great delicacy, but discard everything else, having first wrapped the innards thoroughly. Use a tablespoon to make sure the cavity is empty, removing any blood vessels adjacent to the backbone. Wash the cavity thoroughly, then pat the fish dry with paper towels.

Cleaning through the gills

1 Lay the fish on its back. Make an incision in the bottom of the belly, near the tail. Locate the end of the innards, and snip through it.

2 Cut through the bone under the lower jaw. Open the gill flaps, insert your fingers into the cavity and gently pull out the innards; these will come away through the flaps, leaving the belly intact. Wash the fish thoroughly and then pat it dry.

Boning bony fish such as mackerel and herring

1 Having removed the fins and cleaned the fish through the belly, open the fish out like a book and lay it on a board, with the skin-side up. Press down firmly with your fingers right along the length of the backbone.

2 Turn the fish over and gently pull the backbone away from the flesh. Cut off at the tail and pick out any small loose bones. Rinse the fish and pat dry.

Filleting round fish

1 Lay the fish on a board with the back away from you and the tail toward you. Lift the gill fin and make a diagonal cut behind the fin to the top of the head.

2 Insert the knife about halfway down the fish as close to the backbone as possible. Cut toward the tail, keeping the knife flat to the bone. Lift up the released fillet, turn the knife toward the tail and carefully slide it along the bone to free the fillet completely.

3 Turn the fish over and repeat on the other side. Remove any small pin bones from the fillets with tweezers.

Removing pin bones from fillets

1 There are always some small bones left in a fillet. Run your finger down the fillet to locate them and lift them out with tweezers.

2 Round fish also have tiny pin bones just behind the gill fins. To remove these, make a diagonal cut on either side of the line of bones with a sharp knife. Remove the v-shaped piece of flesh together with the bones.

Flat fish roes

During the breeding season, flat fish contain large roes. In the female fish, these consist of thousands of tiny eggs, which add very little to the flavor of the fish, but weigh quite a lot. So in effect, you are paying for a useless part of the fish.

The soft roes in the male fish, however, are delicious, so do not throw them away. Shallow fry them *à la meunière* in a little butter and serve as a savory or as a garnish for the cooked fish. They are also excellent dipped in egg and bread crumbs and then deep-fried in hot oil.

Gutting/cleaning flat fish

Flat fish are generally sold already cleaned, but it is easy to gut them yourself if necessary. Trim off the fins with sharp kitchen scissors. Make an incision just below the gills, then insert your fingers and pull out the innards, including the roe. Wrap the innards in several layers of newspaper before disposing of them. Retain the roe if you like to eat it.

Filleting flat fish

Four fillets can be obtained from flat fish, two from each side. However, the fillets won't be equal in size because the structure of the fish is not regular.

1 Lay the fish on a board with the dark skin facing up and the head pointing away from you. Using a large sharp knife, cut around the head and right down the center line of the fish, taking the blade of the knife all the way through to the backbone.

2 Working from the head of the fish to the tail, insert the point of the knife under the flesh at the head end. Starting with the left-hand fillet, hold the knife almost parallel to the bones and carefully free the fillet with long stroking movements of the knife.

3 Turn the fish so that the head is toward you and remove the second fillet in the same way.

4 Turn the fish over and repeat the process on the other side.

Skinning whole flat fish

Traditionally, Dover sole are skinned only on the dark side, but other flat fish such as flounder or halibut are skinned on both sides.

1 Lay the fish on a board with the dark skin facing up and the tail toward you. Slit through the skin just below the tail and loosen the skin on both sides.

2 Using a cloth, hold the tail down firmly with one hand. Use the other hand to pull away the skin quickly and firmly toward the head.

Skinning fish fillets

Round and flat fish fillets are skinned in the same way. A really sharp knife is essential for a clean cut.

1 Lay the fillet on a board with the skin side down and the tail toward you. Dip your fingers in salt to stop them from slipping and grip the tail firmly. Angle the knife blade down at 45° toward the skin and cut with a slight sawing action.

2 Working from the tail to the head, cut along the length of the fillet, folding the flesh forward as you go and making sure you keep the skin taut.

Filleting fish

Fish fillets are always a popular choice, because there is no wastage, very few bones and, perhaps most importantly, someone else has done all the hard work. But it is often more practical and cheaper to fillet and skin the fish yourself, with the added bonus that you are left with the head and bones for making stock. Remember to first wash the fish heads thoroughly and then remove the gills before using them for stock.

Preparing fish fillets for cooking

Round and flat fish fillets can be cooked whole and flat, rolled and secured with a toothpick, or cut into cubes.

If you are cooking the fillets whole, trim them neatly with a sharp knife, cutting off any very thin flaps of flesh along the edges.

To roll a fillet, lay it on a board skinned-side upward. Roll the head end (the wider part) toward the tail and tuck the tail underneath. Secure the rolled fillet with a toothpick.

To cube a skinned fillet, use a sharp knife to cut along the length of the fillet, making strips of the desired width. This is easier if you follow the natural long lines of the flesh. Then cut each strip across into cubes.

Boning cod steaks

Cod steaks are often cooked with the bone in, or you may wish to remove it for a special meal.

1 Stand the cod steak upright on a cutting board, then insert a sharp knife at the right hand side at the top of the bone.

2 Cut firmly downward, following the curve of the bone and keeping the knife blade as flat to the bone as possible. Repeat the process on the other side.

3 Lay the steak flat on the cutting board. Carefully lift the flesh from the bone. Make a small cut across the top to release the bone. Fold the flesh into the middle to make a neat, boneless steak.

COOKING FISH

Fish is an extremely versatile food, and there are any number of quick and delicious ways to cook it, "quick" being the operative word, since it is all too easy to overcook the delicate flesh. Almost any cooking method suits fish except boiling, although simmering is fine for hearty soups. Because fish is so delicate, it is always better to undercook rather than overcook it; you can always give it a little extra cooking time, but there is no fixing the dry texture and lack of flavor once it is overdone.

It is impossible to give precise cooking times for fish, because so many factors come into play: the thickness of fillets, for example; whether they are much thinner at one end than the other; the type of fish, and so on. Fish is cooked when the internal temperature reaches about 145°F. You can use a meat thermometer to test this, but with experience you will soon be able to judge by eye.

To test whether fish fillets are cooked, insert a small knife into the center and part the flesh; it should look opaque rather than translucent. Ease the flesh from the bone; it should just come away, not fall off easily. Alternatively, press a fork into the thickest part of the fillet. If the prongs go in only halfway, cook the fish for a little longer. If they sink in, meeting a slight resistance near the bone, then the fish is done.

Always take fish out of the refrigerator at least 30 minutes before cooking to ensure that it cooks evenly.

Cooking without heat
Very fresh fish can be "cooked" without heat by being marinated or soused with lemon juice or white wine vinegar. The acids soften the flesh and turn it opaque. The classic dish of this type is ceviche, where cubes or strips of firm white fish (turbot, cod, halibut, snapper etc.) are marinated in citrus juice, salt and finely chopped chili for at least 2 hours, until the flesh turns pearly white.

Cooking "au bleu"

This old-fashioned method of cooking is mainly used for freshwater fish such as trout, carp, tench or pike, which are still alive or exceedingly fresh. The fish is stunned, cleaned through the gills, then sprinkled with boiling vinegar, which turns the slime on its skin a steely blue color (hence "au bleu").

Enough court-bouillon to cover the fish is heated. The fish is placed in a flameproof dish or fish kettle and the court-bouillon is poured over the fish. The dish or kettle is covered and the fish is simmered gently until it is just cooked. The cooked fish can be served hot or cold. If necessary, the fish should be scaled before being served.

Baking

Whole fish and some chunky fish steaks and fillets, such as cod or halibut, are perfect for baking. Because the flesh is delicate, it is best to bake fish at a lower temperature than would be used for meat, and certainly no higher than 400°F.

Baking *en papillote* (in a parcel) is an extremely healthy way of cooking, because it uses no fat and retains all the flavor of the fish.

Court-bouillon
This flavored stock is invaluable for poaching fish or shellfish. The recipe makes about 4 cups.

1 Slice 1 small onion, 2 carrots and the white part of 1 leek.

2 Place the vegetables in a pan and add 2 parsley stalks, 2 bay leaves, 2 lemon slices, 1¼ cups dry white wine and 6 tablespoons white wine vinegar. Add 2 tablespoons salt, a few white peppercorns and 4 cups water.

3 Bring to a boil, lower the heat and simmer for 20 minutes. Strain and let cool before using.

Braising

This is another excellent cooking method for whole fish or large fillets.

1 Butter a flameproof dish and make a thick bed of thinly sliced or shredded vegetables, such as a mixture of carrots, onions, fennel and celery.

2 Place the fish on top and pour on enough white or red wine and/or fish or chicken stock to come nearly halfway up the fish.

3 Sprinkle on 1 tablespoon of fresh chopped herbs, cover with buttered waxed paper and bring to a boil. Braise the fish at a low temperature on top of the stove or in a preheated oven at 350°F, allowing about 20 minutes for a 2¼ pounds fish; 10–15 minutes for large fillets.

Fish stock

For many recipes, a good fish stock is essential. It is very simple to make. White fish bones and trimmings make the best stock. Ask the fishmonger for these whenever you buy fish; even if you cannot make stock that day, you can freeze them for later use. To make about 4 cups stock, you will need 2¼ pounds white fish bones, heads and trimmings.

1 Wash the fish heads thoroughly and remove the gills. Chop the heads and bones if necessary. Put them in a large saucepan.

2 Coarsely chop the white part of 1 leek (or ½ fennel bulb), 1 onion and 1 celery stalk. Add these to the fish heads and bones in the pan.

3 Add ⅔ cup dry white wine. Toss in 6 white peppercorns and a bouquet garni; add 4 cups water.

4 Bring to a boil, lower the heat and simmer for 20 minutes (not more, or the flavor will become unpleasant). Strain through a muslin-lined sieve.

Frying

Shallow-frying or pan-frying

For this popular method, pieces of fish (fillets, steaks or cutlets) or small whole fish are cooked in a little fat in a shallow pan to caramelize and color the outside. This can either be a prelude to another cooking method or the fish can be fully cooked in the pan. Before frying, the fish can be coated with flour, bread crumbs or oatmeal. Plain fish can be fried without fat using a nonstick pan, but it will have to be cooked carefully to keep it from drying out.

Frying in butter gives the best flavor, but it burns easily, so should be combined with a small amount of oil. Alternatively, use clarified butter or just oil. Heat the fat in the pan until very hot, put in the fish and seal briefly on both sides. Lower the heat and cook the fish gently until done. If the pieces of fish are large or the recipe is more complex, it may be necessary to finish cooking in a medium-hot oven.

Deep-frying

Because fish is delicate, it must be coated in flour or some kind of batter before being deep-fried. This seals in the flavorful juices, so that the fish is deliciously crisp on the outside and moist inside. Most fish is suitable for deep-frying, from tiny whitebait to large chunky fillets.

Use plenty of oil and make sure that it is really hot (350–375°F) before putting in the fish. Use an electric deep-fryer, or test by carefully dropping a cube of bread into the hot oil; if it browns within 30 seconds, the oil is hot enough. Larger pieces of fish should be cooked at a slightly lower temperature than small pieces like goujons. This lets the heat penetrate to the center of the fish before the outside burns.

Do not cook too many pieces of fish at the same time, or the temperature of the oil will drop. Oil used for frying fish should never be used for any other purpose, as it will inevitably impart a fishy flavor.

1 Heat the oil in a deep-fryer to 350°F. Dip the fish in seasoned flour, add to the oil and cook until golden.

2 Drain the fish on a double thickness of paper towels before serving.

Goujons of sole or plaice

The name goujon comes from the French for gudgeon, which are small fresh water fish that are often served crisply fried. Goujons are strips of fish, usually sole of flounder; which are deep-fried and served with tartare sauce. Goujons are the perfect way to persuade children to eat fish, especially if you let them eat it with their fingers.

SERVES FOUR

INGREDIENTS
    8 sole or flounder fillets
    ½ cup milk
    1 cup all-purpose flour
    vegetable oil, for deep-frying
    salt and ground black pepper

1 Skin the fish fillets and cut them into 3 x 1-inch strips. Season the milk with a little salt and pepper. Pour it into a shallow bowl, and place the flour in another bowl or spread it out on a plate.

2 Dip the fish strips first into the milk, then into the flour. Shake off the excess flour.

3 Fill a large saucepan one-third full with vegetable oil. Heat to about 360°F or until a small cube of bread dropped into the oil turns brown in 30 seconds.

4 Carefully lower the fish strips into the hot oil, adding 4 or 5 at a time. Fry for about 3 minutes, turning them occasionally using a slotted spoon, until the strips rise to the surface and turn golden brown in color.

5 Lift out each piece of cooked fish with a slotted spoon and drain them on a double thickness of paper towels. Keep the cooked goujons hot in the oven while you cook successive batches.

Stir-frying

This quick-cooking Asian method is perfect for fish, shrimp and squid.

1 Cut fish or squid into bite-size strips; leave shrimp tails whole, with the tail shells intact. Toss in a little cornstarch to prevent them from falling apart as they cook.

2 Heat a little oil in a wok over very high heat, add a few pieces of fish or shellfish and stir-fry for a few moments.

Searing

This method is best for thickish fillets that have not been skinned or small whole fish such as sardines and red mullet.

1 Smear the bottom of a heavy frying pan or griddle with oil and heat until smoking. Lightly brush both sides of the fish with oil and put it into the hot pan.

2 Sear for a couple of minutes, until the skin is golden brown, then turn the fish over and cook on the other side.

Broiling and Grilling

Fish steaks, thick fillets and relatively small whole fish, such as sardines, red mullet or trout, can be broiled or grilled, as can all types of crustaceans. The broiler should be preheated to very high so that the fish juices are sealed in quickly.

Grilling fish on a barbecue can be a little more tricky, as the bastes or marinades that are used to keep the fish moist can drip onto the coals and cause flare-ups.

All broiled fish will benefit from being marinated for 1 hour in a mixture of oil and lemon juice before being cooked. If the fish is to be cooked whole, make several slashes down to the bone on either side to ensure that the fish cooks quickly and evenly. Brush the broiler rack and fish with oil to prevent sticking. Thin fillets need only be broiled on one side. Do not use a broiler rack. Brush the broiler pan with oil. Place it under the broiler until hot, then pass both sides of the fish through the oil before broiling on one side only; the underside will cook at the same time.

Microwaving

Fish can be cooked successfully in a microwave oven. As long as you do not overcook it, it will emerge moist and full of flavor. Always cover the fish with plastic wrap. Microwave it on full power (100%) for the shortest possible time, as recommended in your handbook, then give it a resting period to let it finish cooking by residual heat. Cooking time depends on the thickness and density of the fish. The following are general guidelines for 1¼ pounds fish, but test before the end of the given time to check that the flesh is still succulent.

Whole round fish, thick fillets, steaks and cutlets: cook for 4–5 minutes, then let stand for 5 minutes.

Flat fish, thin fillets: cook for 3–4 minutes, then rest for 3–4 minutes.

Fish with denser flesh (shark, tuna, monkfish, skate etc): cook for 6–7 minutes: let stand for 5 minutes.

Cook fillets in a single layer, thinner parts toward the center, or tuck a thin tail end underneath a thicker portion.

Fish can also be microwaved whole, provided that they will fit in the oven. Slash the skin in several places to prevent it from splitting. Turn the fish over halfway through cooking.

Poaching

Cooking in a stock or court-bouillon brings out the flavor of fresh fish.

1 A whole fish can be poached in a fish kettle, provided it is not too large, while portions are best placed in a single layer in a shallow heatproof dish.

2 Cover with cold court-bouillon or stock; add a few herbs and flavorings.

3 Lay some buttered waxed paper on top and heat until the liquid just starts to tremble. At this point, thin pieces of fish may be done. Continue to cook thicker pieces at a bare simmer either on top of the stove or in the oven, until the flesh is just opaque. For a 2¼-pound fish, allow 7–8 minutes. To serve the fish cold, let it cool in the poaching liquid.

Butter sauce for poached fish

Poached fish needs very little enhancement other than a simple sauce that has been made from the poaching liquid.

1 Remove the cooked fish from the poaching liquid and keep it hot while you make the sauce.

2 Strain the liquid into a saucepan and place it over medium heat. Simmer gently until the liquid has reduced by half.

3 Whisk in some cold diced butter or a little heavy cream to make a smooth, velvety sauce. Season to taste. Pour the sauce over the fish and serve.

Roasting

This is usually associated with meat, but it is an excellent method of cooking whole fish and "meaty" cuts, such as monkfish tails or swordfish steaks. The oven should be preheated to very hot—450°F—with the roasting pan inside. The fish will then be seared by the heat of the pan and the juices will not escape.

Drizzle a little olive oil onto the fish before roasting. For extra flavor, roast it on a bed of rosemary, fennel or Mediterranean vegetables.

Smoking

Although most of the smoked fish we buy has been commercially smoked, it is easy to smoke your own, adding a new dimension of taste.

Hot smoking

This method cooks and smokes the food at the same time, using a special smoker filled with fragrant hardwood chips (hickory and oak are popular), which give the fish a delicious flavor. Domestic smokers are quite small and very easy to use. Some can be used indoors, but on the whole they are best suited to outdoor use, where the smoke can dissipate easily. For large quantities you can use a kettle grill. Heat the wood chips to 176–185°F, place the fish on the rack, put on the lid and smoke until the fish looks like pale burnished wood.

Cold smoking

This method cures but does not cook the fish. It must first be salted in dry salt or brine, then hung up to drip dry before smoking at 86–95°F.

Tea smoking

This Chinese method of smoking is usually used for duck, but imparts a wonderful flavor to oily fish such as mackerel and tuna, and shellfish such as scallops, mussels and shrimp.

1 Line a wok with aluminum foil and sprinkle in 2 tablespoons each of raw long-grain rice, sugar and tea leaves.

2 Place a wire rack on top of the wok and then arrange the fish in a single layer on the rack. Cover the wok with a lid or more foil and cook over very high heat until you see smoke.

3 Lower the heat slightly (some smoke should still escape from the wok) and cook until the fish is done. A mackerel fillet takes 8–10 minutes, large shrimp 5–7 minutes.

Steaming

Many people assume that steaming will result in bland, flavorless fish. Far from it: this method of cooking enhances the natural flavor, and the fish remains moist and retains its shape, even if you overcook it.

Steaming is the healthiest way of cooking fish. It uses no fat and because the fish is not in contact with the cooking liquid, fewer valuable nutrients are lost.

1 Half-fill the bottom pan of a steamer with water and bring it to a boil. Place the fish in a single layer in the steamer basket, leaving room to enable the steam to circulate freely.

2 Lower the fish into the steamer, making sure that the insert stands well clear of the boiling water.

3 Lay a sheet of waxed paper over the surface of the fish, then cover the pan tightly with a lid or foil and steam until the fish is just cooked through.

4 Fish cooks very quickly in a steamer, but take care that the level of the water does not fall too low. Check once or twice during cooking and keep a kettle of boiling water on hand to add more.

Alternative steamers

There are plenty of steamers on the market, which range from the hugely expensive stainless steel models to modest Chinese bamboo baskets. However, you can easily improvise with a saucepan, any perforated container (a colander or sieve, for example) and some aluminum foil. Make sure that the saucepan is large enough to hold several inches of water.

Whatever the type of steamer, remember that the golden rule of steaming is not to let the boiling liquid touch the steamer basket or the fish or shellfish.

A Chinese bamboo steamer, which can be used in a wok or on top of a large saucepan, is ideal for steaming fish. If desired, arrange the fish on a bed of aromatic flavorings, such as lemon or lime slices and sprigs of herbs. Alternatively, before adding the fish or shellfish, you can place finely shredded vegetables, seaweed or samphire in the bottom of the steamer to give extra flavor.

BUYING, PREPARING AND COOKING SHELLFISH

The term "shellfish" is loosely applied to seafood other than fish. Strictly speaking, it means aquatic invertebrates with shells or shell-like carapaces. This includes the crustaceans—lobsters, crabs, shrimp and similar creatures—as well as some mollusks, such as clams, mussels and oysters. For convenience, however, the category extends to other mollusks too, such as the cephalopods (octopus, squid and cuttlefish) and less well known sea creatures such as sea urchins.

When discussing shellfish, it is impossible to divorce preparation and cooking techniques, since one is bound so closely with the other. Lobsters and crabs, for instance, are cooked live; mussels are opened and cooked in one simple process.

Crustaceans and mollusks need very little cooking to enhance their already superb flavor. Indeed, many mollusks can be eaten raw, provided they are extremely fresh and come from unpolluted waters. Crustaceans of all types must be cooked; unlike fish, the larger specimens can be boiled. Many of the methods used for cooking fish are suitable for shellfish, particularly poaching, frying, broiling and steaming.

CRUSTACEANS

Lobsters and crabs

Buying

Live lobsters or crabs should smell very fresh and still be lively and aggressive when picked up. The tails of lobsters should spring back sharply when they are opened out. Crabs should feel heavy for their size, but you should make sure this is not because there is water inside the shell. Shake them—any sloshing sounds are a bad sign. The shell should not be soft or contain any cracks or holes.

Lobsters in particular command a high price, which reflects the effort involved in catching them. It is a good idea to check that lobsters and crabs have both claws, as one may often be lost in a fight. If a claw is missing, make sure the price is reduced accordingly.

Preparing and cooking a live lobster

1 The most humane way to kill a live lobster is to render it unconscious by placing it in a freezerproof dish or tray and covering it with crushed ice. Alternatively, put the lobster in the freezer for 2 hours.

2 When the lobster is very cold and no longer moving, place it on a cutting board and drive the tip of a large, sharp heavy knife or a very strong skewer through the center of the cross on its head. According to the experts, death is instantaneous.

3 If you can't face stabbing the lobster, put it in a large pan of cold, heavily salted water and bring slowly to a boil. The lobster will expire before the water boils.

4 Alternatively, you can add the comatose lobster to a large pan of boiling water. Plunge it in head first and immediately clamp on the lid. Bring the water back to a boil.

5 Lower the heat and simmer the lobster gently for about 15 minutes for the first 1 pound and then allow 10 more minutes for each subsequent 1 pound, up to a maximum of 40 minutes.

6 When cooked, the lobster will turn a deep brick red. Drain off the water and let cool, if not eating hot.

If cooking two or more lobsters in the same pan, wait until the water comes back to a boil before adding the second one. More than two lobsters should be cooked separately.

Always buy cooked lobsters or crabs from a reputable supplier who cooks them fresh every day. The color should be vibrant, and the crustaceans should feel heavy for their size. Cooked lobsters should have their tails tightly curled under their bodies; avoid specimens with floppy tails, which may have been dead when they were cooked.

Quantities

When calculating how much you should buy, allow about 1 pound per person.

Storing

For practical reasons you will want to cook live lobsters or crabs on the day you buy them, unless you want them to live in your bathtub.

If you cannot put them straight into the pot, live crustaceans can be wrapped in wet newspaper or covered in a very damp dish towel and kept in the coldest part of the refrigerator. If you intend the crustaceans to be unconscious when you kill them, you may want to put them in the freezer for a couple of hours or submerge them in crushed ice.

Removing the meat from a boiled lobster

1 Lay the lobster on its back and twist off the large legs and claws.

2 Carefully crack open the claws with a wooden mallet or the back of a heavy knife and remove the meat, keeping the pieces as large as possible. Scoop out the meat from the legs with a lobster pick or the handle of a small teaspoon.

3 On a cutting board, stretch out the body of the lobster so that its tail is extended. Turn it onto its back and, holding it firmly with one hand, use a sharp, heavy knife to cut the lobster neatly in half along its entire length.

4 Discard the whitish sac and the feathery gills from the head and the gray-black intestinal thread that runs down the tail.

5 Carefully remove all the meat from each half of the tail—it should come out in one piece.

6 Keep the greenish tomalley (liver) and the coral (roe), which are delicious. This roe is only to be found in the female or "hen" lobsters. Like the tomalley, it is usually added to a sauce. The creamy flesh close to the shell can also be scraped out and used in a sauce.

Broiler lobster

Preheat the broiler to high. Boil the lobster for 3 minutes only, then drain, split in half lengthwise and clean.

Lay the halves cut-side up in a broiler pan, brush with melted butter and broil for about 10 minutes, spooning on more melted butter halfway through.

If the lobster has already been killed by stabbing, it can be split in half and broiled for about 12 minutes without being parboiled first.

Barbecuing lobster

Prepare the lobster as for broiling. Brush the cut sides with butter seasoned with garlic or cayenne pepper. Broil cut side down over medium hot coals for about 5 minutes, then turn the halves over and broil them on the shell for 5 more minutes. Turn the lobster halves over once more, brush the flesh with more melted butter and broil flesh-side down for 3–4 more minutes.

Preparing a live crab

To kill a crab humanely, chill it by submerging it in ice, or leave it in the freezer for a couple of hours until it is comatose (see Preparing and cooking a live lobster, page 24). When the crab is no longer moving, lay it on its back on a cutting board, lift up the tail flap and look for a small hole at the base of a distinct groove. Drive an awl or sturdy skewer into this hole, then carefully push the skewer between the mouth plates between the eyes. The crab is now ready for cooking.

Alternatively, if stabbing a crab does not appeal to you, the live crab can be killed and cooked simultaneously. There are two ways of doing this. Either plunge the crustacean into a large pan of boiling salted water, bring the water back to a boil and cook for 10–12 minutes, or place it in a pan of cold salted water and bring it slowly to a boil. The latter method is considered more humane because the crab becomes sleepy as the temperature rises and succumbs well before the water reaches the boiling point. Either way, calculate the cooking time from the moment that the water boils, and do not boil the crab for more than 12 minutes, whatever its size.

Removing the meat from a cooked crab

1 Lay the cooked crab on its back on a large cutting board. Hold the crab firmly with one hand and break off the tail flap. Twist off both the claws and the legs.

2 Stand the crab on its head and insert a heavy knife between the body and shell. Twist the knife firmly to separate them so that you can lift the honeycomb body out.

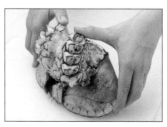

3 Alternatively, hold the crab firmly and use your thumbs to ease the body out of the shell.

4 Remove and discard the feathery, gray gills (these are unattractively but descriptively known as "dead men's fingers"), which are attached to either side of the body.

5 Press down on the top shell to detach the spongy stomach sac—this is found directly behind the mouth. Cut the honeycomb body into quarters with a large heavy knife.

6 Carefully pick out the white meat, using a skewer.

7 Use a teaspoon to scoop out all the creamy brown meat from the back shell, then scoop out the thin solid brown meat from inside the flaps.

8 Crack open the claws and legs with a mallet (or use the back of a heavy knife), then remove the claw meat in the largest possible pieces. Pick or scrape out the leg meat with a lobster pick or a skewer. The smallest legs can be kept whole and used to make a delicious shellfish stock.

Shrimp, Langoustines and Crayfish

Buying

Shrimp are not sold alive, but crayfish must be, as their flesh deteriorates quickly after death and they can become poisonous. All fresh raw shrimp should have crisp, firm shells and a fresh smell. Do not buy them if they smell of ammonia. If you cannot obtain fresh shrimp, buy frozen. Transport them in a freezer bag and get them into your freezer as quickly as possible. Do not buy frozen shrimp that have been thawed—they may have been lying about for some time.

Quantities

If you buy them with the shells on, allow about 11 ounces shrimp per serving. Some crustaceans—Dublin Bay prawns, for example—tend to be sold shelled, without the heads. If you buy Dublin Bay prawns in the shell, remember that there will be a lot of wastage (up to 80 percent) so buy a generous amount. Keep the shells to flavor sauces, stocks and soups.

Storing

Fresh shrimp should be eaten as soon as possible after purchase. Crayfish don't have to be. These freshwater crustaceans—including the Australian yabby—are none too fussy about what they eat, so it is best to purge them after capture or purchase. Place them in a large bowl, cover with a very damp dish towel and leave in the coldest part of the refrigerator for 24 hours.

Poaching langoustines or shrimp

Raw langoustines or shrimp are best poached in sea water. Failing that, use a well-flavored *nage* (fish stock) or heavily salted water. Bring the poaching liquid to a boil in a large deep saucepan, drop in the crustaceans and simmer for only a minute or two, depending on their size. Do not overcook the shellfish, or the delicate flesh will become tough.

Peeling and deveining raw shrimp

Raw shrimp are often peeled before cooking. Raw large shrimp should have their intestinal tracts removed before cooking, a process that is known as "deveining." However, it is not necessary to devein very small shrimp.

1 Pull off the head and legs from each shrimp, then carefully peel off the body shell with your fingers. Leave on the tail "fan" if desired.

2 To remove the intestinal vein from shrimp, make a shallow incision down the center of the curved back of the shrimp using a small knife, cutting all the way from the tail to the head.

3 Carefully pick out the thin black vein that runs the length of the shrimp with the tip of the knife and discard.

Broiling or grilling langoustines or large shrimp

This method is also suitable for crayfish. The shellfish can be raw or cooked.

1 Preheat the broiler or grill to hot. Butterfly the shellfish by laying them on their backs and splitting them in half lengthwise, without cutting right through to the back shell.

2 Open the shellfish out like a book and brush the cut sides all over with a mixture of olive oil and lemon juice.

3 Lay the shellfish in a broiler pan or on the grill. Cook for 2–3 minutes on each side; cooked shellfish for about half this time. To ensure that they keep their shape, you could thread the butterflied langoustines or shrimp onto skewers before cooking them.

Peeling cooked shrimp, langoustines and crayfish

1 Twist off the heads and, in the case of langoustines, the claws.

2 Squeeze the shellfish along their length and pull off the shell and the legs with your fingers.

3 If there are any eggs on the underside of the shrimp, scrape these off with a teaspoon and use them in a sauce.

Fantail shrimp
This way of serving shrimp comes from China. The cooked shrimp, with their bright red tails, are supposed to resemble the legendary phoenix, which in China is a symbol of dignity and good luck. Large shrimp are used.

1 Remove the heads from the shrimp and peel off most of the body shell with your fingers. Leave a little of the shell to keep the tail "fan" intact.

2 Make a long shallow incision in the back of each shrimp and remove the black intestinal cord with the point of the knife.

3 Hold the prepared shrimp by the tails and dip them lightly in a little seasoned cornstarch, and then in a frothy batter before deep frying them in hot oil until the tails, which are free from batter, turn red.

Potted Shrimp
These are very simple to make and will keep for several days. If possible, use fresh, not frozen, brown shrimp. They are tedious to peel, but worth the effort. Serve with buttered brown bread or toast and lemon wedges.

SERVES FOUR

INGREDIENTS
   12 ounces butter
   8 ounces cooked peeled shrimp, defrosted if frozen
   1 bay leaf
   1 large blade of mace or
   $1/2$ teaspoon ground mace
   ground black pepper and cayenne pepper

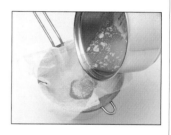

2 Clarify the remaining butter, by placing it in a small saucepan and heating gently over low heat until melted and foaming. Strain through a muslin-lined sieve into a small bowl, leaving the milky solids at the bottom of the pan.

1 Melt 9 ounces of the butter in a small pan. Add the shrimp, bay leaf, mace and seasoning. Heat gently until hot, then discard the bay leaf and mace. Divide the shrimps between four ramekins and let set.

3 Spoon the clarified butter over the potted shrimp, making sure they are completely covered. When cool, transfer the ramekins to the refrigerator and chill for up to 2–3 days, until ready to serve.

MOLLUSKS

Bivalves (mussels, clams, oysters and scallops)

Buying

Like other types of shellfish, mollusks deteriorate rapidly, so you must make sure that they are alive when you cook them. Scallops are an exception, as they are often sold already opened and cleaned. Bivalves such as mussels, clams and oysters should contain plenty of sea water and feel heavy for their size. Do not buy any that have broken shells. If the shells gape, give them a sharp tap on a hard surface. They should snap shut immediately; if they don't, do not buy them, as they will either be dead or moribund.

Quantities

When buying mussels, clams or similar shellfish, allow about 1 pound per person, as the shells make up much of the weight. Four or five scallops will serve one person as a main course.

Storing

Mussels, clams and other bivalves must be eaten within one day of purchase, but will keep briefly when kept in the refrigerator. Put them into a large bowl, cover with a damp cloth and keep them in the coldest part of the refrigerator (at 36°F) until ready to use. Some people advocate sprinkling them with oatmeal and leaving them overnight to fatten up. Oysters can be kept for a couple of days, thanks to the sea water contained in their shells. Store them cupped side down. Never store shellfish in fresh water, or they will die. Frozen bivalves should not be kept in the freezer for more than 2 months.

Preparing

Scrub bivalves under cold running water, using a stiff brush to remove any sand or dirt. Open the shellfish over a bowl to catch the delicious juice. This will be gritty, so must be strained before being used in a sauce or stock. Cockles usually contain a lot of sand. They will expel this if left overnight in a bucket of clean sea water or salted water.

Cleaning mussels

1 Wash the mussels in plenty of cold water, scrubbing them well. Scrape off any barnacles with a knife.

2 Give any open mussels a sharp tap; discard any that fail to close.

3 Pull out and discard the fibrous "beard" that sprouts between the two halves of the shell.

Moules Marinière

1 Chop 1 onion and 2 shallots. Put in a large saucepan with 2 tablespoons butter and cook over low heat until translucent.

2 Add 1¼ cups white wine, a bay leaf and a sprig of fresh thyme. Bring to a boil. Add 4½ pounds cleaned mussels, cover the pan tightly and steam over high heat for 2 minutes. Shake the pan vigorously and steam for 2 minutes more. Shake again and steam until all the mussels have opened. Discard any closed ones.

3 Stir in 2 tablespoons chopped parsley and serve immediately.

Steaming mussels

This method opens and cooks the shellfish all at once. It is also suitable for clams, cockles and razor-shells.

1 Put a few splashes of white wine into a wide saucepan. Add some finely chopped onion and chopped fresh herbs if desired and bring to a boil.

2 Add the mussels, cover the pan and shake over high heat for 2–3 minutes. Remove the mussels that have opened.

3 Replace the lid and shake the pan over high heat for another minute or so. By this time all the mussels that are going to open should have done so; discard any that remain closed.

4 Strain the cooking liquid through a muslin-lined sieve.

5 The cooking liquid can be reheated and used as a thin sauce, or heated until it has reduced by about half. For a richer sauce, stir in a little cream.

6 The mussels can be eaten as they are, or the top shell can be removed and the mussel served on the half shell. Alternatively, they can be broiled, but take care not to overcook them.

Broiling mussels and clams

Steam open the mollusks and remove the top shell. Arrange their half shells in a single layer on a baking sheet. Spoon on a little melted butter that has been flavored with chopped garlic and parsley. Top with fresh bread crumbs, sprinkle with a little more melted butter and cook under a hot broiler until golden brown and bubbling.

Opening clams and razor-shells

The easiest way to open clams or razor-shells is by steaming them, in the same way as you do for mussels. However, this method is not suitable if the clams are going to be eaten raw like oysters.

1 Protect your hand with a clean dish towel, then cup the clam in your palm, holding it firmly. Work over a bowl to catch the juices.

2 Insert a sharp pointed knife between the shells. Turn the knife away from you to open the clam, twisting it to force the shells apart.

3 Cut through the hinge muscle, then use a spoon to scoop out the muscle on the bottom shell. This part of the mollusk should be discarded.

Opening small clams in the microwave

1 Thin-shelled mollusks like small clams can be opened in the microwave. Place them in a large bowl and cook on full power for about 2 minutes.

2 Remove the open mollusks and repeat the process until all have opened. Do not try to open large clams, oysters or scallops this way, as the thick shells will absorb the microwaves and cook the mollusks before they open.

Opening scallops in the oven

The easiest way to open scallops is to place them rounded-side down on a baking sheet and place them in an oven preheated to 325°F for a few moments, until they gape sufficiently for you to complete the job by hand.

1 Spread the scallops in a single layer on a baking sheet. Heat them until they gape, then remove them from the oven.

2 Grasp a scallop in a clean dish towel, flat-side up. Using a long, flexible knife, run the blade along the inner surface of the flat shell to cut through the muscle that holds the shells together. This done, ease the shells apart completely.

3 Lift off the top shell. Pull out and discard the black intestinal sac and the yellowish frilly membrane.

4 Cut the white scallop and orange coral from the bottom shell and wash briefly under cold running water. Remove and discard the white ligament attached to the scallop flesh.

Cooking scallops

Scallop flesh is very delicate and needs barely any cooking; an overcooked scallop loses its flavor and becomes extremely rubbery. Small scallops need to be cooked only for a few seconds, larger ones take a minute or two.

Scallops can be pan-fried, steamed, poached and baked au gratin. They are also delicious broiled.

Wrap scallops in thin strips of bacon or pancetta before broiling them to protect the delicate texture and add extra flavor.

Opening oysters

You really do need a special oyster knife if you are to open—or shuck—oysters successfully. If you don't have one, use a strong knife with a short, blunt blade.

1 Scrub the shells under cold running water. Wrap one hand in a clean dish towel and hold the oyster with the cupped shell down and the narrow hinged end toward you.

2 Push the point of the knife into the small gap in the hinge and twist it back and forth between the shells until the hinge breaks. Pull up the top shell.

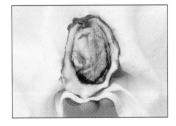

3 Slide the knife along the inner edges of the top shell and sever the muscle that joins the oyster to the shell. Lift off the top shell, leaving the oyster in its juices in the bottom shell.

Cooking oysters

Oysters are best eaten raw with just a squeeze of lemon or a dash of Tabasco sauce. If you prefer to cook them, do so very briefly. They can be poached or steamed for a minute or two and served with a white wine sauce; broiled like mussels or clams; deep-fried in cornmeal batter; or added to meat, fish or shellfish pies or casseroles.

Gastropods (periwinkles, whelks and abalone)

Small gastropods such as periwinkles, whelks and limpets need little preparation other than a quick rinse under cold running water. They are removed from the shell after cooking, either with a small fork or, in the case of periwinkles (which are very rare in the United States), with a dressmaker's pin. Larger gastropods, such as abalone (or their cousins, the ormers) and conch, must be removed from the shell and beaten vigorously to tenderize them before cooking. In some fishmarkets, especially those in California, tenderized abalone is sold in slices.

Cooking abalone or ormers

There are two schools of thought when it comes to cooking abalone. One claims the best way is to marinate the flesh, then cook it briefly in butter; the other claims that if abalone is to be truly tender, it needs long, slow cooking. Both methods work equally well, but only if the abalone has been thoroughly beaten first.

Boiling periwinkles or whelks

Ideally, these tasty shellfish should be boiled in sea water, so if you gather them yourself, take home a bucket of water in which to cook them. Otherwise, use heavily salted water. Bring this to a boil in a pan, add the periwinkles or whelks and simmer for about 5 minutes for periwinkles, 10 minutes for whelks.

To test whether periwinkles or whelks are ready, use a fork or dressmaker's pin to remove the body from the shell. It should come out easily. If not, cook for a little longer, but do not overcook, or the periwinkles will become brittle and the whelks tough.

Cephalopods (octopus, squid, cuttlefish)

Buying

You may have seen Mediterranean fishermen flailing freshly caught octopus against the rocks to tenderize them. It is said that they need to be beaten at least a hundred times before they become palatable. Fortunately for the consumer large octopus are usually sold already prepared, so we are spared this unpleasant task. Small octopuses can be dealt with in much the same way as squid, but even they have tough flesh which needs to be beaten with a wooden mallet before being cooked.

Most fishmongers and supermarkets now sell ready-cleaned squid, but cuttlefish are more usually sold whole. Both are easy to clean, and are prepared in similar ways. When buying fresh squid, look for specimens that smell fresh and salty, have good colour and are slippery. Avoid squid with broken outer skins, or from which the ink has leaked.

Quantities

The amount of octopus or squid that will be needed will depend on how substantial a sauce you are going to serve. As a general guide, 2¼ pounds octopus, squid or cuttlefish will be more than enough for six people.

Storing

As for fish.

Cleaning and preparing octopus

1 Cut the tentacles off the octopus and remove the beak and eyes. Cut off the head where it joins the body and discard it. Turn the body inside out and discard the entrails.

2 Pound the body and tentacles with a mallet until tender, then place in boiling water and simmer very gently for at least 1 hour or until tender. Serve with a flavorful sauce.

Baby Octopus and Red Wine Stew
Baby octopuses are tender and delicious, particularly cooked in a stew with the robust flavors of red wine and oregano. Unlike large octopuses, they need no tenderizing before cooking.

SERVES FOUR

INGREDIENTS
2 pounds baby octopuses
1 pound onions, sliced
2 bay leaves
4 tablespoons olive oil
4 garlic cloves, crushed
1 pound tomatoes, peeled
    and sliced
1 tablespoon each chopped fresh
    oregano and parsley
salt and ground black pepper

Put the octopuses in a saucepan of simmering water with a quarter of the sliced onion and the bay leaves. Cook gently for 1 hour. Drain the octopuses and cut into bite-size pieces. Discard the heads. Heat the olive oil in a saucepan, add the remaining onions and the garlic cloves and sauté for 3 minutes. Add the tomatoes and herbs, season with salt and pepper and cook, stirring, for about 5 minutes until pulpy, then cover the pan with a lid and cook very gently for 1½

Cleaning and preparing squid

1 Rinse the squid thoroughly under cold running water. Holding the body firmly in one hand, grasp the tentacles at the base with the other, and gently but firmly pull the head off the body. As you do this the soft yellowish entrails will come out.

2 Use a sharp knife to cut off the tentacles from the head of the squid. Reserve the tentacles but discard the hard beak in the middle.

Squid ink

This can be used as a wonderful flavoring and coloring for homemade pasta and risotto, or to make a sauce. Having removed the ink sac, put it in a small bowl. Pierce it with the tip of a knife to release the thick, granular ink. Dilute this with a little water and stir until smooth. Use the ink right away, or freeze for later use.

There is ink in an octopus too. It is found in the liver and is very strongly flavored. Like squid ink, it should be diluted in water before being used.

3 Remove and reserve the ink sac, then discard the head.

4 Peel the purplish-gray membrane off of the body.

5 Pull out the "quill." Wash the body under cold running water.

6 Cut the body, flaps and tentacles to the required size.

Cooking squid

Squid is often cut into rings and deep-fried. It can also be stewed, stuffed and baked, or sliced and stir-fried.

1 For stir-frying, slit the body from top to bottom and turn it inside out. Flatten it and score the inside lightly with a knife to make a criss-cross pattern.

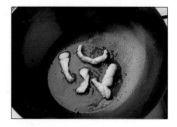

2 Cut each piece lengthwise into ribbons. These will curl when stir-fried.

Cleaning and preparing cuttlefish

Cut off the tentacles and remove the beak from the cuttlefish. Along the length of the body you will see the dark line of the cuttle bone. Cut along this line and remove the cuttle bone. Prepare in the same way as squid. The body is usually left whole.

Sea urchins

There are several edible varieties of sea urchin. They are particularly popular in France, where they are served raw, or lightly cooked in salted water and eaten like boiled eggs. The tops are sliced off and fingers of bread are then dipped into the coral flesh.

A CATALOG OF
FISH AND SHELLFISH

The almost infinite variety of edible sea and freshwater fish has

always been an inspiration to cooks, who love them for their

fresh flavor, versatility and nutritious qualities. There is a host

of delicious shellfish, each with its own unique flavor—

all evoke the unmistakable tang of the sea. Once, we were

limited to eating only fish and shellfish from local waters, but

now, thanks to modern transportation methods, a whole new

world of exciting species is available to cooks. This chapter is

designed to help you to identify the fish and shellfish you may

find on the fishmonger's slab and to give you an

indication of how they can be cooked.

SALTWATER FISH

There are two main categories of saltwater fish: round and flat. Those that live on or near the sea bed are known as demersal fish. Flat fish are demersal fish, spending most of their time sitting on the sea bed and doing very little swimming. Consequently, they have delicate white flesh with little muscle tone. The nutritious oil of "white" fish is concentrated in the liver.

In "oily" fish, this oil is dispersed throughout the flesh. Oily fish tend to swim in schools near the surface of the sea; they are known as pelagic fish.

ROUND WHITE FISH

THE SEA BASS AND GROUPER FAMILY

This large and important family of fish is known as *perciformes* because they all share some of the characteristics of perch. They have at least some spiny fins, a V-shaped tail and pectoral fins set high on the body. The pelvic fins have one spiny ray each.

Various species of perciformes are found in the Indian and Pacific oceans and the Caribbean, and also in Mediterranean and Atlantic waters.

Right: Sea bass

Scaling sea bass
The skin of sea bass is excellent to eat and it becomes deliciously crisp when broiled or pan-fried. It does, however, have very hard scales, so it is essential to scale sea bass before cooking. Ask your fishmonger to do this, or follow the instructions in the section on Buying and Preparing Fish.

Sea bass *(Dicentrarchus labrax)*

One of the finest of all fish, sea bass are as good to look at as they are to eat. They have an elegant, sleek shape rather like a salmon, and a beautiful silvery body with a darker back and a white belly. They can grow to a length of 36 inches and weigh up to 15½ pounds, although the average weight is 2¼–6½ pounds.

Habitat Sea bass are voracious predators that live in small schools close to rocky coasts in Great Britain and the Mediterranean. They can also be found in salt water lakes and large river estuaries. They can be caught in traps or trawled, but the best are line-caught. Because sea bass are in such demand, wild fish have become prohibitively expensive. They can, however, be farmed successfully, and there are sea bass farms all over the Mediterranean.

Other names The French for sea bass is *bar*; due to their ferocity, they are also known as *loup de mer* (sea wolf). In Italian, they are *spigola* or *branzino*; their Spanish name is *lubina*.

Buying Sea bass are available all year round, as whole fish or as fillets. They are best in spring and early summer, before they spawn. Line-caught, wild sea bass have the finest texture and flavor, but farmed fish are an acceptable and much cheaper alternative. Look for bright, silvery skin and clear eyes. Allow about 7 ounces per serving.

Cooking Sea bass have very few small bones and fine, firm flesh that holds its shape well during cooking. They are versatile fish with a delicate flavor and can be cooked by almost any method— broiled, baked, braised, poached, shallow or stir-fried or steamed over seaweed or samphire. A whole poached sea bass, skinned and served cold with mayonnaise, makes a great party dish. Plainly cooked sea bass can be served with any number of sauces, from *beurre blanc* to fresh tomato coulis and Asian sesame dressing. A classic French dish is *bar au fenouil*, grilled sea bass served on a bed of fennel twigs flamed with Pernod.

Sea bass are highly prized in China, where they are braised with ginger and scallions, while the Japanese slice the flesh wafer-thin and use it raw for *sashimi*.

Alternatives Few fish can equal sea bass for flavor, but good substitutes in most recipes are gray mullet, porgy, grouper and John Dory.

Other varieties

Dicentrus punctatus
(speckled bass) takes its Latin name from the small black spots on its back and sides. It is found mainly in the southern Mediterranean and is very similar to sea bass. Two other varieties come from North America and southern seas: striped bass and black bass. Both are excellent fish, but neither tastes quite as good as sea bass.

Stone bass/Wreckfish *(Polyprion americanum)*

This ugly cousin of the sea bass lives in deep Atlantic waters, often amid wrecked ships at the bottom of the sea, which is how it came by its alternative name. This makes it difficult to catch; it can only be line-fished at a depth of more than 500 feet, so it is seldom found at stores and markets. Its Italian name is *cernia di fondale* (bass from the deep). It has dark skin and large, bony fins, and the end of its tail is straight, not V-shaped like the tails of other types of bass.
Cooking If you do find stone bass for sale, it is likely to be as fillets or steaks, which can be cooked in the same way as any other white fish.

Comber *(Serranus)*

These smaller members of the grouper family have reddish or brownish skin with wide vertical markings. *Serranus scriba* is so called because its markings are said to resemble scribbles.
Cooking Comber have delicious firm white flesh. The whole fish can be poached, steamed, braised or baked. Fillets and steaks can be broiled, pan-fried or steamed.

THE SEA BREAM FAMILY

There are approximately two hundred species of sea bream, some of which, unusually for seafish, are vegetarian. They have tall, compact bodies and slightly snub noses.
Habitat Sea bream are found in all warm and temperate coastal waters, including the Atlantic, up to the Bay of Biscay.

Above: Sea bass fillets

Gilt-head bream *(Sparus aurata)*

This beautiful fish is considered the finest of all sea bream. It has silver scales, a gold spot on each cheek and a golden crescent in the middle of its head from which it takes its name. Its dense, juicy white flesh has been highly prized for thousands of years; the ancient Greeks and Romans considered it a fish fit for feasting and it was sacred to Aphrodite, the goddess of love. One wonders what she would have made of the fact that gilt-heads are hermaphrodites, starting as male and becoming female as they mature.
Other names Gilt-heads are also known as royal bream. Sometimes in English, as in French, they are called *daurade* (also spelt *dorade*). The Italian name is *orata*, Spanish *dorada*.
Buying Gilt-heads grow to a length of 24 inches and can weigh up to 6½ pounds. They are sold whole or as fillets. There is a high percentage of wastage, which makes this quite an expensive fish. Nowadays, gilt-heads are farmed successfully in the Mediterranean, which makes them a little less costly. Fresh gilt-head bream should have bright, shiny scales.
Cooking All bream have numerous wide scales that must be removed before cooking, or the diner will experience a most unpleasant mouthful. Whole gilt-head bream can be treated like sea bass or sole—baked, broiled, poached,

steamed in seaweed or braised. The flesh should be scored in several places on both sides before the fish is broiled or baked whole, to ensure even cooking. The dense flesh is robust enough to withstand spicy or aromatic flavors. A classic French dish is *daurade rôtie*, where the fish is covered with alternate strips of pork fat or bacon and anchovy fillets, then wrapped in waxed paper and baked.

Gilt-head fillets can be pan-fried, broiled or baked. Very fresh fish can be used raw to make *sashimi*.

Red bream *(Pagellus bogaraveo)*

This tall rosy-red fish has a pronounced black spot above the pectoral fin on each shoulder. It grows to about 20 inches and is usually sold already filleted. Red bream lives deep in the sea and feeds on crustaceans and mollusks, which make it particularly tasty. It is found in northern European waters, but swims southward in winter to spawn, and is much sought after in Spain and Portugal.
Other names Young red bream have small blue spots on their backs and are sometimes known as blue-spotted bream. In French, red bream is rather rudely called *dorade commune* (common bream); the Italians call it *pagro*, *pagello* or *occhialone*, meaning "big eye." The Spaniards call it *besugo*.
Cooking Extremely fresh red bream can be eaten raw as *sashimi*. Whole fish and fillets should be cooked in the same way as snapper, bass or red mullet.

Black bream *(Spondyliosoma cantharus)*

This large bream is sometimes found in the North Sea. It is actually dark gray, with beautiful golden stripes running from head to tail. Unlike the gilt-head, it is unisexual and monogamous. Like gilt-head bream, it can be baked, broiled, poached, steamed in seaweed, or braised. The flavor and texture are similar but not as fine.

Ray's bream *(Brama brama)*

These large fish live in depths of 328 feet and below, but come up to the surface in summer, sometimes with tragic consequences, as the eponymous John Ray found when he discovered huge numbers of the fish stranded on the coast of Britain in the 17th century. Ray's bream are brownish-gray, with firm flesh and a good flavor. They should be cooked in the same way as other bream.

Dentex *(Dentex dentex)*

These relatives of the sea bream are particularly popular in Mediterranean countries, in whose waters they are found. They are also found to a lesser extent in the East Atlantic. Their color varies with their age; young dentex are gray, changing first to reddish pink, then to a beautiful steel blue with a sprinkling of dark spots.

Above, from front: gilt-head bream, red bream and black bream

Other names *Denté* in French, *dentice* in Italian and *dentón* in Spanish.
Cooking Although dentex can grow up to 39 inches in length, they are best eaten when about 12 inches long. Fish this size can be broiled whole or baked with herbs. Larger specimens should be cut into steaks and broiled or fried.

Porgy *(Pagrus pagrus)*

The eponymous hero of Porgy and Bess took his name from these rosy-tinted North American relatives of the bass, variations of which are also found in the Atlantic coastal waters around Africa. Porgies grow to a length of up to 30 inches and can be cooked whole or as steaks—baked, broiled, poached, steamed, or braised, using any of the recipes for bream.

Unusual species of bream

Among the many varieties of bream, there are a number whose names describe their appearance. The **two-banded bream**, a fish that makes very good eating, has two distinct vertical black bands fore and aft.
Annular bream, which is the smallest of its group, has a dark ring around its tail, as does **saddled bream**, while **sheepshead bream** has an upturned snout.
The small varieties, such as annular bream and saddled bream, are used for making soup.
A classic Tuscan dish, *sarago e parago*, uses two different kinds of small bream, boned and stuffed with ham and rosemary, then grilled over a wood fire.

THE COD FAMILY

This large family of fish includes haddock, hake, ling, whiting and many other related species of white-fleshed fish. Most of them come from the Atlantic and other cold northerly waters, although hake is found in the warmer Mediterranean and is very popular with the Spaniards and Portuguese.

Cod *(Gadus morruha)*

Long, torpedo-shaped fish with vibrant yellowish-brown mottled skin and a whitish belly, cod have a large head with a snub nose, a protruding upper jaw and a whiskery barbel on the chin that acts as a sensor as they search for food on the sea bed. They can live to over twenty years and grow to a length of 20 feet (weighing up to 110 pounds), although such specimens are sadly rare, and most commercially fished cod weigh between 6½ and 17½ pounds.

Habitat Cod prefer to live in cold water with a high salt content. They hatch in huge numbers (a single female can lay up to five million eggs) close to the surface of the water, but gravitate down to the sea bed where they feed on crustaceans, mollusks and worms. Large cod also feed on smaller fish. Cod can be caught in trawler nets or line-caught. Trawled fish are often damaged in the nets.

For years, cod was so plentiful that it was regarded as an inferior fish, fit only to be fried with potatoes or masked with an unpleasant floury white sauce. All too often, its succulent, flaky white flesh was overcooked, making it watery or dry. Today, overfishing has depleted stocks so much that now it has become relatively scarce and therefore more highly appreciated. As the great French chef Auguste Escoffier predicted in the 19th century: "If cod were less common, it would be held in as high esteem as salmon," (at that time, regarded as the king of fish) "for, when it is really fresh and of good quality, the delicacy and delicious flavor of its flesh admit of its ranking among the finest of fish."

Other names In France, fresh cod is called *cabillaud*. In Italy, it is *merluzzo* and in Spain, *bacalao* (which can also mean salt cod).

Buying Cod is most commonly trawled or netted, but it can also be line-caught. The first two methods can damage the delicate flesh, so try to buy the superior line-caught fish, if possible.

When buying a whole small cod or codling, the skin should be shiny and clear. There is a lot of wastage in whole cod, which makes these fish very expensive, so they are more usually sold as steaks and fillets. Shoulder steaks have the finest flavor. Try to buy thick cuts from the shoulder or middle of the fish, and always check that the flesh is very white. Never buy cod with discolored patches on the flesh. The fresher the fish, the firmer and flakier the flesh will be.

Cooking Cod holds its texture well and can be cooked in many different ways, but it is vitally important not to overcook it. The flavor is robust enough to take quite strong and spicy seasoning. Whole fish can be poached in a court-bouillon and served cold with mayonnaise, green sauce or tartare sauce. Cod can also be baked or roasted or braised in white wine.

Above: Cod fillet and steaks

Most cooking methods are suitable for cod fillets and steaks, except for broiling, which can destroy the flaky texture. They can be poached, steamed, braised in tomato sauce or topped with a crust of bread crumbs and herbs and baked. They are also delicious floured and sautéed, or coated with batter and deep-fried. Cod makes an excellent substitute for more exotic fish in curries. A classic English dish is poached cod with parsley sauce. Fresh and smoked cod fillets can be used to make fish cakes, croquettes, fish pies, salads and mousses.

Cod can be salted or dried (see Dried and Salted Fish). The roe is often smoked and used to make *taramasalata*. Frozen cod is usually frozen at sea to retain freshness and flavor, but is never as good as fresh fish. It is available as steaks, fillets, breaded cuts and fish fingers. The liver produces cod liver oil, which tastes disgusting but is good for you.

Alternatives Any firm-fleshed white fish can be substituted for cod, including flat fish such as brill, halibut and turbot.

Above: Cod

Above: Haddock

Coley *(Pollachius virens)*

Traditionally regarded as cod's poor relation, fit only for feeding to the cat, coley has unappealing grayish flesh, which is responsible for its low price. Long and slim, the fish has a protruding lower jaw and no barbel. The skin on the back is dark gray, lightening to mottled yellow on the sides and almost white on the belly. Coley generally weigh 11–22 pounds, but smaller fish do appear on the fishmonger's slab.
Habitat Coley live in huge schools in both deep waters and near the surface. They prefer cold, salty water. They are voracious predators who prey on herring and have cannibalistic tendencies.
Other names Coley are also known as saithe, coalfish and pollock (not to be confused with pollack). In French, they are *lieu noir*, in Italian *merluzzo nero* and in Spanish *abadejo*.
Buying Coley are sometimes sold whole, weighing 2¼–8¾ pounds, but are more usually sold as steaks, cutlets and fillets. The unattractive gray flesh looks off-putting, but whitens during cooking. It should feel firm to the touch. Coley must be extremely fresh, or the flesh will become woolly and unpleasant.
Cooking Coley is less fine than cod in texture and flavor. Rubbing the grayish flesh with lemon juice helps to whiten it, but the color can also be masked by coating the fish in batter or using it in a fish pie, casserole or fish cakes. It will withstand robust flavors and can be baked, braised, broiled or fried. Smoked coley has an excellent flavor, but is seldom available commercially. It is worth trying if you have a home smoker.

Alternatives Haddock, cod or any firm-fleshed white fish can be used instead of coley.

Haddock *(Melanogrammus aeglefinus)*

These are generally smaller than cod, growing up to 39 inches long and weighing 2¼–4½ pounds They have dark brownish-gray skin with a black lateral line and a black spot above the pectoral fin (purportedly the thumb print of St. Peter). Their eyes are large and prominent. They live close to the sea bed and prefer water with a high salt content.

Haddock is often considered to be interchangeable with cod, but its white flesh has a more delicate flavor and a softer, less flaky texture.
Habitat Haddock are schooling fish that live at the bottom of cold northern seas in Europe and North America. They feed on mollusks, worms and other small fish and spawn in the coldest, saltiest water they can find, off the coast of Norway and the Faroes, for example.
Other names In North America, young haddock and cod are known as scrod. In French, the fish is called *aiglefin* (from the Latin name). Confusingly, the French word for smoked haddock is *haddock*. In Italian, haddock is *asinello*; in Spanish it is *eglefino*.
Buying Fresh haddock is at its best in winter and early spring, when the cold has firmed up the flesh. You may find whole small haddock (weighing 1–4½ pounds) at the fishmonger's; but the fish is usually sold as fillets. Before you buy, prod the flesh to make sure that it is firm.
Cooking Fresh haddock is a versatile fish, which can be cooked in the same way as cod. When cooking whole haddock, leave the skin on to hold the delicate flesh together.

Haddock is the perfect fish for deep-frying, and it makes wonderful fish and chips. It also makes excellent fish lasagne and pie, especially when the fresh fish is mixed with an equal amount of smoked haddock.

Below: Haddock fillets

Hake *(Merluccius merluccius)*

This most elegant member of the cod family is a long, slim fish with two spiny dorsal fins, bulging eyes and a protruding lower jaw without a barbel. The head and back are dark steely gray and the belly is silvery white. The inside of the mouth and gills is black. A mature fish can grow up to 39 inches, but the average length is 12–20 inches.

Habitat Hake are found in most temperate and cold waters. By day, they live near the sea bed, but at night they move to the surface to hunt oily fish such as herrings, mackerel and sprats.

Other names The French have several names for hake: *merlu, colin* and *merluchon* (small immature fish). The Spanish call it *merluza*. In Italian, it is *nasello*. In North America, hake is often known as whiting, although it is far superior to the European whiting.

Buying Due to overfishing, hake are becoming quite scarce and expensive. Hake can be trawled or caught on long lines. Try to buy line-caught fish, which has a better texture. Hake must be very fresh, or it becomes flabby. The flesh has a pinkish tinge; it will always feel soft to the touch, but should never feel limp. Whole fish should have bright eyes and smell of the sea.

When calculating how much hake to buy, allow for 40 percent wastage for whole fish. Keep the head, as it makes particularly delicious soup or fish stock.

Hake is usually sold as cutlets or steaks. Those cut from near the head have the best flavor. The fish has few bones, and these are easy to remove. Avoid buying fillets, as they tend to disintegrate during cooking.

Cooking Whole hake can be poached, baked or braised in wine, lemon juice and fresh herbs or tomato sauce. Like all fish, it should never be overcooked. Steaks can be broiled, coated in egg and bread crumbs and deep-fried or sautéed in olive oil and garlic. They can also be layered with potatoes and onions, or with tomatoes and cheese

Above: Ling

and baked *au gratin*. Light buttery sauces go well with hake, as does caper sauce. Shellfish such as mussels and clams are perfect partners. A popular Spanish hors d'oeuvre is *escabeche*— marinated hake served cold.

Alternatives Haddock or cod can be substituted for hake in any recipe.

Other varieties North American silver hake is a small, streamlined fish with an excellent flavor. Varieties of hake are also found in the warmer waters of South America and southern Africa, but don't taste as good as northern hake.

Ling *(Molva molva)*

This fish has a long, slender greenish-brown body with a silver lateral stripe, no scales and a barbel on the lower jaw. It is the largest relative of the cod, growing to a length of 6 feet.

Habitat Common ling live in the Atlantic, often in proximity to rocks, where they feed on round and flat fish, small octopus and crustaceans. A smaller relative is found in the Mediterranean.

Other names Mediterranean ling are sometimes known as blue ling. They have larger eyes and a shorter barbel than common ling, and are esteemed for their superior flavor. Both varieties are known as *lingue* in French, *molva occhiona* in Italian and *maruca* in Spanish. Rock ling are available in Australia. In Scandinavian countries, ling is salted, dried and sold as *lutfisk* or *klipfisk* (see Dried and Salted Fish).

Buying As with all fish, the best ling are line-caught. You may find small whole ling on the fishmonger's slab, but the fish is more commonly sold as fillets or middle-cut cutlets. Ling is available most of the year, except in high summer.

Cooking Ling has firm flesh with a fairly good flavor and is sometimes substituted for monkfish. Whole fish can be baked or braised, or made into casseroles, soups and curries. Fillets and cutlets can be broiled or pan-fried, and served with a flavorful sauce.

Alternatives Any member of the cod family can be substituted. For a more extravagant substitute, use monkfish or conger eel.

Pollack *(Pollachius pollachius)*

These attractive fish have steely gray backs and greenish-yellow bodies with a curved lateral line. They have a protruding lower jaw and no barbel. Pollack are smaller than cod, growing to a length of less than 39 inches.

Habitat Pollack can live in schools near the surface of the sea, where they feed on sprats and herrings, or close to the bottom where they eat deep-sea shrimp and sand-eels.

Other names Its yellow color gives pollack the name of *lieu jaune* in French, *merluzzo giallo* in Italian and *abadejo* in Spanish.

Buying Pollack are at their best in autumn and winter. They are usually sold as fillets, cutlets or steaks. If you need a whole fish, look for a superior line-caught specimen.

Above: Hake

Above: Pouting

Cooking Pollack has a drier texture and less pronounced flavor than cod, so it benefits from a creamy, highly flavored sauce. It is good for fish pies and soups and can be baked, braised, deep-fried or sautéed. It is suitable for any recipe for cod, haddock, hake or ling.

Pouting *(Trisopterus luscus)*

This sulky-sounding fish is a poor (and cheap) relation of the whiting and is often caught in the same nets. It is comparatively small (about 10 inches long), with light brown papery skin.
Other names It is also known as pout. In French it is *tacaud*, in Italian *merluzzo francese* and in Spanish *faneca*.
Buying Pouting goes bad extremely quickly and must be eaten very fresh. Your nose will soon tell you if the fish is past its prime. If possible, buy a whole fish and ask the fishmonger to fillet it. Then cook it as soon as you can, as the fillets will rapidly deteriorate.
Cooking As for whiting.

Whiting *(Merlangus merlangus)*

Similar in appearance to haddock, whiting are small fish (generally about 12–16 inches long). They have greenish-gray skin, a silvery belly and a black spot at the base of the pectoral fin. The head is pointed, with a protruding upper jaw and no barbel.
Habitat Whiting are found all over the Atlantic, from Iceland to northern Spain. They feed on crustaceans and small fish such as sand-eels and herrings and are often found near rocky shores.
Other names Its old name was merling. The French call it *merlan*, the Italians *merlano* and the Spanish *merlán*.
Buying The fact that it is abundant all year and has soft, rather unexciting flesh means that whiting is cheap and tends to be undervalued. However, really fresh whiting is well worth buying. Whole fish should be scintillatingly shiny. Fillets should be pearly white and feel soft but definitely not flabby. Stale

whiting may have a woolly texture and taste unpleasant, so make sure that you buy only absolutely fresh fish. Whiting are small, so allow two fillets per serving. You may find whiting boned through the back, leaving the two fillets attached.
Cooking The whiting's meltingly tender flesh makes it an ideal basis for a soup, as it contributes a velvety texture. It is also excellent for quenelles and fish mousses. Whiting is a versatile fish that can be coated in bread crumbs or battered and fried. it can also be pan-fried, broiled or gently poached in wine or court-bouillon and served with a lemony sauce or flavored butter. Whatever cooking method you use, make sure the whiting is well seasoned.
Alternatives Flounder or sole can be used, and all the members of the cod family.

Whiting en colère

A once immensely popular dish was *merlan en colère* ("angry whiting"). Whole fish were baked with the skin on, then curled around so that their tails could be stuck through their eye sockets or into their mouths. Presumably the name came from the assumption that the fish was chasing its own tail in anger. Mercifully, this method of serving whiting has fallen out of favor.

Below: Whiting

THE GURNARD FAMILY

Gurnard are curious, almost prehistoric-looking fish with cylindrical bodies, high, armor-plated heads with wide mouths, and strange pectoral fins with the three lowest rays divided into "fingers." They use these to explore the sea bed. Another curiosity is the grunting noise they emit, caused by vibrating the swim bladder—for what purpose, no one has yet discovered.

Below: Gurnard

Gurnard weigh between 3¾ ounces and 4½ pounds. There are several types, which are distinguished by their color; all have lean white flesh with a firm texture but rather insipid taste. They are rich in iodine, phosphorus and protein.
Habitat Gurnard are found in the Atlantic and Mediterranean. They live on or near the sea bed, using their "fingers" to seek out the crabs, shrimp and small fish that live in the sediment.
Other names Also known as sea robin and gurnet. The French name, *grondin*, echoes the grunting sound they make. In Italian, they are *capone* (meaning large head); in Spanish, *rubios*.

Grey gurnard *(Eutrigla gurnardus)*

These fish have brownish-gray backs and silvery bellies. They grow to a maximum length of 18 inches. The lateral line is scaly and should be removed before cooking.

Red gurnard *(Aspitrigla cuculus)*

The most attractive member of the gurnard family, this pinkish-red fish has bony extensions to the lateral line, which give it the appearance of vertical

Above: Tub gurnard

stripes on its back. It has the finest flavor of all the gurnards and is sometimes substituted for red mullet.

Tub gurnard *(Trigla lucerna)*

This larger gurnard is orangey-brown with bright orange pectoral fins. It is an excellent swimmer and sometimes leaps right out of the water, high above the surface, which explains its alternative name of flying gurnard.
Buying Gurnard are bony fish with an unexceptional flavor, so they tend to be cheap. They are usually sold whole—ask the fishmonger to remove the spiny fins and the skin. Beware, especially in France, of buying red gurnard masquerading as red mullet *(rouget)*. The latter is vastly superior.
Cooking Small gurnard are best used in soups and stocks. Larger fish can be braised or baked on a bed of vegetables with a little white wine. Take care when eating whole gurnard, as they are very bony. Fillets can be coated in bread crumbs and fried, or steamed and served with a Mediterranean sauce.
Alternatives Red or gray mullet can be used in any gurnard recipe, and will generally give a better result.

Scorpion fish *(Scorpaena scrofa, Scorpaena porcus)*

Like gurnard, scorpion fish have huge heads and armor-plated cheeks. Their enormous scaly heads have loose folds of skin above and between the eyes. The dorsal fin is made up of large poisonous spines. The smaller brown scorpion fish has a finer flavor than its larger cousin.
Habitat Scorpion fish are found throughout the Mediterranean and off the coast of North Africa. They also live in Atlantic waters, ranging from the English Channel to Senegal.
Other names The French for scorpion fish is *rascasse* (*chapon* in the south of France). Italians call it *scorfano*; in Spanish it is *cabracho* or *rascacio*.
Buying Scorpion fish are usually sold whole. You should allow for a huge amount of wastage; a 4½ pounds fish will only serve four people.
Cooking Scorpion fish is best known as an essential ingredient in bouillabaisse. Whole fish can be baked or braised with fennel; scorpion fillets can be cooked *à l'antillaise*, braised with tomatoes, potatoes and red peppers.
Alternatives Monkfish, snapper, John Dory or gurnard can be used in a pinch.

Above: Scorpion fish

THE MULLET FAMILY

Over a hundred species of mullet are found in temperate and tropical seas. These belong to two main groups, gray and red, which are unrelated and very different in appearance and flavor.

Gray mullet (family Mugilidae)

Varieties of gray mullet are found all over the world. These beautiful silvery fish resemble sea bass, but have larger scales and small mouths, suited to their diet of seaweed and plankton. They live in the vicinity of the muddy sea bed, so they sometimes smell and taste rather muddy. A good gray mullet has lean, slightly soft, creamy white flesh with quite a pleasant flavor.

Habitat Gray mullet are found in coastal waters and estuaries all over the world.

Varieties The finest is the golden mullet (*Liza aurata*), which has a thin upper lip and gold spots on its head and the front

Below: Red mullet are considered one of the finest seafish.

of the body. It is one of the smallest mullets, growing only to about 18 inches. In French, it is known as *mulet doré*. Thick-lipped mullet (*Crenimugil* or *Chelon labrosus*) has, as its name suggests, thick lips and a rounded body. This mullet is sometimes farmed. The thin-lipped mullet (*Liza ramada*) has a golden sheen, a thin upper lip and a pointed snout, which gives it its French name of *mulet porc*. The largest mullet is the common or striped gray mullet (*Mugil cephalus*), which can grow up to 28 inches. This fish has a brown body, silvery back and a large head. Its eyes are covered by a transparent membrane. In French it is called

Above: Silver-skinned gray mullet are found all over the world

mulet cabot. There is also a small Mediterranean mullet whose main claim to fame is its ability to leap out of the water to escape predators. This is the leaping gray mullet (*Liza saliens*).

Buying Except in France, you are unlikely to find any differentiation between the varieties of gray mullet at the fishmonger. If possible, choose fish that come from the high seas rather than estuaries, as the latter often have a muddy taste and can be flabby. Gray mullet are usually sold whole—ask the fishmonger to scale and skin them for you. Keep the roes, which are delicious. Larger fish may be sold filleted.

Cooking Gray mullet must be scaled before being cooked. Any muddiness can be eliminated by soaking the fish in several changes of acidulated water. Whole fish are very good stuffed with fennel and grilled. Slash the sides and add a splash of aniseed-flavored alcohol before cooking the fish, and serve with a buttery sauce. Mullet roe is a delicacy and can be eaten fresh, fried in butter or used in a stuffing for a baked fish. When salted and dried, mullet roe is the authentic basis of taramasalata and *bottarga* or *boutargue*.

Red mullet (*Mullus surmuletus and Mullus barbatus*)

These are among the finest of all saltwater fish. They are small (up to 16 inches long), with pinkish-red skins streaked with gold. Their Roman-nosed heads have two long barbels on the chin. They have lean, firm flesh. The flavor is robust and distinctive.

Other varieties *Mullus surmeletus* is more correctly known as *surmullet*; it has rosy red skin and is larger than *Mullus barbatus*, which has three yellowish stripes along each side and grows to a length of 12 inches.

Goatfish Types of red mullet known as goatfish because of their long, beard-like barbels are found in the warm Pacific and Indian Oceans. They are smaller (up to 8 inches) and less colorful than cold-water mullet, and they have drier, less tasty flesh.

Habitat Red mullet are found in Atlantic and Mediterranean waters. They live on sandy or rocky areas of the sea bed, feeding on small sea creatures.

Other names Red mullet are usually cooked complete with their livers and sometimes all their guts. These impart a gamey flavor, giving the fish the nickname "woodcock of the sea." In America, all red mullet are known as "goatfish," regardless of size or place of origin. The French for mullet is *rouget*; depending on the variety, it is *rouget barbet*, *rouget de roche* or *rouget de vase* (*Mullus barbatus*). In Italian, red mullet is *triglia*, in Spanish, *salmonete de roca* (*Mullus surmuletus*) or *salmonete de fango* (*Mullus barbatus*).

Buying Red mullet has delicate flesh that is highly perishable, so it is essential to buy extremely fresh fish. They should have very bright skin and eyes and feel very firm. The scales should be firmly attached, not flaking off the skin. Because they are small, red mullet are usually sold whole, but large fish are sometimes filleted. The flesh is quite rich, so a 7 ounces fish will be ample for one person. Ask the fishmonger to scale and gut it for you, and keep the liver, which is a great delicacy.

Cooking The best ways to cook red mullet are broiling and pan-frying. Score the sides before broiling a whole fish to ensure even cooking. Red mullet marry superbly with Mediterranean flavors such as olive oil, saffron, tomatoes, olives, anchovies and orange. They can be cooked *en papillote* with flavorings such as fennel or basil, or made into mousses and soufflés. Very small, bony red mullet are often used in bouillabaisse.

THE WRASSE FAMILY

This large family of fish is notable for its varied and dazzling colors. Wrasse range from steely blue to green, orange and golden; in some species, the sexes have different colors. All wrasse have thick lips and an array of sharp teeth. They are small fish, seldom growing larger than 16 inches in length.

Habitat Wrasse are found in both Atlantic and Mediterranean waters. They live near rocky coasts, feeding on barnacles and small crustaceans.

Varieties The most common is the ballan wrasse (*Labrus berggylta*), which has greenish or brownish skin, with large scales tipped with gold. Male and female cuckoo wrasse (*Labrus mixtus*) have strikingly different coloration; the males are steely blue with almost black stripes, while the females are orangey-pink with three black spots under the dorsal fin. The name of the five-spotted wrasse (*Symphonus quinquemaculatus*) is self-explanatory, while the brown spotted wrasse is completely covered with spots. Rainbow wrasse (*Coris julis*) have spiny dorsal fins and a red or orange band along their body.

Right: Common wrasse

Below: Brown spotted wrasse

Other names In French, wrasse is variously known as *vielle*, *coquette* and *labre*. In Italian, it is *labridi*; in Spanish *merlo*, *tordo* or *gallano*.

Buying Wrasse are available in spring and summer. Look for scintillating skin and bright eyes. Ask the fishmonger to scale and clean the fish. Allow at least 14 ounces per serving.

Cooking Most wrasse are fit only for making soup, but some larger varieties, such as ballan wrasse, can be baked whole. Make a bed of sliced onions, garlic, smoked bacon and potatoes, bake at 400°F until soft, then add the wrasse, moisten with white wine and bake for 10–15 minutes.

OILY FISH

Fish such as herrings, mackerel and sardines have always been popular because they are cheap and nutritious, but now they are considered the ultimate "good for you" food. In recent years they have received excellent press, due to their healthy properties. Not only do they contain protein and vitamins A, B and D, but the Omega-3 fatty acids in their flesh are known to reduce the risk of clogged arteries, blood clots, strokes and even cancer. People who eat fish regularly tend to live longer—the Japanese, among the world's greatest fish eaters, have one of the lowest death rates from heart disease.

Oily fish are pelagic fish, which swim near the surface of the sea and live in schools that can be quite enormous. The largest family of oil-rich fish are the *clupeiformes*: herrings and their relatives—sardines, anchovies, sprats and pilchards. Other oily fish are smooth-skinned mackerel and tuna.

Below: Herring

THE HERRING FAMILY

Herring *(Clupea harengus)*

There are numerous different varieties of herring, each confined to its own sea area—the North Sea, Baltic, White Sea (an inlet of the Barents Sea), the coast of Norway and many colder coastal areas. Herring are prodigiously fertile fish, which is just as well, since they have been overfished for centuries and are becoming more scarce.

Herring are slender silver fish with a central dorsal fin and large scales. They seldom grow to a length of more than 14 inches. Their oily flesh can be cured in many ways, including smoking, salting, drying and marinating in vinegar and spices.

Habitat Herring live in huge schools in cold northerly waters, where they feed on plankton. They are migratory fish that come inshore to spawn. They sometimes change their habitual route for no apparent reason, so that there may be a glut in a particular area for several years, but no herring at all the next year.

Boning a whole herring
Herring must be scaled before cooking; the scales virtually fall off by themselves, so this is easy to do. Whether or not you leave the head on is a matter of choice.

1 First, scale the herring, then slit the belly with a sharp knife and remove the innards.

2 Lay the fish on a cutting board, belly-side down. With the heel of your hand, press down firmly all along the backbone.

3 Turn the herring over and lift off the backbone. You will find that most of the small side bones will come off with it.

Varieties Herring are mostly known by the name of the region where they are located—North Sea, Norwegian, Baltic, for instance. Each variety has its own spawning season, which influences the eating qualities of the fish.

Buying Like all oily fish, herring must be absolutely fresh, or they will taste rancid. They are at their best before they spawn. Look for large, firm fish with slippery skins and rounded bellies containing hard or soft roes; hard roes are the female eggs, soft roes the male milt. Soft herring roes are considered a particular delicacy. By running your hands along the belly of the fish, you will be able to tell whether the roes are hard or soft.

Once they have spawned, herrings lose weight and their flesh becomes rather dry. If the fishmonger cleans them for you, be sure to keep the roe. As herrings contain numerous soft bones, you might ask him to bone or fillet them for you. They can be gutted either through the belly or through the gills, leaving the roe inside.

Above: Herring fillets

Cooking The oiliness of the flesh makes herrings particularly suitable for broiling and grilling. Score whole fish in several places on both sides to ensure even cooking. Herring benefit from being served with an acidic sauce such as gooseberry or mustard to counteract the richness.

Whole herrings are excellent baked with a stuffing of bread crumbs, chopped onions and apples. They are also good wrapped in bacon and broiled, or broiled with a mustard sauce. Both whole herrings and fillets are delicious rolled in oatmeal and then pan-fried in bacon fat. Serve them with a squeeze of lemon juice.

Herring fillets can be made into fish balls, or cooked in a sweet-and-sour sauce made with ketchup, wine vinegar, honey and Worcestershire sauce. They are also delicious soused in a vinegary marinade flavored with herbs and spices.

Fillets are also traditionally made into rollmops or smoked to make kippers—these processes are explored fully in the chapters on Pickled and Smoked Fish.

Alternatives Sardines, sprats and mackerel can be cooked in the same way as herrings.

Herring roes

Soft roes have a creamy, melting texture. They can be tossed in seasoned flour, gently fried in butter and served as they are, or deviled with cayenne pepper and Worcestershire sauce and served on hot toast. They also make a delicious omelet filling. Poached in stock and mashed, they can be used as a spread, in a stuffing for whole baked herrings or added to a sauce or savory tart filling. Hard roes have a grainy texture, which people tend either to love or loathe. They can be baked or braised under the fish to add extra flavor.

Above: Soft herring roes

Anchovies (*Engraulis encrasicolus*)

These small slender fish seldom grow to more than 6¼ inches; the average length is only 3¼–4 inches. They have steely blue backs and shimmering silver sides, and the upper jaw protrudes markedly. Most anchovies are sold filleted and preserved in salt or oil, but if you are lucky enough to find fresh fish, you are in for a treat.

Habitat Anchovies are pelagic fish and are found in tightly packed schools throughout the Mediterranean, in the Black Sea (where, sadly, pollution has depleted stocks) and the Atlantic and Pacific Oceans.

Other names In French, anchovy is *anchois*, in Italian *acciuga* or *alice*, in Spanish *boquerón*.

Buying Ideally, fresh anchovies should be cooked and eaten straight from the sea. The best anchovies come from the Mediterranean and are at their peak in early summer. By the time they have been exported, however, they will have lost much of their delicate flavor. When buying fresh anchovies, look for scintillating skins and bright, slightly bulging eyes.

Preparing You are unlikely to find a fishmonger willing to clean anchovies for you, but they are easy to prepare at

Above: Anchovies

home. To gut, cut off the head and press gently along the body with your thumb to squeeze out the innards. To fillet, run your thumbnail or a stubby blunt knife along the length of the spine from head to tail on both sides and lift off the fillets.

Freezing Since fresh anchovies are hard to come by, it is worth freezing them when there are plentiful supplies. Remove the heads and clean the fish, then pack them head-to-tail in a shallow freezer box, separating the layers with

sheets of plastic wrap. Cover the box with a lid and freeze. Defrost before using.

Cooking Whole anchovies can be broiled or fried like sardines, or coated lightly in egg and flour and deep-fried. They make an excellent *gratin* when seasoned with olive oil and garlic, then topped with bread crumbs and baked. Fillets can be fried with garlic and parsley, or marinated for 24 hours in a mixture of olive oil, onion, garlic, bay leaves and crushed peppercorns. Anchovy extract and anchovy paste are useful ingredients.

Sardines and Pilchards (*Sardinia pilchardus*)

It is a common misconception that sardines and pilchards are different fish; in fact, a pilchard is merely a larger, more mature sardine. Even the largest pilchards grow only to 8 inches, while sardines may be only 5–6 inches long. They are slim fish, with blue-green backs and silvery bellies. They have thirty scales along the mid-line on either side. Their flesh is compact and has a delicious, oily flavor. Canned sardines and pilchards are very popular staples because they are so convenient and easy to prepare.

Left:
Sardines

Habitat Sardines take their name from Sardinia, where they were once abundant. They are pelagic fish, and are found throughout the Mediterranean and Atlantic. Various related species are also found in other parts of the world.

Other names Sardines are easy to recognize on foreign menus: they are *sardine* in French, *sardina* in Italian and Spanish, and *pilchard* or *sardine* in German. Confusingly, the French use the word *pilchard* when speaking of canned herring.

Buying Sardines are at their best in spring and early summer. They do not travel well, so try to buy fish from local waters and avoid any damaged or stale-looking specimens. Small sardines have the best flavor, but larger fish are better for stuffing. Depending on the size, allow 3–5 sardines per serving.

Cooking Sardines should be scaled and gutted before being cooked. This is easy to do; just cut the head almost through from the backbone and twist, pulling it toward you. The innards will come away with the head. Whole sardines are

superb simply broiled plain or grilled, which crisps the skin. They can be coated in bread crumbs, fried and served with tomato sauce, made into fritters or stuffed with capers, salted anchovies or Parmesan and baked. They make an excellent sauce for

Below: Pilchards

Above: Sprats

pasta and are also delicious marinated and served raw.

Alternatives Large anchovies or sprats can be used instead of small sardines.

Sprats *(Sprattus sprattus)*

These small silvery fish look very similar to sardines or immature herrings, but are slightly squatter. Once, the sprat was an important fish, but they are seldom sold fresh these days, being mostly smoked or cured, or sold as fishmeal.

Habitat They are abundant in the Baltic, North Sea and the Atlantic, and, since they can tolerate low salinity, are also found in fjords and estuaries. In addition to being sold fresh, sprats are available smoked or canned in oil.

Other names Sprats are *sprat* in French, *papalina* in Italian and *espadin* in Spanish. Smoked sprats are called *brisling* in Norway.

Cooking Sprats can be cooked in the same way as anchovies and small sardines. They have very oily flesh and are delicious when fried in oatmeal or deep-fried in batter.

Raw sprats can be marinated in vinaigrette; they are often served as part of a Scandinavian smorgasbørd.

Above: Whitebait

shake them in a plastic bag containing flour seasoned with salt and cayenne pepper. Deep-fry until very crisp.

"Blue" fish

Although they are not related to each other, several species of particularly oily fish are known collectively as "blue" fish. All have very smooth, taut skin with virtually undetectable scales and firm, meaty flesh. Varieties of blue fish are found in almost all temperate and tropical seas.

Mackerel *(Scomber scombrus)*

These streamlined fish are easily identified, thanks to their beautiful greenish-blue skin. They have wavy bands of black and green on their backs, while the bellies are silvery. The smooth, pale beigey-pink flesh is meaty, with a distinctive full flavor.
Habitat Mackerel are pelagic fish, often found in huge numbers in the North Atlantic, North Sea and Mediterranean. They spend the winter near the bottom of the cold North Sea, not feeding at all.

Below: Mackerel

Whitebait

This name is given to tiny silver fish—only about 2 inches in length—that are caught in summer as they swim up estuaries. The name can refer to immature sprats or herrings, or to a mixture of both fish.
Other names Whitebait are *blanchaille* in French; this name is also used to describe tiny freshwater fish. The Italian name for them is *bianchetti*; the Spanish *aladroch*.
Buying Whitebait do not need to be cleaned. They are available fresh in spring and summer, and frozen all year round. Allow about 4 ounces per person when serving them as an appetizer.
Cooking Whitebait are cooked whole, complete with heads. They are delicious deep-fried and served with brown bread and butter. Prepare them for cooking by dunking them in a bowl of milk, then

Below: Jack mackerel, which are not true mackerel, are common in New Zealand

Other names Larger mackerel are known as *maquereau* in French; small specimens are called *lisette*. In Italian, mackerel is called *sgombro*, and in Spanish it is known as *caballa*.

Buying Mackerel are delicious when extremely fresh, but not worth eating when they are past their prime. They are in their prime in late spring and early summer, just before spawning. Look for firm fish with iridescent skin and clear, bright eyes. Small mackerel are better than large fish.

Larger specimens are sometimes sold filleted, and either sold fresh or smoked. Mackerel is a popular canned fish, and may be canned in either oil or tomato sauce.

Cooking Whole mackerel can be broiled, grilled, braised or poached in court-bouillon, white wine or cider. Make several slashes on both sides of each fish before cooking them over direct heat. Like herrings, they need a sharp sauce to counteract the richness of the flesh; classic accompaniments are sorrel, horseradish or mustard sauce. Fillets can can be cooked in the same way as herring—either coated in oatmeal and fried, or braised with onions and white wine. Raw mackerel fillets can be marinated in sweet-and-sour vinaigrette to make an appetizer.

Below: Mackerel fillets can be cooked in the same way as herring—they are especially good coated in oatmeal and pan-fried.

Bluefish
(Pomatomus saltatrix)

Found in the Mediterranean and American Atlantic waters, bluefish are highly aggressive and are often fished for sport. They have shiny blue-green backs and masses of very sharp teeth. Bluefish are very popular in Turkey, where they are displayed in fish markets with their bright red gills turned inside out like elaborate rosettes to indicate their freshness. The flesh of bluefish is softer and more delicate than that of mackerel, but they can be cooked in the same way.

Right: Bluefish in a Turkish market with their bright red gills displayed.

Other varieties of mackerel
Chub mackerel *(Scomber japonicus colias)* are similar to Atlantic mackerel, but are also found in the Mediterranean and Black Sea. They have larger eyes and less bold markings on their backs. **Spanish mackerel** *(Scomber colias)* have spots below the lateral line. The rarer *Orcynopsis unicolor* is found near the coast of North Africa. It has silvery skin with spots of gold.

Horse mackerel *(Trachurus trachurus)* or **scad** and similar fish such as **jack mackerel** and **round robin** vaguely resemble herrings and are not, despite their name, true relatives of mackerel. They are perfectly edible, but their flesh is rather insipid and they tend to be bony. They can all be cooked in the same way as mackerel.

THE TUNA FAMILY

Tuna has been a popular food for centuries. The fish were highly prized by the Ancient Greeks, who mapped their migratory patterns in order to fish for them. The Phoenicians preserved tuna by salting and smoking them, and in the Middle Ages they were pickled. A school of immense tuna fish traveling through the high seas is a magnificent sight, although satellite tracking has robbed the experience of some of its excitement. These beautiful, torpedo-shaped fish can grow to an enormous size (up to 1,540 pounds). They have immensely powerful muscles and firm, dark, meaty flesh. There are many varieties of tuna, but thanks to centuries of overfishing, only about half a dozen varieties are sold commercially.

Habitat Tuna are related to mackerel and are found in warm seas throughout the world, as far north as the Bay of Biscay.

Other names Tuna is also known as tunny fish. In French, it is *thon*, in Italian *tonno*, in Spanish *atun*. In Japan, where raw tuna is eaten as *sashimi*, it is called *maguro*.

Buying Tuna is usually sold as steaks. It is a very substantial fish, so allow only about 6 ounces per serving. Depending on the variety, the flesh may range from pale beigey-pink to deep dark red. Do not buy steaks with heavy discolorations around the bone or that are dull-looking and brownish all over. The flesh should be very firm and compact.

Below: Tuna steaks

Cooking Tuna becomes grayish and dry when overcooked, so it is essential to cook it only briefly over high heat, or to stew it gently with moist ingredients like tomatoes and bell peppers. It has become fashionable to sear it fleetingly, leaving it almost raw in the middle; if this is not to your taste, cook the tuna for about 2 minutes on each side—no more.

The following cooking methods are suitable for most types of tuna. Steaks can be seared, broiled, baked or braised. They benefit from being marinated for about 30 minutes before cooking. Tuna marries well with Mediterranean vegetables such as tomatoes, peppers and onions, as well as olives. Most varieties can be eaten raw as *sashimi*, *sushi* or *tartare*, but they must be absolutely fresh. Thinly sliced raw tuna can be marinated in vinaigrette or Asian marinades. Tuna fillets are delicious cut very thin, dusted with flour and cooked like veal *scaloppine* in butter. Broiled fresh tuna makes a superb alternative to canned in a classic Salade Niçoise.

Albacore *(Thunnus alalunga)*

Also known as longfin, due to its long pectoral fins, this tuna is found in temperate and tropical seas, although only the smaller specimens venture into the North Sea. Albacore has pale, rosy flesh whose color and texture resemble veal. Once known as "Carthusian veal," it could be eaten by monks on days when eating meat was not permitted. It is frequently used for canning.

Other names Albacore is also known as "white" tuna. In French it is *thon blanc* or *germon*; in Italian *alalunga* and in Spanish *atun blanco* or *albacora*.

Cooking Because its rosy-white flesh is so akin to veal, albacore is often cooked in similar ways—as cutlets or larded with anchovy fillets and pork back fat, and braised.

Above: Bigeye or blackfin tuna steaks

False albacore *(Euthynnus alletteratus)*

This comparatively small tuna (weighing about 33 pounds) is found only in warmer waters, generally off the coast of Africa. It is highly sought-after in Japan, where it is used for *sashimi*.

Bigeye *(Thunnus obesus)*

This fat relative of the bluefin is found in tropical waters. It has rosy flesh and is substituted for bluefin when that superior tuna is unavailable. It is sometimes known as blackfin tuna. Other languages make the rather rude reference to its obesity: In French, it is *thon obèse*, in Italian, *tonno obeso* and in Spanish, *patudo*.

Bluefin *(Thunnus thynnus)*

Considered by many to be the finest of all tuna, bluefin are also the largest, and can grow to an enormous size (up to 1,540 pounds), although the average weight is about 264 pounds. Bluefin have dark blue backs and silvery bellies. Their oily flesh is deep red and has a more robust flavor than albacore. Bluefin is the classic tuna for *sushi* and *sashimi*.

Habitat Bluefin are found in the Bay of Biscay, the Mediterranean and tropical seas. They are very strong swimmers and a dense school powering its way through the sea is an awesome sight.

Left: Bluefin tuna

Other names In Australia, the fish is known as Southern bluefin. Due to its bright red flesh, bluefin is *thon rouge* in French. In Italian it is merely *tonno*; in Spanish it is known as *atun*.

Buying Bluefin tuna is extremely expensive, largely because the Japanese will pay almost any price for it. It has an almost gamey flavor and is best when it has been kept for a week. Once the flesh has turned from bright red to light brown, however, it should be avoided at all costs—the tuna is past its prime.

Bonito *(Sarda sarda)* and Skipjack *(Katsuwonus pelamis)*

These fish fall somewhere between mackerel and tuna. There are two main types of bonito: Atlantic *(Sarda sarda)* and skipjack or oceanic. The Atlantic bonito is also found in the Mediterranean and Black Sea; skipjack is most commonly found in the Atlantic and Pacific Oceans.

Bonito are inferior to true tuna in quality and taste, with pale flesh which can sometimes be rather dry. Skipjack are usually used for canning. They are popular in Japan, where they are known as *katsuo* and are often made into dried flakes *(katsuobushi)*, which is a main ingredient of *dashi* (stock).

Other names
Skipjack have dark blue parallel lines along their bellies and are sometimes known as "striped tuna." This gives them the French name *bonite à ventre rayé* (striped belly). In Italian they are *bonita*, in Spanish, *listado*.

Frigate mackerel *(Auxis rochei)*

Despite its name, this small fish is a tuna that is found in the Pacific and Indian Oceans. It grows to only about 20 inches and has very red, coarse flesh. Small ones can be cooked whole.

Yellowfin *(Thunnus albacores)*

These large tuna are fished in tropical and equatorial waters. Weighing up to 550 pounds, they resemble albacore, but their fins are yellow. They have pale pinkish flesh and a good flavor.

Other names Confusingly, the French and Italians call yellowfin *albacore* and *tonno albacora* respectively. In Spanish, it is *rabil*.

Buying Since yellowfin tuna come from warm oceans, in Europe they are generally sold frozen as steaks. Make sure that they have not begun to thaw before you buy. Frozen yellowfin is available all year round.

Cooking Very fresh yellowfin can be eaten raw as *sashimi* or *sushi*, but is better cooked in any recipe that is suitable for tuna.

Salade Niçoise
Tuna is the essential ingredient of this substantial Provençal salad, whose other components consist of whatever produce is fresh and available. Although the salad can be (and frequently is) made with drained canned tuna, it is infinitely nicer to use fresh seared or broiled fish. Arrange some coarsely shredded Romaine lettuce in a salad bowl and add the tuna, some quartered hard-boiled eggs, thickly-sliced cooked new potatoes, tomato wedges, crisply-cooked green beans, some pitted black olives and a few anchovy fillets. Just before serving, toss the salad in a little garlic-flavored vinaigrette.

Above: Bluefin tuna steaks

FLAT FISH

All flat fish start life as pelagic larvae, with an eye on each side of their head like a round fish. At this stage, they swim upright near the surface of the sea. As they mature, the fish start to swim on one side only and one eye moves over the head on to the dark-skinned side of the body. Later, they gravitate to the sea bed and feed on whatever edible creatures pass by. Because they do not have to chase their food, their flesh is always delicate and white, without too much muscle fiber. They have a simple bone structure, so even people who are nervous of bones can cope with them. With the exception of flounder, flat fish are seldom found outside European waters. Dover sole, turbot and halibut possibly rank as the finest fish of all.

Brill (Scophthalmus rhombus)

Similar to turbot in appearance and taste, brill is regarded as the poor

Above: Brill

relation, although it has fine softish white flesh with a delicate flavor. Brill can grow to about 30 inches and can weigh up to 6½ pounds, but are often smaller. The fish have slender bodies and there are small, smooth scales on the dark gray skin on the top. The underside is creamy or pinkish white.

Habitat Brill live on the bottom of the Atlantic, Baltic Sea and Mediterranean.

Buying Many people prefer turbot to brill; others think that brill is every bit as good as its plumper friend. Brill is considerably cheaper than turbot and available almost all year round, as whole fish or fillets. Brill lose condition after spawning and can contain a great deal of roe just before, so avoid

Left: Dab

buying them at that time. There is a high percentage of wastage in all flat fish, so you will need a 3–3½ pounds fish for four.

Cooking Brill can hold its own against robust red wine and is often cooked in a *matelote* (fish stew) or red wine sauce. Small fish (up to 4½ pounds) are best cooked whole; they can be baked, braised, poached, steamed, pan-fried or broiled. Whole poached brill is excellent garnished with shrimp or other shellfish. Fillets of brill *à l'anglaise* are coated in egg and bread crumbs and then pan-fried in butter.

Other names In French, brill is *barbue*, in Italian, *rombo liscio*, "smooth turbot;" its Spanish name is *rémol*.

Alternatives Any halibut, sole or turbot recipe is suitable for brill.

Dab (Limanda limanda)

There are several related species of dab, none of which has much flavor. European and American dabs are small lozenge-shaped fish, which seldom grow to more than 14 inches. They have brownish, rough skin and a lateral line.

Habitat Dabs are found in shallow water on the sandy bottom of the Atlantic and off the coast of New Zealand.

Other names The so-called false dabs are more elongated than their European counterparts. In America, dabs are known as sand dabs. In French, they are *limande*, in Italian *limanda*; in Spanish *limanda nordica*.

Buying Dabs are only worth eating when they are very fresh. Near the seaside, you may find them still alive and flapping on the fishmonger's slab; if not, make sure they have glossy skins and a fresh smell. Dabs are usually sold whole, but larger fish may be filleted.

Cooking Dabs have rather soft, bland flesh. Pan-fry them in butter or broil them. Fillets can be coated in egg and bread crumbs and fried.

Above: Halibut

Below: Halibut Steaks

Halibut *(Hippoglossus hippoglossus)*

Halibut are the largest of the flat fish, sometimes growing up to 6½ feet and weighing well over 440 pounds, although they normally weigh between 6½ pounds and 33 pounds. Halibut have elegant, elongated greenish-brown bodies, a pointed head with the eyes on the right-hand side, and pearly white undersides. The flesh is delicious with a fine, meaty texture.

Habitat Halibut live in very cold, deep waters off the coasts of Scotland, Norway, Iceland and Newfoundland. They migrate to shallower waters to spawn. A warm water variety is found in the Pacific. These fish are voracious predators, which will eat almost any type of fish or crustacean, and will even devour birds' eggs that roll off cliffs.

Other names Beware of Greenland halibut *(Reinhardtius hippoglossoides)*, which is a vastly inferior fish. True halibut is called *flétan* in French and *halibut* in Italian and Spanish.

Buying: Whole young halibut, called chicken halibut, weigh 3¼–4½ pounds, and one will amply serve four. Larger fish are almost always sold as steaks or fillets. Go for steaks cut from the middle rather than from the thin tail end, and allow 6–7 ounces per serving. Fresh raw halibut can be used for *ceviche*, *sashimi* and *sushi*.

Cooking Chicken halibut can be baked, braised, poached or cooked *à la bonne femme*, with shallots, mushrooms and white wine. The flesh of large halibut can be dry, so should be braised or baked with wine or stock.

Alternatives Brill can be substituted for halibut in any recipe. Turbot or John Dory can also be used.

Flounder *(Platichthys flesus)*

Another large family of fish, species of flounder are found in many parts of the world, from Europe to New Zealand. The mottled grayish-brown skin has orange spots and is rough. Flounders can grow to 20 inches, but they usually measure only 10–12 inches.

Below: Flounder

They sometimes hybridize with plaice, which they resemble, having a similar soft texture and undistinguished flavor.

Habitat Flounders live close to the shore and are sometimes found in estuaries. They spend their days on the sea bed, not feeding, but become active at night.

Other names Many types of flounder are found in America, where they are variously known as summer, winter and sand flounders. Other varieties have such descriptive names as arrowtooth, black, greenback and yellowbelly. In France, they are called *flet*, in Italy, *passera pianuzza*, in Spain, *platija*.

Buying Like dabs, flounders must be extremely fresh. Apply the same criteria.

Cooking As for dabs, brill or plaice.

Megrim *(Lepidorhombus whiffiagonis)*

Small yellowish-gray translucent fish with large eyes and mouths, megrim seldom grow to more than 20 inches in length. They have dryish, rather bland flesh and are not considered worth eating.

Habitat Found mostly to the south of the English Channel.

Other names Megrim rejoices in the alternative names of whiff or sail-fluke. In France, it is called *cardine franche*, in Italy *rombo giallo* (although you are unlikely to find it on a restaurant menu in either country). In Spain, where it is quite popular, it is called *gallo*.

Buying Megrim are either sold whole or as fillets. The flesh can be a little dry. They need to be extremely fresh, so make sure you smell them before you buy. Allow a 12 ounces fish, or at least two fillets per serving.

Cooking Whole fish can be coated in batter or bread crumbs and deep-fried, or poached or baked. Their flesh can sometimes be rather dry, so use plenty of liquid. Fillets are best crumbed and deep-fried. Remove the coarse skin before frying or broiling.

Alternatives Lemon sole, plaice, dab or witch (Torbay sole).

Above: Megrim

Plaice *(Pleuronectes platessa)*

These distinctive-looking fish have smooth, dark grayish-brown skin with orange spots. The underside is pearly white. The eyes are on the right hand side; a ridge of bony knobs runs from behind them to the dorsal fin. Plaice can live for up to 50 years and weigh up to 15½ pounds, but the average weight is 14 ounces–2¼ pounds. They have soft, rather bland white flesh, which can sometimes lack flavor.

Habitat Plaice are found in the Atlantic and other northerly waters, and in the Mediterranean. They are bottom-feeding fish which, like flounder, are most active at night.

Other names In France, plaice are *plie* or *carrelet*, in Italy, *passera* or *pianuzza*, in Spain, *solla*.

Buying Plaice must be very fresh, or the flesh tends to take on the texture of cotton balls. These fish are available all year, whole or as fillets, but are best

Above: Plaice

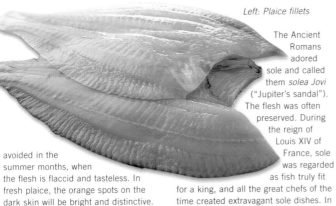

Left: Plaice fillets

avoided in the summer months, when the flesh is flaccid and tasteless. In fresh plaice, the orange spots on the dark skin will be bright and distinctive. Dark-skinned plaice fillets are cheaper than white-skinned, but there is no difference in flavor. There is a lot of wastage on plaice, so you should allow a whole 12–16-ounce fish per serving, or 6-ounce fillet.

Cooking Any sole or brill recipe is suitable for plaice. Deep-fried in batter, plaice is a classic fish and chip stand favorite. Whole fish or fillets can be coated in egg and bread crumbs and pan-fried. Steamed or poached plaice is highly digestible. For plaice *à la florentine*, bake a whole fish or white-skinned fillets in stock and white wine, lay it on a bed of lightly-cooked spinach, cover with a cheese sauce and broil until bubbling and browned.

Alternatives Flounder, dab, sole and brill can all be substituted for plaice.

Sole/Dover sole *(Solea solea)*

Arguably the finest fish of all, Dover sole have a firm, delicate flesh with a superb flavor. Their oval bodies are well proportioned, with grayish or lightish brown skin, sometimes spotted with black. The eyes are on the right-hand side. The nasal openings on the underside are small and widely separated, which distinguishes these sole from lesser varieties. Dover sole can weigh up to 6½ pounds, but the average weight is 7 ounces–1 pound, 6 ounces.

The Ancient Romans adored sole and called them *solea Jovi* ("Jupiter's sandal"). The flesh was often preserved. During the reign of Louis XIV of France, sole was regarded as fish truly fit for a king, and all the great chefs of the time created extravagant sole dishes. In the earlier part of the 20th century, it was the mainstay of English fish cooking.

Habitat Dover sole are found in the English Channel and the Atlantic and also in the Baltic, Mediterranean and North Seas. They come inshore to spawn in spring and summer. For the most part, they spend their days buried in the sand on the sea bed and hunt for food at night.

Other names Sand or partridge sole *(Pegusa lascaris)* are very similar in appearance to Dover sole and are sometimes sold as "Dovers," although they are smaller and inferior fish. Their distinguishing feature is a much larger nasal opening on the underside. Another species, known as "tongues," *(Dicologlossa cuneata)* are smaller still (only 3–4 inches in length). In France, these fish are sometimes sold as baby Dover sole or called *séteaux* (or *cétaux*) or *langues d'avocat* ("lawyers' tongues"). In French, Dover sole is *sole*, in Italian, *sogliola*, in Spanish, *lenguado*.

Buying Sole are at their best three days after being caught, so if you are sure that you are buying fish straight from the sea, keep them for a couple of days before cooking. The skin should be sticky and the underside very white. Nowadays, whole sole are graded by weight; an

Above: Dover sole (top) and lemon sole

Below: Turbot

Other names In America, lemon sole are known as yellowtail flounder. In France, they are *limande-sole*, in Italy *sogliola limanda*, in Spain, *mendo limón*.

Buying Lemon sole are available all year round and are sold whole or as fillets. They must be very fresh and should have a tang of the sea.

Cooking Lemon sole are best cooked simply; use them in any dab, plaice or Dover sole recipe.

Turbot *(Psetta maxima)*

What turbot lacks in looks, it makes up for in texture and taste. Highly prized since ancient times, it was called *le roi de carême* ("the king of Lent") in the Middle Ages. All the great chefs of the time created sumptuous recipes for turbot, marrying the fish with langoustines, truffles, lobster sauce and beef marrow.

Turbot have tiny heads and large, almost circular bodies with tough warty brown skin like a toad. Unusually, the white underside is sometimes pigmented with gray. They can grow to 40 inches in length and can weigh as much as 26½ pounds. The flesh is creamy white, with a firm, dense texture and a superb sweet flavor.

8-ounce fish will serve one person. If you want to serve two, buy a fish weighing at least 1½–1¾ pounds (which will yield four decent-size fillets, but could prove costly). It is best to buy a whole fish; if you ask the fishmonger to fillet it for you, keep the bones and trimmings to make fish stock (and help justify the cost).

Cooking There are umpteen recipes for sole, but a plain lightly-broiled fish served with a drizzle of melted butter and lemon juice is hard to beat. Skin both sides before cooking. Small sole can be coated in egg and bread crumbs and pan-fried or deep-fried; larger specimens can be poached, steamed or cooked in butter *à la meunière*. Fillets can be fried, poached in wine or served with an elaborate sauce, or given an Asian twist with soy sauce, lemongrass and ginger. They can be steamed and rolled up around a stuffing or used to line a mold, which is then filled with shellfish mousse.

Alternatives
Nothing tastes quite like Dover sole, but lemon sole, plaice and other flat fish can be cooked in the same way.

Lemon sole *(Microstomus kitt)*

Despite the name, lemon sole is related to dab, plaice and flounder. These fish are oval in shape, with the widest part well toward the head. They have smooth reddish brown skin with irregular marbling and a straight lateral line, very small heads and bulging eyes. The flesh is soft and white, similar to that of plaice but slightly superior. It is a good alternative to the more expensive Dover sole.

Habitat Lemon sole are found in the North Sea and Atlantic Ocean and around the coast of New Zealand. They lead largely stationary lives on the stony or rocky sea bed and vary enormously in size depending on local conditions.

Turbot kettle
In the days of affordable luxury, a whole huge turbot might be steamed in a magnificent diamond-shaped copper turbot kettle with handles on the points and a grid for lifting out the cooked fish.

Nowadays you will only find one of these kettles in the kitchen of a stately home or a fine restaurant. Modern turbot kettles are made of stainless steel or aluminum.

Above: Chicken turbot

Habitat Turbot live on the sea bottom in the Atlantic, Mediterranean and Black Seas, and have been introduced to New Zealand coastal waters. They can be farmed successfully, and this has improved both the quality and the size of the fish.
Other names The name is the same— *turbot*—in French, *rombo chiodato* (studded with nails) in Italian; *rodaballo* in Spanish. Small young turbot, weighing up to 4½ pounds, are called chicken turbot.
Buying Turbot is extremely expensive; a really large wild fish can cost several hundred dollars. Farmed fish are cheaper, but can be fatty.

people. There is a high percentage of wastage, so if your fishmonger fillets a whole turbot for you, ask for the bones and trimmings to make a superb stock.
Cooking It is neither practical nor economical to cook a whole turbot that weighs more than about 3–3½ pounds in a domestic kitchen. To cook a chicken turbot, broil it or poach in white wine and fish stock, using a large frying or roasting pan. Traditionally, turbot was poached in milk to

Below: Witch

keep the flesh pure white, then served with hollandaise sauce. Almost any cooking method is suitable for turbot, except perhaps deep-frying, which would be a waste; it is essential not to overcook it. Creamy sauces such as lobster, parsley and mushroom go well with plainly-cooked turbot. Chunks of poached turbot dressed with a piquant vinaigrette, make a superb salad.
Alternatives Nothing quite equals turbot, but brill, halibut, John Dory and fillets of sole make good substitutes.

Witch *(Glyptocephalus cynoglossus)*

This member of the sole family has an elongated body like a sole, with a straight lateral line on the rough, gray-brown skin. The flesh tastes rather bland, and resembles megrim.
Other names Also known as Torbay sole, witch flounder and pole flounder. In French, it is *plie grise*, in Italian *passera cinoglossa*, in Spanish, *mendo*.
Buying Witch are available all year round, usually only near the coast where they are caught—mostly off the southwest coast of England. They are only worth eating when very fresh.
Cooking Because these fish taste rather dull, it is important to season them well before cooking. Witch are best broiled, but any sole recipe is suitable.

Turbot should have creamy white flesh; do not buy fish with a blue tinge. It is available all year round, sold whole, as steaks and fillets. A chicken turbot weighing about 3–3½ pounds will feed four

MIGRATORY FISH

Certain species of fish undertake an astonishing annual mass migration from one area to another to spawn or feed. They follow a specific route, although how they know which route to take remains a mystery. Each year salmon and sea trout migrate from the sea to spawn in the fresh water of the river; having spawned, they return to the sea, and so the pattern continues. Eels, on the other hand, travel from rivers and lakes to spawn in sea water, entailing a journey of thousands of miles. The whole process is truly one of nature's miracles.

EELS *(Anguillidae)*

There are more than twenty members of the eel family. All are slim, snake-like fish with smooth slippery skin and spineless fins. Most have microscopic scales, but these are not visible to the naked eye. The *Anguillidae* family are freshwater fish, but other species, such as conger, moray and snake eels, are marine fish. Eels have fatty white flesh with a rich flavor and firm texture.

Eels have been a popular food since Roman times, and were highly prized in the Middle Ages. Their mysterious life cycle gave rise to all sorts of improbable myths; one popular belief was that they were loose horsehairs that came to life when they touched the water. The less fanciful but equally amazing truth was only discovered by a Danish scientist at the end of the 19th century.

Habitat Freshwater eels are born in the Sargasso Sea. Each female lays up to 20 million eggs and both she and her male partner die immediately after the eggs have been laid and fertilized. The eggs hatch into minuscule larvae, which are carried on the ocean currents to the coasts of Europe and America, then back to the rivers where their ancestors matured. This journey takes a year for American eels and between two and three years for European eels. No one has yet fathomed how the babies know which direction to take, since they have never seen "home." When the baby elvers enter the estuaries in huge

Above: Young eels

flotillas, they are tiny transparent creatures not more than 3¼ inches long. As they mature, their skin color changes to yellow, then to green and finally to silver. At this stage, the eels begin the long journey back to the Sargasso Sea, where they spawn and immediately die.

Varieties Tiny elvers are known as glass eels (*civelles* or *piballes* in French). Adult European eels (*Anguilla anguilla*) and American eels (*Anguilla rostrata*) are *anguille* in French, *anguilla* in Italian and *anguila* in Spanish. The Japanese eel (*Anguilla japonica*) and Australian eel (*Anguilla australis*) are both known as the shortfinned eel, while *Anguilla dieffenbachii* is the longfinned eel.

Buying You may find tiny elvers for sale in the spring—these are a great delicacy and are extremely expensive. One-third of a pound consists of up to two thousand tiny elvers.

Adult eels are at their plumpest and best in autumn when they have turned silver with almost black backs. Females weigh three times as much as males, so a female silver eel is highly prized.

Farmed eels are available all year round. Eels should be bought alive, as they go bad very quickly once dead. Ask the fishmonger to skin them for you and to chop them into manageable lengths.

Skinning an eel

You will probably prefer to ask your fishmonger to kill and skin your eel, but if this is not possible, this is how to do it yourself. Grip the eel in a cloth and bang its head sharply on a hard surface to kill it. Put a string noose around the base of the head and hang it firmly on a sturdy hook or door handle. Slit the skin all around the head just below the noose. Pull off the top of the skin, turn it back to make a "cuff," then grip with a cloth or two pairs of pliers and pull the skin down firmly toward the tail. Cut off the head and tail. Alternatively, kill the eel and chop it into sections, leaving the skin on. Broil the pieces, skin-up, turning frequently until the skin has puffed up on all sides. When cool enough to handle, peel off the skin.

Cooking Tiny elvers can be tossed in seasoned flour and deep-fried; soak them first in acidulated water to remove the mud. Eel is a versatile fish that can be fried and served with parsley sauce. It is good poached or braised in red wine. If you broil it, marinate it first, then wrap it in bacon to keep it moist. Eel is excellent in soups and casseroles, such as *matelote*, and the rich flesh marries well with robust Asian flavors. Two classic English eel recipes are jellied eels and eel pie with mashed potatoes and green "liquor." Eels are also delicious smoked.

Conger eel *(Conger conger)*

These marine eels can grow to an enormous size—sometimes up to 9 feet, although the average length is 2–5 feet. They are ferocious carnivores with long, thick scaleless bodies and very bony firm white flesh, which is quite good to eat.

Habitat Conger eels are found in temperate and tropical seas, living in rocky crevices and wrecks. Many live in deep water, but some prefer to lurk in shallow inshore waters, causing panic among unfortunate swimmers who inadvertently disturb a large specimen.

Other names In French conger eel is *congre*, in Italian *grongo*, and in Spanish, *congrio*.

Below: Conger eel steaks

Buying Conger has the merit of being cheap. It is available from early spring to autumn and is usually sold cut into chunks or steaks. Ask for a middle cut from near the head end; the tail end is extremely bony. If you are offered a whole conger, ask the fishmonger to fillet it and keep the head and bones for soup or stock.

Cooking Conger is best used for soups or hearty casseroles. Its dense flesh makes it good for terrines. Thick middle cuts can be roasted, poached or braised and served with a *salsa verde*.

Above: Fierce-looking conger eel, which is a ferocious carnivore.

Moray eel *(Muraena helena)*

These eels are even more fearsome than the conger eel. They grow to only about 6 feet, but are extremely vicious and will not hesitate to bite. Moray eels have long, flattened bodies and thick, greenish leathery skin with a pattern of light spots and no scales. The white flesh is rather tasteless and very bony.

Habitat Most species of moray eel are found in tropical and sub-tropical waters, but some occur in the Atlantic and Mediterranean. These eels typically anchor the tail end of their bodies in rock crevices and corals and wait with their mouths agape for catching prey that comes too close.

Buying Morays are mostly fished for sport and are seldom found in fishmongers. When they are available, they are sold in chunks.

Cooking Morays are really fit only for soup, and are often used in the traditional *bouillabaisse*. They can be cooked gently in cider, then the flesh removed from the bone and used in fish pies or fish cakes. The tail end is full of sharp bones. Avoid it, unless you are making stock.

Right: Atlantic salmon

THE SALMON FAMILY

Known as "the king of fish," salmon is probably the most important of all fish, prized by sportsmen and gastronomes alike. Various species are found throughout the world, but the finest by far is the Atlantic salmon. All salmon spawn in fresh water. Some species spend their lives in landlocked waters, but after two years, most salmon migrate upstream to the sea to feed before returning to spawn in the rivers where they were born. This arduous trek makes them sleek and muscular. Once they return to fresh water, they stop feeding, only starting again when they go back to the sea.

Salmon have suffered from over-fishing and environmental disturbance, and wild fish have become rare and expensive. Once, it was possible to land salmon weighing 44 pounds or more, but such magnificent fish have now disappeared. Fortunately, salmon can be farmed successfully, although early salmon farms produced fish with flabby, bland flesh, often riddled with sea lice, which attacked and further decimated the wild stocks. Lessons have been learned, and it is now possible to buy healthy, well-flavored farmed salmon.

Atlantic salmon *(Salmo salar)*

These magnificent fish have silvery-blue backs, silver sides and white bellies. In comparison to their large, powerful bodies, their heads are quite small. The heads and backs are marked with tiny black crosses. Salmon's fine fatty flesh is deep pink and firm with a superb, rich flavor.

Habitat Atlantic salmon are found in all the cold northern waters of Europe and America. They are spawned in rivers, then undertake the exhausting journey back to the sea, returning to the river to spawn in their turn. When young salmon, which are 4–8 inches long, first migrate to the sea, they are called smolts. After a year or two of voracious feeding, they reach a weight of

Below: Salmon steaks

2¼–4½ pounds and make their first spawning run; these young fish are called grilse. The males develop elongated hooked jaws; this is just to help them fight the strong currents, since they do not feed during the spawning run. Some fish may spawn only once or twice in their lifetimes, others up to four times.

Salmon were a popular food in the Middle Ages, when they were braised with spices, potted or salted, or made into pies and pâtés. Once they became rarer, they were regarded as a luxury and chefs vied to marry them with extravagant ingredients such as lobster, crayfish and cream. Only recently has salmon once again become affordable.

Other names The deep, cold lakes of Canada and North America are home to landlocked salmon; these are variously known as ouananiche, lake salmon and sebago. In French, salmon is *saumon*, in Italian *salmone*; in Spanish, *salmón*.

Buying Salmon are sold whole, as steaks, cutlets, fillets and large middle and tail cuts. The best (and most expensive) salmon are wild fish. Ethical fishmongers will tell you which are wild and which farmed and charge accordingly. Wild salmon are sleeker, with firmer, lustrous skin and deep pink flesh. They are available from spring to late summer. Late-spawning fish that return to the sea in autumn are known as kelts because they have not eaten for many months; kelts are thin and in poor condition and are not worth buying. Grilse—young salmon with an average weight of 3 pounds—are cheaper than large wild fish and will provide a generous meal for two. Scottish and Irish wild salmon are the finest of all; Atlantic salmon that comes from Greenland and Scandinavia is less highly regarded.

The quality of farmed salmon can be variable. The flesh should be firm and dark pink with creamy marbling and not too much fat, not flabby and pale or grayish. Salmon heads are surprisingly heavy, so if you buy whole salmon, allow about 12–14 ounces per serving. If buying steaks or cutlets you will only need about 7 ounces per person. If the fishmonger removes the head, keep it to make stock or soup.

Cooking There is almost no limit to the ways in which you can prepare and cook salmon. It can be eaten raw as a *salmon tartare*, *sashimi* or in *sushi*. It can be marinated in oil, lemon juice and herbs or salted and marinated to make *gravad lax*. It can be poached, pan-fried, seared, broiled, baked or braised, or enveloped in pastry as in *saumon en croûte* or *coulibiac*. Poached salmon is delicious hot or cold; a whole fish poached in *court-bouillon* makes a superb festive dish served with plain or green mayonnaise and dressed with cucumber. It is also excellent with a spicy salsa. Hot poached salmon cries out for hollandaise or rich seafood sauce or *beurre blanc*. If you do not have a fish kettle large enough for a whole salmon, wrap the fish in foil, moisten with white wine and herbs, then bake.

Salmon fillets can be thinly sliced and flash-fried, or sandwiched together with fish or shellfish mousse or vegetable purée and baked or braised. They are delicious made into fish cakes, kedgeree, pâté and mousse. Try them in butter flavored with mace, or as *rillettes*. Steaks can be cooked in red wine, poached, baked *en papillote* with white wine and herbs or Asian flavorings, broiled, pan-fried or grilled. Salmon is also delicious cold- or hot-smoked. It can be cured in salt and is one of the world's most popular canned fish.

Alternatives Sea trout and good quality brown or rainbow trout can be used instead of salmon.

Pacific salmon *(Onorhynchus)*

Five species of Pacific salmon are found around the Pacific coast from California to Alaska, and another is found in northern Japan. Even the largest, the Chinook or king salmon, is smaller and slimmer than its Atlantic counterpart. Other Pacific salmon include the sockeye or red salmon, chum or dog salmon and pink salmon. None is as fine as the Atlantic salmon, and all are frequently sold canned.

Sea trout *(Salmo trutta)*

Although they are closely related to the brown trout, sea trout differ from other species in that they migrate to the sea like salmon. They closely resemble salmon, but have smaller, less pointed heads and squarer tails. Sea trout seldom grow to more than 6½ pounds, which makes them more manageable for cooking. They have fine, dark pink flesh, which is beautifully succulent and has a delicate, mellow flavor.

Other names Sea trout are also known as salmon trout or sewin. In French, they are *truite de mer*, in Italian, *trota di mare*, and in Spanish, *trucha marina*.

Buying Sea trout are always wild, but they do not cost as much as wild salmon. They are sold whole; a 4½-pound fish will serve 4–6 people. They should be very bright and silvery with an almost golden sheen.

Cooking As for salmon.

Above: Sea trout

Exotic Fish

Thanks to modern transportation, unusual exotic fish from tropical seas all over the world are now available at European and North American markets. Warm water fish never have quite as good a flavor as those from colder climes, but they add variety to a fish diet and are often very beautiful to look at. Do not be alarmed by the prospect of cooking unfamiliar fish; they can be cooked in the same way as other species, and lend themselves to exotic flavorings, so you can experiment with new taste sensations.

Barracouta/Snoek *(Thyrsites atun)*

This long thin fish has smooth blue-gray skin with silver sides and belly, a flat dorsal fin running almost the length of the body and a series of spines near the tail. Barracouta can grow to 6½ feet long, but are generally 24–36 inches in length. The lower jaw protrudes and there is a single lateral line. The dryish flesh is dark, but whitens on cooking. Barracouta have long, irregular bones. The fish are often canned, which softens the bones and makes them more palatable.
Habitat Barracouta are widely distributed in temperate regions of the southern hemisphere.
Other names In Australia and New Zealand, the name barracouta is often shortened to "couta." In South Africa, these fish are always known as snoek.
Buying Barracouta are not sold fresh in the northern hemisphere, but you may find them canned or smoked.
Cooking Barracouta can be broiled, fried or baked. They are often pickled in vinegar and spices, and marry well with Asian flavors. Smoked barracouta is absolutely delicious.

Barracuda *(Sphyraena barracuda)*

These fearsome-looking game fish have long slender bodies, forked tails and sharp teeth capable of delivering a vicious bite. They strike fear into the hearts of divers, who often encounter these alarming fish on coral reefs.

Above: Barracuda

There are about twenty species of barracuda. The largest is the great barracuda, which has dark bars and scattered black blotches on its greenish skin. This fish can grow to over 3¼ feet in length. Other species include the yellowtail and the small Pacific and Mexican barracudas. All have meaty, rich, oily flesh, which has the reputation of being toxic. Play it safe by not eating raw fish; properly cooked, it is perfectly acceptable.
Habitat Barracuda are found in warm waters, mainly in the Pacific and Caribbean, but sometimes in warmer Atlantic seas. Young fish travel in schools, but older specimens are solitary. They are full of curiosity and will follow divers around the reefs, or even walkers along the shore, which gives them the probably undeserved reputation of being predatory.

Below: Barramundi

Other names In French, barracuda is known as *brochet de mer*, because it resembles pike. Italians call it *luccio marina*, while in Spain it is *espeton*.
Buying Small barracuda up to 6½ pounds are best. Ask the fishmonger to scale and fillet them. Larger fish are often sold already filleted. Barracuda is available all year round.
Cooking The rich flesh of barracuda lends itself well to Asian and exotic spices and flavorings. It is oily, so avoid cooking with butter, cream or too much oil. Small whole barracuda can be broiled, grilled or baked. Fillets and steaks can be curried or marinated in spices and broiled or baked.
Alternatives Any firm-fleshed oily fish, such as tuna or bonito.

Barramundi *(Lates calcifer)*

This beautiful giant perch has an elongated silver body with a dark gray back, a curved lateral line and a protruding lower jaw. Barramundi can grow to an enormous size, often

weighing more than 44 pounds; the record catch so far weighed 550 pounds. The best size for eating is about 22 pounds, although whole baby barramundi (or "barra") are popular in Australia. The chunky white flesh has a delicious, quite delicate flavor.

Habitat Barramundi are found in Indo-Pacific waters, from Japan to the East Indies. They often swim close to the shore and are sometimes found in estuaries and brackish water.

Other names Barramundi are sometimes known as giant perch.

Buying You are unlikely to find barramundi outside the Antipodes and Asia. Small fish are sold whole, and larger specimens are sold as steaks or fillets. Look for bright skin and white flesh.

Below: Flying fish

Cooking Whole fish can be broiled, grilled, braised, baked or fried. Cook fillets and steaks in the same way as bream, snapper, grouper and mullet.

Flying fish *(Exocoetidae)*

These are the fish that gave their name to the exocet missile, due to their habit of gliding amazing distances through the air at about 40 miles per hour. They are supported by a disproportion-ately large, highly-developed, wing-like, spineless pectoral fin. Flying fish begin their "flight" below the water, at high speed, bursting through the surface into the air. Only then do they expand their pectoral fins, which allow them to glide for about 30 seconds before dropping tail-first back into the water. Flying fish may look spectacular, but their flavor is less exciting than their appearance.

Habitat Various species of flying fish are found in the Caribbean, Pacific and warm Atlantic waters. They are attracted by bright lights and are sometimes lured by fishermen who hang a lamp over the side of the boat to encourage the fish to "fly" into their nets.

Other names The French call flying fish *exocet*, the Italians, *pesce volante*, the Spanish, *pez voador.*

Buying Flying fish are usually displayed whole so that customers can admire their exotic shape. Large fish are sometimes filleted. They do not travel well, so are best eaten near the shores where they are caught.

Cooking Whole fish or fillets can be dusted in seasoned flour and deep-fried, baked au gratin or braised with tomatoes, onions and zucchini.

Fugu fish—delicious or deadly
Ranking high amongst the ugliest fish in the world is the puffer or fugu fish, the eating of which constitutes a kind of Japanese roulette, since the internal organs (roe, liver, kidneys etc, depending on the species) contain a toxin five hundred times more deadly than cyanide. Nonetheless, fugu are regarded as a great gastronomic treat in Japan, where chefs train for many years to learn how to prepare this potentially deadly luxury. One slip of the knife and the lethal poison may be released into the flesh, resulting in instant death to the poor unfortunate who eats it.

Happily, it is now possible to farm fugu fish that are free from toxins, so the health of the gourmet population of Japan should be more secure in the future.

Left: Strawberry Grouper

Grouper (Epinephelus)

Groupers are members of the extensive sea bass family. Dozens of species of these carnivorous fish are found in all the warm seas of the world; all have firm white flesh and make good eating. They look extremely gloomy, with upturned protruding lower lips, giving them the appearance of permanently sulky teenagers. They have beautiful coloring, often with mottled skin. One of the largest is the giant grouper, which can weigh more than 660 pounds; even larger is the Queensland grouper, which can weigh over half a ton, and has been known to attack and terrorize divers. Smaller species include the red, black, yellowmouth and Malabar groupers.

Below: Mahi mahi steaks

Habitat Warm water groupers inhabit all warm seas, from Africa to the Caribbean. Most inhabit rocky shores, but many live on deepwater reefs.

Other names In Australia, grouper are called rock or reef cod. In France, *merou*; in Italy, *cernia*, in Spain, *mero*.

Varieties There are two basic types of grouper; red and black. Red groupers have reddish-brown skin with attractive yellowish markings. Black groupers range from pale gray to very dark.

Buying Grouper are available all year round. Fish weighing up to 11 pounds are sold whole, or may be filleted or cut into steaks. You are unlikely to find any distinction made between the different varieties of grouper. All taste very similar and are interchangeable.

Cooking Grouper can be cooked in all the same ways as sea bass. It goes well with spices and Caribbean flavorings.

Alternatives Sea bass and bream can be substituted for grouper.

Mahi mahi/Dolphinfish (Coryphaena hippurus)

These strange and beautiful fish have long, tapering streamlined bodies, with a high ridge of fin running down the body from the head to the forked, swallow-like tail. They are among the fastest swimmers, with a top speed of 50 miles per hour. Their skin changes color as they swim, from green and gold to silver and gray, with gold and blue spots. The average weight is about 5½ pounds, but fish have been known to grow to ten times that weight. The flesh is firm and white, with an excellent sweet flavor.

Habitat Mahi mahi are found in almost all the warm seas of the world. They are very inquisitive fish, and are easy to catch, since they are drawn to objects floating on the water.

Other names Mahi mahi is the Hawaiian name for these fish, which are also known as dorade or dolphinfish, though they are not related to dolphins. In French, they are *coryphene*, in Italian *lampuga* and in Spanish, *llampuga*.

Buying Available from spring through to autumn, mahi mahi is sold as steaks or fillets. Do not buy frozen fish, as it is completely lacking in flavor.

Cooking The Hawaiians eat mahi mahi raw, but it is best broiled or fried. It marries well with spicy flavors and is delicious served with a piquant salsa.

Alternatives Monkfish, John Dory, cod or any firm-fleshed fish can be substituted.

Above: Mahi mahi

Above and left: Parrot fish come in a wide variety of colors.

Alternatives Red snapper, bream and John Dory can all be used instead of parrot fish.

Pomfret *(Stromateus* spp*)*

These small silvery fish look like coins as seen through the eyes of Salvador Dali. Their almost circular bodies have very pointed dorsal and anal fins and curved forked tails, not unlike those of flat fish. Scales are almost absent, and the white flesh is fairly soft, with a mild flavor. Together with their close relation, the American butterfish, pomfret make good eating.

Parrot fish *(Scarus* spp*)*

Perfectly adapted to living in proximity to coral reefs, parrot fish have hard, parrot-like beaks (evolved from fused teeth) with which they nibble the coral. There are almost a hundred species of parrot fish. All have compact, brightly colored bodies and large scales. They come in an incredible variety of vibrant hues—green, blue, red and multi-colored. The largest is the rainbow parrot fish, which can grow up to 3½ feet, but most are only 12 inches long. Like many types of exotic fish, parrot fish look much better than they taste.

Habitat Parrot fish are found in tropical and sub-tropical seas. They live in large numbers around coral reefs, crushing the coral to reach the soft sea creatures inside, or scraping algae from surrounding rocks.

Other names In French, they are *perroquet,* in Italian, *pesce pappagallo,* in Spanish, *vieja.*

Buying Many supermarkets now stock parrot fish. Make sure that the colors are clear and bright; avoid fish that look faded. The average fish from the fish market

or fishmonger's slab will feed one person; a larger 1¾–2¼-pound fish will serve two. Larger fish are sometimes sold filleted, or can be filleted on request.

Cooking Parrot fish can be rather bland, so spice them up with tropical flavors, such as coconut milk, garlic, chili and lemongrass. Whole fish can be baked or braised; they look pretty and taste good served with a spicy salsa.

Above: Pomfret

Habitat A variety of pomfret is found in the Mediterranean, but the best-flavored fish come from the Indian and Pacific oceans. Butterfish are found off the northwest coast of America.

Buying Pomfret are available most of the year, either fresh or frozen. Small fish weighing about 14 ounces are sold whole and will feed one person. Fillets from small fish are rather thin, so it is best to choose a larger fish if possible and ask the fishmonger to fillet it.

Other names Pomfret from the northwest Atlantic are known as butterfish, and in America also go by the names of dollar fish, and pumpkinseed fish, due to their shape, which in Europe is likened to that of the chestnut. In France, they are called *castagnole du Pacifique*, in Italy *pesce castagna* and in Spain, *castagneta*.

Buying Pomfret are available most of the year. A small whole fish weighing about 14 ounces will feed one person. Fillets from small pomfret are rather thin, so if possible, buy a larger fish and ask the fishmonger to fillet it for you.

Cooking Whole pomfret can be broiled, fried, baked, poached or steamed. This fish goes well with spices and Asian flavors such as coconut, lemongrass and tamarind. Beloved of Indian chefs, pomfret makes excellent curries and is often cooked in a tandoor as tikka masala. Because the fillets are thin and the flesh is soft, pomfret fillets should be cooked only briefly.

Alternatives Trout can be used instead of pomfret, as can any flat fish.

Pompano (Alectis ciliaris) and Jack (Seriola)

This large family of fish comprises more than two hundred species. All are oily fish, similar to mackerel, but with a stronger flavor. The dark flesh becomes lighter on cooking. Jacks vary enormously in size and shape, but all have forked tails and virtually scaleless iridescent skin. Among the most common jacks and pompanos are the small leatherjacket, the larger yellowtail, the amberjack and crevalle jack. The best of all for culinary purposes is the Florida pompano, which has white, meaty flesh, while the oddest-looking is the lookdown, a small glum-looking fish with a flat, thin body and a high domed forehead.

Habitat Pompano and jacks are found in warm seas all over the world. They travel in schools, either around coral reefs or, like Florida pompano, close to the shore.

Other names In Australia and New Zealand, yellowtail jack are known as kingfish. In French, jack is *carangue*, in Italian, *carango*; in Spanish, *caballa*. Pompano is *palomine* in French, *leccia stella* in Italian and *palometa blanca* in Spanish.

Buying Pompano and jack are available all year round. They are usually sold whole, but may be filleted. Outside Florida, you are likely to find only farmed pompano, but this is of excellent quality.

Cooking Jack can be cooked in the same way as mackerel. The robust flesh lends itself to spicy Asian flavors such as chili, ginger and cilantro. Pompano and jack can be stuffed with bread crumbs or crab meat and baked, grilled or broiled. They can be cooked *en papillote*, steamed or poached in court-bouillon flavored with Asian ingredients such as soy sauce or Thai fish sauce and fresh ginger. The Japanese use the fillets raw as *sashimi*.

Below: Yellowtail jack or kingfish

Below: Yellowtail jack steaks

will feed two people, while a 4½-pound fish makes a good meal for four people.
Cooking Snapper is a versatile fish that can be baked, broiled, poached, steamed and pan-fried. It lends itself to exotic and Caribbean flavors, such as chili, mango and coconut.
Alternatives Gray mullet, bream, John Dory and sea bass can be substituted.

Tilapia *(Tilapia)*

Members of the enormous *Cichlids* family, tilapia have only one nostril on either side of their heads. The female is considerably smaller than the male, and scientists have now successfully bred tilapia that produce offspring that are almost exclusively male. Tilapia are freshwater fish, but can also live in salt water and are found in tropical seas. There are many varieties, with colors ranging from gray to bright red. Their flesh is white and moist, with a pleasant, sweet flavor.
Habitat Tilapia are found in warm tropical waters, both fresh and salt. They are farmed all over the world.
Other names In Egypt and Israel, tilapia are sometimes marketed as St. Peter's fish (not to be confused with John Dory).
Buying Tilapia are available all year round. Small fish are sold whole, but larger fish are filleted. A small whole fish (about 12 ounces) will serve one person; a 1½ pounds fish serves two.
Cooking Whole tilapia can be stuffed and baked, broiled or grilled. The bland flesh benefits from Chinese flavorings and spices. Fillets can be coated in egg and bread crumbs or batter and deep-fried.
Alternatives Carp, bream and zander can be used instead of tilapia.

Above: Red and emperor snappers

Snapper *(Lutjanidae)*

More than 250 species of snapper are found in warm seas throughout the world. The best-known and finest to eat is the American red snapper (*Lutjanus campechanus*), which is bright red all over, including the eyes and fins. The silk snapper is similar, but has a yellow tail. Other species include the pink snapper, or *opakapaka*, mutton snapper, which is usually olive green with vertical bars (but can change color), the yellowtail snapper and the African and Indo-Pacific. All have domed heads with large mouths and big eyes set high on the head. Most snappers weigh between 3¼ and 5½ pounds, although mutton snappers can weigh up to 22 pounds, while yellowtails average only 9 ounces. Snappers have firm, flaky well-flavored white flesh.
Habitat Red snapper come from deep waters around Florida and Central and South America. Other varieties are found in warm waters from the Atlantic to the Caribbean and Indo-Pacific.
Other names Snapper from the Indian Ocean and Arabian Sea are known as job or jobfish. In French, they are called *vivaneau*, in Italian, *lutianido*, in Spanish, *pargo*.
Buying Snapper are available all year round. Many fish sold as red snapper are a different, inferior species; true American red snapper have red eyes. A whole fish weighing about 2¼ pounds

Above: Tilapia

CARTILAGINOUS FISH

This unusual group of fish, called *chondrichthyes*, have no bones. Their skeletons are made entirely of cartilage. Many of these very ancient fish exist only as fossils, but about 500 species are still living, including edible fish such as shark, dogfish, ray and skate. Cartilaginous fish are thought to have evolved from freshwater fish that adapted to life in the sea. Unlike other fish, they have no swim bladders to control buoyancy, but in compensation have developed very large livers, whose high oil content helps the fish to float. This oil is often extracted and used for medicinal purposes.

Almost all cartilaginous fish have long snouts and mouths set well back on the underside of the head. They have several rows of teeth, arranged one behind the other. As one row wears away, they start to use the next. They have stiff fleshy fins and no scales, but their bodies are covered with backward-facing denticles, which give them a rough texture. Once these fish die, the urea they contain turns into ammonia, imparting an unpleasant smell and taste, so it is essential that they are eaten very fresh.

THE SHARK FAMILY

The shark family is a large one, ranging in size from the small dogfish to the huge basking shark, which can weigh up to 8,800 pounds, and whose liver alone weighs 1,100–1,540 pounds. Edible sharks include porbeagle, blue shark, mako, tope and dogfish. They are an unattractive bunch, with a bad reputation, but some of them make excellent eating. Shark flesh is firm and slightly sweet, with a meaty texture.
Buying Shark is sold as steaks, loin or fillets. The flesh has a faint smell of ammonia, which disappears during cooking if the shark is fresh. However, after a week or so, it becomes very pungent and nothing will get rid of it.
Cooking Shark meat is a match for robust and aromatic flavors and is excellent in curries. Steaks can be broiled, pan-fried or grilled. They can

be dry, so marinate them in olive oil and lemon juice, or cover them with pork back fat before cooking.

Steaks can also be braised or baked *au gratin* in a mornay sauce and glazed under the broiler. Shark makes a good addition to a fish soup or casserole and can be served cold in salads, dressed with a lemony mayonnaise. It is also ideal for home-smoking.
Alternatives Any meaty fish can be used instead of shark in recipes; try monkfish, swordfish and tuna.

Blue shark *(Prionace glauca)*

This migratory shark has exceedingly sharp teeth and is regarded as a man-eater. It has a sleek indigo-blue back, shading to bright blue on the sides and a snow white belly. It seldom grows to more than 13 feet in length. The very white flesh is not especially good, but the fins are used to make Asian shark's fin soup.
Other names In French, blue shark is *peau bleu*, in Italian, *verdesca*, in Spanish, *tintorera*.

Above: Shark loin can be bought in one piece or cut into steaks. The meat can be dry, so is best marinated.

Dogfish *(Scyliorhinus caniculus)*

Three species of these small members of the shark family are commonly eaten: the lesser spotted dogfish, the spur-dog or spiny dogfish *(Squalus acanthius)* and the larger, more portly nursehound *(Scylorhinus stellaris)*. The first has gray-brown skin with numerous brown spots, the second has gray skin, while the nursehound's skin is reddish. The thick rough skin is almost always removed before sale to disguise the shark-like appearance of these fish. Lesser spotted dogfish grow to about 32 inches, spur-dogs to 4 feet and nursehounds to 4 feet, 9 inches; the fish you find at the market are usually half that size. The flesh is white or pinkish with a firm texture and a good flavor. It is, of course, boneless.
Habitat Different varieties of dogfish are found in cool temperate waters all around the world.

Above: The lesser spotted dogfish, which is generally sold skinned but not filleted, is more commonly known as huss or even rock salmon.

Filleting dogfish

The central cartilage in dogfish is very easy to remove, and there are no small bones. It is usually sold as a whole skinned fish. To fillet it, use a sharp knife with a long blade to cut down through the flesh on either side of the cartilage, using the full length of the blade and keeping it as close to the cartilage as possible. The fillets will fall off.

Other names Dogfish are variously known as huss, flake, rigg and even rock salmon, although this last is a complete misnomer. Spur-dogs are also known as spinebacks or spiky dogs. In French, they are *petite* or *grande roussette*, depending on their size, or, misleadingly, *saumonette* (little salmon). In Italian they are *gattopardo* (leopard), in Spanish, *pata-roxa*.

Buying Dogfish are sold skinned, often as fillets. They are cheap and available all year round. They must be very fresh, so sniff before you buy to make sure they do not smell of ammonia.

Cooking Dogfish has good firm flesh and can be cooked in the same ways as monkfish and skate. It is excellent in

Shark à la Créole
Shark is a very popular fish in the Caribbean and the southern United States. This recipe reflects the mixture of the two cultures.

For 4 people you will need 4 shark steaks. First, make a marinade with the juice of 2 limes, 2 crushed garlic cloves, 2 seeded and chopped red chilies, salt and ground black pepper. Dilute the marinade with 1 tablespoon water and pour into a nonmetallic dish. Add the shark steaks, turn them over in the marinade so that they are coated, then cover and let marinate for several hours in a cool place or in the refrigerator.

When ready to cook, slice 2 red onions, 4 shallots and 4 tomatoes. Remove the seeds from 2 red or green fresh chilies and chop the chilies finely. Heat 2 tablespoons oil in a shallow saucepan, add the vegetables and chilies and brown. Drain the shark steaks and lay them on top of the vegetables. Cover and cook gently for about 20 minutes, until tender. Squeeze on the juice of a lime and garnish with chopped parsley. Serve with creole rice and black-eyed peas.

casseroles and chunky soups and is the perfect fish for fish and chips. This fish can also be broiled or grilled with a good coating of olive oil, or cooked and flaked and used in salads. Dogfish is delicious smoked.

Mako shark *(Isurus oxyrinchus)*

Part of the family of mackerel sharks, mako are swift surface swimmers with streamlined blue-gray bodies and bright white bellies, which grow to 6½–9¾ feet. They are found in subtropical and temperate–warm seas. Prized by game fishermen, they have a habit of raiding and damaging fishing nets and lines. Mako sharks have firm white flesh. They are usually sold as loins or fillets, but the flesh tends to be flavourless, so it will benefit from a robust marinade.

Other names In French, *taupe bleu*, in Italian, *squallo mako* or *ossirina*, in Spanish, *marrajo*.

Porbeagle *(Lamna nasus)*

These stocky, dark mole-gray sharks are closely related to the great white shark. They are surface swimmers, found in cold and temperate seas, but little is known about their growth or longevity. Porbeagles are widely regarded as the finest of all the sharks for eating, with firm, meaty pink flesh which is sometimes likened to veal. It is usually sold as loin or fillets.

Other names In French, porbeagle is known as *taupe* or *veau de mer*; in Italian it is *smeriglio*, in Spanish, *cailón*.

Cooking Porbeagle so closely resembles veal that it can be sliced into thin cutlets, dipped in egg and bread crumbs and then pan-fried like *scallopine alla milanese*. It can also be used in any other shark recipe.

Tope *(Galeorhinus galeus)*

These small gray sharks have pointed upward-tilting noses and serrated triangular teeth. Although edible, they do not taste particularly good and are best cut into chunks and used in mixed fish soups and casseroles.

Other names In French it is *milandre*, in Italian *cagnesca*, in Spanish, *cazón*.

Above: Porbeagle, which is sometimes sold at fishmongers and markets by its French name, taupe.

Below: Tope

Ray and Skate *(Raja)*

Although they are different members of the same family, it is virtually impossible to distinguish between ray and skate on the fishmonger's slab, since only the "wings" are sold, never the whole fish. These fish have large, kite-shaped bodies with long thin tails and enlarged flattened pectoral fins (the wings). The skin is grayish-brown and smooth, bumpy or even thorny, depending on the species. Ray and skate have short snouts and large mouths on the underside with sharp slashing teeth. They can be

Below: Skate wing

differentiated by the shape of the snout; in skate, this is pointed. The largest rays can grow to 8 feet and weigh up to 220 pounds.

The thornback ray (*Raja clavata*) is considered to have the best flavor, but gastronomically speaking, there is little to distinguish between the edible skates and rays. They have moist, meaty pinkish flesh with a fine texture and good flavor. Normally, only the wings are eaten, but the cheeks are regarded as a delicacy, as are the small medallions from the tail known as "skate knobs." The liver also makes good eating.

Habitat Rays and skates are found in cold and temperate waters. They are lazy bottom-living fish that hide on the sea bed waiting for their prey to pass by. They have evolved a way of breathing without opening their mouths. Most rays lay eggs, each enclosed in a four-horned black sac known as a "mermaid's purse."

Other names Among the edible rays and skates are the common skate (*raie* in French, *razza* in Italian; *raya* in Spanish), thornback ray or roker, rough skate and butterfly skate.

Buying Skate is available most of the year, but is best in autumn and winter. Smaller wings are sold whole; if you want a larger piece, ask for a middle cut. The wings are covered with a clear slime, which regenerates itself even after death. To test for freshness, gently rub off the slime and make sure that it reappears. Even fresh skate smells faintly of ammonia. This is normal, and the smell will disappear during cooking.

Cooking Before cooking skate, wash it well in cold water to eliminate the ammoniac smell. If the skin is still on, leave it and scrape it off after cooking. The classic skate dish is *raie au beurre noir* (with black butter). Poach the wings in water acidulated with a little vinegar or *court-bouillon* for about 10 minutes, then drain and sprinkle with capers. Brown some butter (do not let it burn and blacken) and pour it over the fish. Skate can also be broiled, deep-fried in batter or curried, and makes a delicious salad. Its gelatinous quality makes it good for soups and fish terrines and mousses.

Alternatives Fillets of brill, sole, John Dory or turbot can be used instead.

Skinning cooked skate

1 Lay the fish on a board. With a blunt knife, scrape off the skin from the thicker part toward the edge.

2 Discard the skin. Scrape the flesh off the cartilage in the same way.

DEEP SEA AND GAME FISH

Deep in the world's oceans live several varieties of fish that never come close to the shore. Many have odd shapes and vibrant colors, which consumers seldom see, since the fish are filleted on board the boats that travel far out to sea to trawl the fish. Most edible deep-sea fish are found around the coasts of New Zealand, South Africa and South America. The Caribbean is home to huge game fish, such as marlin, and avid fishermen will pay vast sums for a day's sport. Little is known about the life cycles of these monsters of the deep, but it is certain that, as stocks of the more common inshore fish decline, we will see more and more deep-sea fish appearing at fishmongers and supermarkets.

Antarctic sea bass *(Dissostichus eleginoides)*

Not a true sea bass, this fish is also known as toothfish, icefish and Chilean sea bass. It has only recently been fished commercially and little is known about it. The white flesh has a good texture and a pleasant flavor, but it does not compare to true sea bass.
Habitat Antarctic sea bass inhabits the southern oceans from Antarctica to the Falklands and Chile.
Buying Available all year round as fillets.

Below: Hoki fillets are very long and thin. The flesh is pinkish white, and has a flaky texture that is similar to hake when cooked.

Prod the flesh to make sure that it is firm. When buying Antarctic sea bass, make sure that you are not paying for real sea bass, which is much more expensive.
Cooking Cook Antarctic sea bass in the same way as cod or any round white fish. A well-flavored sauce will enhance the rather bland flavor.

Grenadier/Rattail *(family Macrouridae)*

There are about fifty species of these unusual-looking fish. They may be the most abundant of all fish, although since they live at depths of between 656 feet and 19,700 feet, it is hard to be sure. Grenadiers have large pointed heads that contain sensors to help them navigate in the dark ocean depths, and bodies that taper into filament-like tails (hence their other name). The swim bladders of grenadiers vibrate to produce a grunting sound. Despite their odd appearance, grenadiers are good to eat. The white flesh has a delicate, fairly moist texture.
Habitat Grenadiers are distributed throughout the world. They live at great depths, feeding on luminous creatures that they can detect even in the dark.
Buying Grenadier fillets are available all year round. You may find fresh fish, but in the northen hemisphere it is more common to find the fish frozen.
Cooking Fillets can be deep- or pan-fried or brushed with oil and broiled. They benefit from a creamy sauce and are good baked *au gratin*.
Alternatives Cod, hake, hoki or any fairly firm white fish can be used instead.

Hoki *(Macruronus novaezelandiae)*

Although hoki resemble grenadiers in appearance, they are actually related to hake and have the same white flesh and flaky texture. They have blue-green backs with silvery sides and bellies, and their tadpole-like bodies taper to a point. The average length of a hoki is 24–39 inches.
Habitat Hoki occur in large numbers around the coasts of Southern Australia and New Zealand; a similar species is found around South America. They live at depths of 1,640–2,626 feet.
Other names In Australia, hoki are inaccurately called blue grenadier. In New Zealand, they are sometimes called whiptail or blue hake.
Buying Hoki is available all year round, as fillets, loins and other cuts. It is frequently used to make fish fingers.
Cooking The delicate white flesh is suitable for most cooking methods, particularly frying. It can sometimes taste insipid, so is best served with a robust tomato-based sauce or a creamy sauce. Hoki can be cubed for kebabs and is an excellent fish for smoking.
Alternatives Hake, monkfish and huss can be substituted for hoki.

Marlin *(family Istiophoridae)*

More commonly fished for sport than for commerce, marlin are magnificent-looking billfish, renowned for their speed and endurance. The name billfish comes from their greatly elongated upper jaw, which forms a bill or spear. They have beautiful slender bodies with smooth iridescent skin and a high dorsal fin, which they fold down when speeding through the water.

There are several species of marlin, the best-known being blue, black (the largest marlin), white (the smallest) and striped. All can attain enormous weights of up to 660 pounds but the average size is 352–440 pounds. The deep pink flesh is high in fat and has a fairly firm texture with a disappointingly undistinguished flavor.
Habitat Marlin are found in warm seas throughout the world. Unusually for predators, they have no teeth, but use

their bill to stun schooling fish, and then to spear them.

Other names In French, marlin are *makaire*, in Italian *pesce lancia*, in Spanish *aguja*.

Buying Marlin are available in summer usually as loins and steaks. Try to buy cuts from smaller fish if possible. In the United States, marlin is almost always sold smoked rather than fresh.

Cooking Cook as swordfish, or cut into cubes and marinate to make ceviche.

Alternatives Swordfish, shark, and tuna can be used instead of marlin.

Sailfish *(Istiophorus* spp*)*

The sailfish resembles marlin, but looks even more spectacular. It has a beautiful streamlined body with a golden back spotted with blue, and a high, wavy blue dorsal fin which it unfurls like a sail to travel through the water at up to 60 miles per hour. Sailfish are tremendous fighters and will perform amazing aerial acrobatics when hooked.

Habitat As for marlin.

Other names Sailfish are *voilier* in French, *pesce vela* in Italian and *pez vela* in Spanish.

Buying Available in summer as loins and steaks. Buy cuts from smaller fish.

Cooking As for marlin.

Below: Marlin steaks

Orange roughy *(Hoplosthetus atlanticus)*

These ugly, but very delicious fish have orange bodies and fins and massive heads with conspicuous bony ridges and cavities. Although they are not large (the average weight is about 3–3½ pounds), they are always cleaned and filleted at sea. The pearly white flesh is similar in texture to that of cod, but has a sweet shellfish flavor.

Habitat For many years, orange roughy were believed to inhabit only Icelandic waters. In the 1970s, however, large numbers were found on the opposite side of the world in the deep waters around New Zealand and most of the world's stocks now come from there.

Other names In Australia roughy is sometimes known as sea perch. In French it is *hopostète orange*, in Italian *pesce specchio* (mirror fish); and in Spanish *reloj*.

Buying Orange roughy is available all year round, usually as fillets. If you are

Above: Orange roughy fillets

Above: Redfish

lucky enough to find fresh fish, you are in for a treat; most is frozen at sea.
Cooking Orange roughy holds together well when cooked, and its crab-like flavor marries well with other seafood. It can be used for soups and stews, and is good poached, pan-fried, roasted or steamed. It can also be dipped in batter or egg and bread crumbs and fried.
Alternatives Cod, haddock or any firm white fish can be substituted.

Redfish/Ocean perch *(Sebastes marinus)*

These beautifully-colored red fish were once the most important deep-sea fish, with vast catches being landed every year in northern fishing ports. As new varieties of fish have become widely available, however, their popularity has declined. Redfish can grow to about

11 pounds. The flesh is white and moist, with a sweet flavor.
Habitat Redfish inhabit the cold, deep waters of the Atlantic and Arctic Oceans. Related species *(Helicolenus* spp*)* are found in the Pacific.
Other names Redfish are known as ocean perch or Norway haddock. In French, they are *rascasse* (not to be confused with their relative, the scorpion fish), in Italian, *scorfano* (ditto), in Spanish, *gallineta nórdica.*
Buying Redfish are available all year round, sold whole or as steaks and fillets. A whole fish weighing 14 ounces–1 pound, 6 ounces will feed one person; a 2¼–3½ pounds fish will feed two.
Cooking Redfish is suited to all cooking methods. It marries well with Mediterranean flavors and spices, and is very good baked in a creamy sauce.
Alternatives Hake or cod can be used instead of redfish.

Blackened Redfish
A favorite recipe from New Orleans is blackened redfish, a spicy Creole dish. Fillets of redfish are thickly coated on both sides with a mixture of dried herbs and spices—crushed peppercorns and coriander seeds, cayenne pepper, paprika, dried thyme and oregano—then seared on both sides in a very hot frying pan or griddle until the spice crust is blackened and charred and the fish is cooked.
The contrast between the aromatic, crunchy crust and the tender white fish is delicious.
However, this fierce cooking method produces plenty of smoke, so remember to open the kitchen window.

Above: Swordfish

Stuffed Swordfish Rolls
Swordfish steaks can be pounded lightly between two sheets of plastic wrap and used to roll around a stuffing. Choose ½ inch thick steaks and pound them lightly using a meat mallet or rolling pin until they are only ¼ inch thick.

Make a stuffing using finely grated Parmesan cheese, bread crumbs and chopped fresh herbs bound together with an egg. Roll the swordfish steaks around the stuffing and secure with wooden toothpicks.

Place the swordfish rolls in a shallow, heavy pan and pour in about 1¼ cups well-flavored tomato sauce. Bring gently to a boil, then reduce the heat and simmer gently for about 30 minutes, turning once. Remove the swordfish rolls from the sauce and discard the toothpicks, then return to the sauce and serve hot.

Swordfish *(family Xiphiidae)*

Famous as both a culinary and game fish, swordfish differs from other billfish in having neither scales nor teeth. In all other respects, it is as dramatic and graceful to look at, as it powers through the water with only the curve of its dorsal fin visible above the surface. Its long

Below: Swordfish steaks

"sword" represents up to one-third of its total length and appears to be a powerful weapon, but no one is certain whether it is actually used to kill its prey, or merely to stun small fish. Swordfish can grow to an enormous size, sometimes weighing up to 1320 pounds. Their excellent white, meaty flesh is very low in fat and tends to dryness, so it needs careful cooking.
Habitat Swordfish are migratory fish that are widely distributed in warm, deep waters around the world. They occasionally migrate into northern European seas, but are more commonly found in the Mediterranean.

Frozen fish is also available, but is best avoided. Because swordfish is so meaty and substantial, 5–5½ ounces will provide an ample portion for one person. Try to buy fairly thick steaks, as thinner ones are more apt to dry out during cooking.
Cooking It is essential not to let swordfish dry out during cooking, so baste it frequently with olive oil when broiling or grilling and serve with a drizzle of extra virgin olive oil or some herb butter. Swordfish makes excellent kebabs and can withstand a robust or spicy sauce. It is delicious marinated in a mixture of olive oil and lemon juice that has been flavored with garlic and fresh herbs, then seared in a very hot ridged pan or grilled. Swordfish can also be braised with Mediterranean vegetables such as bell peppers, tomatoes and eggplant. Broiled or grilled.

Swordfish are particularly good served with a spicy, fresh tomato salsa made using chopped fresh cilantro.
Alternatives Shark and tuna can be used instead of swordfish.

Other names In French, swordfish is *espadon*, in Italian it is *pesce spada*, in Spanish, *pez espada*.
Buying Fresh swordfish is available all year round, usually sold as steaks.

MISCELLANEOUS FISH

Right: Garfish

A few fish do not slot neatly into any obvious category. The only connection between the fish described in this chapter is that they are all exceptionally good to eat. They are a strange-looking collection, from the hideously ugly monkfish to the slimline but no more beauteous John Dory and the needle-like garfish with its unappealing phosphorescent green bones. Monkfish and John Dory are seldom sold whole, so there is an enormous amount of wastage, which sadly makes these gastronomically excellent fish extremely expensive to buy.

Garfish/Needlefish *(family Belonidae)*

There are more than fifty species of needlefish. Most inhabit tropical seas, but some, like the garfish, are found in cooler waters, and one species is found only in fresh water. Many people find the needle-like appearance of the garfish off-putting, despite (or perhaps because of) their vibrant silver and blue-green coloring and their long spear-like beaks.

Needlefish can grow to 6½ feet, but are more commonly up to 32 inches in length. Their bones are a phosphorescent green even when cooked (this coloration is completely harmless), and even their flesh has a greenish tinge, although this whitens on cooking. Despite these physical disadvantages, garfish are good to eat, with firm flesh from which the backbone can easily be removed, since you can hardly miss it.
Habitat Garfish inhabit the Atlantic Ocean and Mediterranean Sea, sometimes straying into fresh water. Other needlefish are found in the

tropics, the Black Sea and the Pacific Ocean, while the Atlantic is also home to the saury, another sub-species. When they are frightened or being chased by predators, needlefish sometimes leap out of the water and launch themselves through the air like dangerous missiles. It has been known for fishermen to be severely injured by their needle-sharp beaks.
Other names The French for garfish is *aiguille* or *orphie*, the Italian is *aguglia*, and the Spanish is *aguja*. Saury is also known as skipper, because of its habit of skipping over the water to escape from predators. Saury and needlefish are *balaou* in French, *costardello* in Italian and *paparda* in Spanish.
Buying Garfish are sold whole. If you do not want to serve it that way, ask the fishmonger to clean the fish and cut it into 2-inch chunks.
Cooking To cook a whole garfish, wash it thoroughly inside and out, rub the cavity with lemon juice, then curl the fish around and stick the pointed beak into the tail end so that it forms a ring. Brush with a marinade of olive oil, lemon juice, garlic and chopped parsley and broil or grill for about 15 minutes, basting frequently.

Chunks of garfish or saury can be coated in seasoned flour and pan-fried in butter and oil, or stewed with onions and tomatoes. They are gelatinous fish, so make excellent soups and stews or fish couscous.

John Dory *(family Zeidae)*

These fish were sacred to Zeus, hence the Latin name of *Zeus faber*. The olive-brown bodies of these fish are so slim that they look almost like upright flat fish. Dories have extremely ugly faces and spiny dorsal fins from which long filaments trail. Their most distinguishing feature is a large black spot ringed with yellow right in the middle of their bodies; this is said to be the thumbprint of St. Peter. The story goes that the saint lifted a John Dory in the Sea of Galilee, leaving his thumb- and fingerprints on either side, and found in its mouth a gold coin, which he used to pay the unpopular tax collectors. This delightful fable is highly unlikely, since John Dory are not found in the Sea of Galilee, which is a freshwater lake. John Dory is also known as "St. Peter's fish." Despite its unattractive appearance, John Dory is one of the most delicious of all fish, with firm, succulent white flesh that is on a par with turbot and Dover sole.
Habitat Dories are found in the Atlantic; those from American coastal waters are known as American dories *(Zenopsis ocellata)*, while fish from the eastern Atlantic, from Britain and Norway to Africa, and from the Mediterranean are European dories *(Zeus faber)*. Another species, from the southern hemisphere *(Zeus japonica)*, inhabits the Indo-Pacific oceans.
Other names The name John Dory is said to come from the French *jaune doré* (golden yellow), which describes

the golden sheen of very fresh dories. Another theory is that it comes from the Italian *janitore* (janitor). However, most countries celebrate the St. Peter legend in describing the fish. The French call it *St. Pierre*; the Italians, *San Pietro*; the Spanish, *pez de San Pedro*.

Buying Thanks to its large head, almost two-thirds of a dory's weight is wastage, which makes it a very expensive fish. Small dories weighing 2¼–4½ pounds are sold whole; a 2¼ pounds fish will feed two people. For fillets,

buy the largest fish you can afford, otherwise the fillets will be too thin. Allow 5–7 ounces per serving.

Cooking Whole fish can be broiled, braised, baked, steamed or poached; boiled dory served with mayonnaise is a popular Venetian and Catalan dish. Its succulent flesh goes well with Mediterranean flavors such as tomatoes, fennel, red bell peppers, olives and saffron. Fillets can be cooked in the same way as sole, brill and turbot. They are superb served with a red wine, white wine or creamy sauce. Small fillets can be used in substantial fish soups such as bouillabaisse and *cacciucco*, or used in combination with other fish in a mixed grill or *panaché*.

Alternatives Brill, sole, halibut and turbot can be used instead of John Dory.

Bouillabaisse
One of the world's great classic dishes is the Provençal fish soup, bouillabaisse. More of a stew than a soup, this dish was originally cooked on the beach by fishermen, using those fish that had little market value, such as spiny scorpion fish. This fish is regarded as the most important ingredient in bouillabaisse. The soup can also contain monkfish, weaver fish, John Dory and other Mediterranean fish, plus small crabs and other shellfish, all cooked with tomatoes, potatoes and onions and flavored with garlic, olive oil and saffron. Sometimes, the cooking liquid is served on its own as soup, accompanied by garlicky croutons, with the fish served as a separate course. Nowadays, bouillabaisse is no longer an ad hoc fishermen's stew, but a very expensive treat served in top restaurants.

Left: John Dory

Monkfish/Anglerfish (Lophius piscatorius)

This extraordinarily ugly fish has an enormous head equipped with a "rod and lure" to catch its food, hence its alternative name of anglerfish. It has a huge mouth fringed with lethally sharp teeth and a dangling "rod" (actually the first spine of the dorsal fin) on its nose. Its comparatively small body has brown, scaleless skin. On the fishmonger's slab, the only part of a monkfish you are likely to see is the tail, since the head is almost always removed because of its extreme ugliness, disproportionate weight and the fact that only the cheeks are worth eating. The tail is quite another matter; it is one of the finest of all fish, with a superb firm texture and a delicious sweetness, much like lobster meat. In fact, some unscrupulous caterers have been known to pass off monkfish as lobster or scampi. The only bone the tail contains is the backbone, which makes it especially easy to prepare and pleasant to eat. Monkfish liver, if you can find it, is considered to be a great delicacy.

Habitat Monkfish are found in the Atlantic and Mediterranean. They lurk on the sea bottom dangling their "fishing rods" to lure passing fish. They are extremely predacious and will sometimes swim up to the surface to prey on small birds.

Varieties The best monkfish are *Lophius piscatorius* and the similar *L. budegassa*, which is highly prized in Spain.

American monkfish or goosefish *(L. americanus)* is considered inferior, while New Zealand monkfish *(Kathetostoma giganteum)* is truly a poor relation.

Other names Monkfish is also known as monk or angler. In French, it is *lotte* or *baudroie, crapaud* or *diable de mer* ("sea toad" or "devil"). In Italian, it is *coda di rospo* or *rana pescatrice* ("fishing frog"), in Spanish, *rape.*

Buying Monkfish is available all year, but is best in spring and summer before spawning. It is sold as whole tails, fillets or medallions. Generally speaking, the larger the tail,

Below: Monkfish

the better the quality; avoid thin, scraggy tails. For tails with the bone in, allow about 7 ounces per person. A 3¼-pound tail will serve four to six people. Ask the fishmonger to skin the tail and remove the membrane.

Cooking One of the best ways to cook a whole monkfish tail is to treat it like a leg of lamb; tie it up with string, stud with slivers of garlic and thyme or rosemary leaves, anoint with olive oil

and roast in a hot oven. This dish is known as *gigot de mer.* Monkfish can also be grilled, made into kebabs, pan-fried, poached and served cold with garlicky mayonnaise, or braised with Mediterranean vegetables or white wine, saffron and cream. It goes well with other seafood such as salmon, red mullet

and shellfish, and is classically used in bouillabaisse and other hearty fish soups. Thin fillets are delicious marinated in olive oil and lemon juice, then coated with flour and sautéed in butter.

Alternatives Nothing has quite the same nice firm texture as monkfish, but conger eel, John Dory, shark or cod can all be used instead.

Below: Monkfish cheeks, round nuggets of monkfish flesh, are sometimes available from specialist fishmongers.

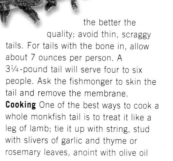

Preparing monkfish tails
The tails are the best part of the monkfish. Because of their high water content, fillets should be cooked with very little liquid. They are easy to prepare.

1 Grasp the thick end of the tail firmly with one hand and peel off the skin with the other, working from the thick to the thin end.

2 Carefully pull off the thin, dark or pinkish membrane.

3 Fillet the tail by cutting through the flesh on either side of the backbone with a sharp knife (there are no small bones). The bone can be used to make stock.

Opah *(Lampris regius)*

Variously called moonfish, sunfish or mariposa, this beautiful, slim, oval fish has a steel blue back shading into a rose pink belly, with silver spots all over its body. It has glorious red fins, jaws and tail, and, unusually, is the only member of its family. It is toothless and scaleless, and can grow to an enormous size. Some specimens weigh over 440 pounds and measure more than 6½ feet, though the average weight of those caught is about 44 pounds. The flesh is salmon pink, with a flavor similar to tuna.
Habitat Opah are found in warm waters throughout the world, but so far only

Above: Monkfish tail can be filleted and then roasted like a leg of lamb in a hot oven with olive oil, herbs and garlic.

solitary specimens have been caught, and little is known about them.
Other names In French, opah is *poisson lune*, in Italian, *lampride* or *pesce rè*, in Spanish, *luna real*.
Buying Should you be lucky enough to find opah on the fishmonger's slab, ask for it to be cut into steaks or fillets.
Cooking Treat opah in the same way as salmon or tuna, taking great care not to overcook, and serve with a creamy sauce or mayonnaise.
Alternatives Tuna, shark or salmon.

FRESHWATER FISH

Nothing can beat the taste of a freshwater fish, caught, cleaned and cooked within a couple of hours of being pulled from the lake or river, especially if you have caught it yourself. The flesh of freshwater fish is fragile, so generally speaking, they are only really good to eat when they are absolutely fresh. Sadly, many of the world's rivers and lakes are so polluted that supplies of good, untainted fish are low, so many of the freshwater fish we buy are farmed. A major problem with all freshwater fish is that they often contain numerous small, very fine bones, which many people find disconcerting. Apart from trout and zander, you will find few of the fish in this chapter on the fishmonger's slab; most are eaten by the anglers who catch them for sport. If you are lucky enough to be given a freshly caught fish, you will relish the experience.

Barbel *(Barbus)*

These "bearded" fish (the Latin name means "beard") live in fast-flowing rivers. They have brown backs, yellowish sides and white bellies. Barbel have rather tasteless flesh and are extremely bony, so they are not regarded as prime river fish. They are popular in the Loire and Burgundy regions of France, where they are typically poached or braised with a red wine sauce.

Cooking Barbel need strong flavors to enhance their intrinsic blandness. Small young fish can be grilled and served with a well-seasoned butter; larger fish (weighing up to 4–4½ pounds) are best used in a stew, such as *matelote*.

Bream *(Abramis brama)*

The appearance of bream, with their flat oval greenish-brown bodies covered with gold scales, is more attractive than their taste. The bony flesh is soft and bland, and can sometimes taste muddy, since bream live in the silt near the bottom of pools and slow-flowing rivers. Despite this, bream was an extremely popular fish in the Middle Ages. It was caught in fishponds around the country and used in numerous recipes.

Above: Carp rouge

Cooking Bream is best used in braised dishes and stews. It should be soaked in acidulated water for several hours before being cooked to eliminate the taste of silt.

Carp *(Cyprinus carpio)*

Carp are members of the minnow family, which contains more than 1,500 different species. They are among the hardiest of all fish and can live for hundreds of years. Although they can grow to over 77 pounds, most of the carp caught weigh only about 4½ pounds; anything larger than this and the keen angler is in seventh heaven. There are three main varieties of carp; the very scaly common carp; the scaleless leather carp, and the mirror carp,

Above: Bream

Right: Carp

Carp roe
This roe has a delicate texture and flavor and is much sought after in France, where it is poached and served in pastry shells or ramekins, or made into fritters, omelets and soufflés. A classic dish is *tourte de laitances* (soft roe or milt), which combines puréed carp and pike with soft carp roes; the mixture is then baked in a puff pastry tart.

---

which has only a few large irregularly spaced scales that can easily be removed with a fingernail. All carp are handsome fish with compact, meaty flesh that varies in taste according to how the fish is cooked.

Originally natives of Asia, carp were highly prized by Chinese emperors as ornamental pets and as food; they frequently featured on festive banquets. Travelers along the Silk Routes brought them to Europe, where they proliferated in unpolluted fresh water and became a staple food of Eastern European Jews who lived far from the sea, but could cultivate carp in ponds. The tongues were regarded as a delicacy. Carp are still immensely popular in Chinese cuisine; the lips are considered the finest part and they command high prices in restaurants.

Habitat In their natural state, carp like living in muddy and polluted waters, which they seem to prefer to clean streams and lakes. Nowadays, they are extensively farmed

in clean ponds. In the wild, they are considered the most difficult of all freshwater fish to catch; despite being toothless, they are powerful fighters, and can demolish fishing tackle.

Other names In French, carp is *carpe*, in Italian and Spanish, *carpa*.

Buying Most commercially available carp are farmed and weigh 2¼–4½ pounds. A 4½ pounds fish will amply serve four. Look for a plump fish, preferably containing roe or milt, which are considered a delicacy. You may find live carp for sale; if so, ask the fishmonger to prepare the fish, gutting it and removing the bitter gall bladder from the base of the throat. If you buy a common carp, ask the supplier to scale it for you.

Preparing If you have to scale carp yourself, pour boiling water over the fish to loosen the scales before scraping them off.

Cooking Carp is a very versatile fish, which can be delicious if prepared with interesting flavorings. It can be stuffed with fish mousse or forcemeat and baked, and is also excellent braised,

opened out and broiled or deep-fried, or poached in a sweet-and-sour sauce. A traditional German or Polish Christmas Eve dish is carp cooked in beer or white wine. It marries well with Asian flavors such as ginger, soy sauce and rice wine, and makes a good addition to fish stews and soups that have been well flavored with plenty of tomatoes and garlic.

Carp can be cooked *au bleu*, as described in the chapter on Buying and Preparing Fish, or stewed with red wine and mushrooms to make a *meurette*. A classic dish is *carpe à la Juive*, a sweet-and-sour cold dish made with whole or thickly-sliced carp braised with onions, garlic, vinegar, raisins and almonds. When cooked, the whole fish (or the sliced reformed into the original shape), is left to go cold in the sauce, which solidifies into a flavorful jelly.

Alternatives Catfish, perch and zander can be substituted for carp.

Catfish *(Ictalurus* spp*)*

These fish take their name from the long whiskery barbels that help them to locate their prey in the muddy waters where they live. There are dozens of species, ranging from tiny fish to gigantic specimens weighing several hundredweight. Catfish are extremely hardy and can live out of

Above: Catfish

water for a considerable time. These fish are found all over the world, but the best fish for eating are the American species known as bullheads, which have firm, meaty, rather fatty white flesh and very few bones.

Habitat Catfish are bottom-living fish that feed on live and dead prey. They inhabit muddy waters throughout the world and are successfully farmed in America and Canada.

Other names In French, catfish is *silure*, in Italian, *pesce gatto*, in Spanish, *siluro*.

Buying Catfish is sold skinned and usually filleted. Its chunky flesh is filling, so 6 ounces is ample for one person. Sniff the fish before you buy to make sure that it smells fresh and sweet. Avoid fillets from very large fish, which can be rather coarse.

Cooking The classic Southern cooking method for catfish is to coat it in cornmeal, deep-fry it and serve with tartare sauce. It can also be broiled or pan-fried in butter, baked, or cooked like eel, whose flesh it resembles. The tough skin must be removed before cooking. Catfish makes a good addition to fish soups and stews with hearty flavorings such as garlic and tomatoes, or Caribbean spices.

Alternatives Any trout or perch recipe is also suitable for catfish.

Char *(Salvelinus alpinus)*

These trout-like fish are members of the salmon family. They have attractive silvery-green sides dotted with pale spots, and rose-pink bellies.The white flesh is firm and succulent, with a delicate flavor. Sadly, these fish, which once inhabited cold lake waters in large numbers, are becoming increasingly rare in the wild. They can, however, be farmed successfully. The most common varieties are Arctic char, char, brook trout and lake trout. All can be distinguished from trout by their smaller scales and rounder bodies.

Habitat Arctic char are found in cold-water lakes in North America, Canada, Britain and Iceland. Other species inhabit the lakes of northern France and the Swiss Alps. Brook and lake trout (which are actually char) live in the

Potted Char

When char proliferated in the Lake District in England in the 18th and 19th centuries, potted char became a popular delicacy. It was often sold in white china pots that were decorated with painted fish.

1 To make potted char, flake some leftover cooked fish, removing all skin and bones.

3 Put the prepared fish into ramekins. Cover with plastic wrap and chill until the mixture is firm.

2 Weigh the boned fish. Melt an equal amount of butter in a saucepan. Flavor the butter with nutmeg or mace and salt and pepper. Pour the butter onto the flaked fish.

4 Seal with a thin layer of clarified butter and cover again; it will keep in the refrigerator for a week. Salmon, trout, whitefish and grayling can be prepared in the same way.

lakes of North America; Dolly Varden is found from Western North America to the Asian coast.

Other names Char is *omble chevalier* in French, *salmerino* in Italian, and *salvelino* in Spanish.

Buying You may be lucky enough to find wild char in summer and early autumn. Farmed Arctic char from Iceland and America are available all year round. Small fish are sold whole; larger char may be cut into steaks.

Cooking Char can be cooked in the same ways as trout and salmon trout. It can be poached, baked, braised, fried, broiled or grilled.

Grayling *(Thymallus arcticus)*

A relative of trout, grayling is an attractive silvery fish with a small mouth and a long, high dorsal fin spotted with gold. These small fish (rarely weighing more than 2½ pounds) have firm white flesh with a delicate trout-like flavor; they are said to smell of thyme when first caught, but their scent and flavor are fleeting, so they should be eaten within hours of being caught.

Habitat Grayling are found in lakes from Europe to North America and the northern coasts of Asia, but as these become more polluted, their numbers are declining.

Other names In France, grayling is called *ombre*, in Italy, *temolo*, in Spain, *salvelino* or *timalo*.

Cooking Grayling must be scaled before cooking. Pour boiling water over the fish and scrape off the scales with a blunt knife. These fish are excellent brushed with melted butter and broiled or pan-fried, preferably on the shore where they were caught. To enhance the faint aroma of thyme, put a few fresh thyme leaves inside the fish. Grayling can also be baked and potted like char.

Gudgeon *(Gobio gobio)*

Small fish with large heads and thick lips, gudgeon have delicious, delicate flesh. They live at the bottom of lakes and rivers all over Europe and, freshly caught and crisply fried, gudgeon were once a common sight in cafés on riverbanks in France.

Other names Gudgeon are *goujon* in French, a name that has come to have a much wider application. Nowadays, deep-fried strips of any white fish are known as *goujons*.

Cooking Gudgeon must be gutted and wiped clean before cooking. Coat them in flour or very light batter and deep-fry until very crisp and golden. Sprinkle with salt and serve with lemon wedges.

Roach *(Rutilis rutilis)*

These members of the minnow family have greenish-gray skin and golden eyes. They can weigh as much as 4–4½ pounds. Their white flesh is firm and has quite a good delicate flavor. Their greenish roe (which turns red on cooking) is excellent to eat. Roach are not the easiest fish to eat, because they contain so many bones. Use tweezers to remove as many bones as possible before cooking.

Habitat Roach inhabit sluggish waters in Europe and North America. Unusually for members of the minnow family, they are also sometimes found in brackish coastal waters.

Other names In French, roach is *gardon*, in Italian, *triotto*, in Spanish, *bermejuela*.

Cooking Small roach can be fried with other tiny fish. If you can cope with the bones, larger fish can be broiled or pan-fried, or baked in white wine.

Pike-Perch/Zander *(Stizostedion lucioperca)*

Zander (sometimes spelt sander) look like a cross between perch and pike, but have a much more delicate and appealing flavor than the latter. They have greenish-gray backs with dark bands, and hard, spiny dorsal fins and gills. Zander can grow quite large,

Above: Roach

sometimes weighing up to about 11 pounds, and fillets from fish this size are delicious and meaty. American pike-perch are known as walleye. Zander can be farmed successfully, and are cooked in the same way as perch.

Perch *(Perca fluviatilis)*

These beautiful fish have greenish-gold skins and coral fins. Their humped backs have a spiky dorsal fin, which makes them difficult to handle. Perch are highly prized for their firm, delicate white flesh and are considered to be one of the finest freshwater fish. They grow slowly and can reach a weight of 6½ pounds, but the average weight is only about 1¼ pounds.

Above: Zander

Habitat Perch are found in sluggish streams, ponds and lakes throughout Europe and North America, and as far north as Siberia.

Other names The American yellow perch is very similar to the common perch and is often simply called "perch." In French, perch is *perche*, in Italian, *pesce persico* ("Persian fish"), in Spanish, *perca*.

Cooking Unless perch are scaled the moment they are caught, this is a nearly impossible task. The only solution is to plunge the fish into boiling acidulated water for a few moments, then peel off the entire skin. Small perch can be pan-fried or deep-fried in oil. Fillets can be pan-fried and served with a buttery sauce such as hollandaise, béarnaise or *beurre blanc*. Larger fish can be baked, poached or broiled, or stuffed with seasoned bread crumbs and braised in wine.

Pike *(Esox lucius)*

Described by Isaac Walton in *The Compleat Angler* as the tyrants of fresh water, pike are indeed fearsome creatures, with their elongated upturned noses and jaws equipped with hundreds of sharp teeth. Pike can grow to an enormous size, sometimes up to 5 feet. The larger the fish, the better the sport for anglers, but fish this size are not good to eat, as the flesh is dry and tough; the best size for eating is 2¼–4½ pounds. Pike have soft white flesh that is full of lethally sharp bones. Despite this, they are highly regarded in France. During the spawning season, pike roes can become toxic, so they should never be eaten.

In the Middle Ages, pike were highly prized in France and were cultivated in the fish ponds of the Louvre for the delectation of the king. Monks also farmed the fish to enjoy on meatless days. The voracious appetites of these fish earned them the nickname *grands loups d'eau* (great water wolves).

Habitat Pike lurk in the streams and ponds of Eastern Europe, Britain and France. They are solitary, aggressive predators who like nothing better than to eat a duckling or water rat. Their close relations, muskellunge and pickerel, are found in the United States and Canada. Fish from fast-flowing streams taste better than those that are fished from ponds.

Other names The large American pike, muskellunge (a corruption of the French for "long mask," *masque allongé*) is also known as musky. In France, pike is called *brochet* (pickerel is *brocheton*), in Italy, *luccio (luccio giovane)*, in Spanish, *lucio (lucio joven)*.

Above: Pike are large, fearsome-looking freshwater fish.

Pike Quenelles

The most famous recipe involving pike is *quenelles de brochet*, featherlight oval fish dumplings poached in water or fish stock. To make enough for four people, you need 1 pound skinned pike fillets, 4 egg whites, 2 cups chilled heavy cream, salt, white pepper and nutmeg.

1 Purée the fish until smooth, adding the egg whites one at a time until completely amalgamated. Chill.

2 Whip the cream until stiff, then fold it into the fish mousse. Season and chill for at least an hour.

3 To cook, bring a pan of water or fish stock to a bare simmer. Shape the fish mousse into ovals using two tablespoons dipped in hot water and drop them into the trembling (not boiling) liquid, a few at a time.

4 Poach for about 10 minutes, until the quenelles are cooked through, but still creamy in the center. Lift the cooked quenelles out of the water with a perforated spoon and drain on paper towels.

5 The quenelles are delicious served with a creamy sauce. Alternatively, cover them with a rich béchamel and bake *au gratin*.

Buying Pike are at their best in autumn and early winter. The best fish to buy are small whole fish weighing 2½–4½ pounds, which will feed four to six people. Large pike are sold cut into steaks; these can be tough.

Cooking Scale pike before cooking. Pour on a little boiling water—not too much, as the natural coating on the fish keeps it tender. Whole fish can be stuffed and baked or braised. Small pike are good cooked *au bleu*, or poached in a *court-bouillon* and served with *beurre blanc*. Pike is also traditionally cooked *à la Juive*, like carp. Sorrel, horseradish and similar sharp-flavored ingredients make excellent accompaniments. Fillets and steaks are best marinated for several hours before cooking to offset any dryness. They can then be pan-fried, braised or baked with white wine and served with a creamy shellfish sauce. They can be made into mousses, terrines and fish cakes.

Shad *(Alosa)*

The largest member of the herring family, shad is a migratory fish that spawns in fresh water. It resembles a fat silvery-green herring and can weigh up to 11 pounds. The three main species of shad are the allis, thwaite and American. They resemble fat silvery-green herrings. Although the white flesh has a fine, rich flavor, it is full of fine bones, which make eating the fish rather difficult. The best part of the shad is the large-grained roe, which has the wonderfully crunchy texture of caviar and is said by some to have aphrodisiac qualities.

Habitat Allis and thwaite shad are caught in the Loire and Garonne rivers in France during the spawning season. American shad is found all along the US coast from Canada to Florida. In the 19th century, American shad were introduced to the Pacific and are now fished from Alaska to southern California. Pollution and overfishing for the highly-prized roe have decimated the numbers of shad in this region.

Other names In French, shad is *alose*, in Italian, *alosa*, in Spanish, *sábalo*.

Buying Shad are at their best in spring when they are full of roe. They are usually sold whole. A 3–3½-pound fish will amply serve four. Ask the fishmonger to clean and scale the fish and persuade him, if you can, to bone it for you. Make sure you keep the roe, which is also good to eat.

Cooking Once the fish is cooked, make a series of incisions about 4 inches apart along its length and pull out as many bones as possible with your fingers. Whole shad can be stuffed with fish mousse (whiting is traditionally used), spinach or sorrel and baked, or poached and served on a bed of sorrel with *beurre blanc*. Fillets and steaks are good broiled, deep-fried or pan-fried and served with tomato sauce; check for small bones before serving. Shad roes are delicious briefly poached, then creamed with butter, cooked finely chopped shallots, cream, egg yolks and lemon juice. Serve them on toast as a rich appetizer or savory, or use them to garnish a cooked shad.

Sturgeon *(family Acipenseridae)*

You have only to see a sturgeon to know that it is a "living fossil," part of a family of fish that were abundant in prehistoric times. The bodies of these long thin fish are armor-plated with several rows of bony scales that extend along their length. They have long, shovel-shaped snouts, with four whiskery barbels that are used for detecting food. Sturgeons are noted for their longevity, sometimes living more than 150 years, growing to a length of 29½ feet and weighing up to 3,080 pounds. There are about two dozen species of sturgeon, among them European, Beluga, Sevruga, Oscietra and the sterlet, which is found in Russian rivers. They have firm white flesh with a rich texture. Sturgeon can, however, be dry and somewhat indigestible. The fish is often sold smoked, but its real glory is its roe (caviar), the ultimate luxury food (see Dried and Salted Fish). In Russia, the bone marrow (*vésiga*) of the fish is dried and used in the classic recipe, *coulibiac*.

Habitat Sturgeon are migratory fish that live in the sea but swim into rivers to spawn. Once plentiful in European and American rivers, they are now found mainly in the rivers that feed the Black and Caspian Seas. Recently, they

Below: Sturgeon steaks

have been successfully farmed in France and California.

Other names In French, sturgeon is called *esturgeon*, in Italian it is *storione*, and in Spanish, *esturión*.

Buying Wild sturgeon is at its best in spring and early summer. Farmed fish is available all year round. It is sold as steaks or large cuts.

Cooking Sturgeon needs careful cooking to make it palatable, and should be marinated or barded with canned anchovy fillets to keep it moist. Its texture is similar to veal and it is often cooked in the same ways, as breaded fillets or braised steaks. It can be poached in white wine (or, for a touch of luxury, champagne), or baked in a creamy sauce with onions. In Russia, sturgeon is traditionally poached with vegetables and served hot with tomato sauce, or cold with a piquant garnish of

Above: Brown and rainbow trout

mushrooms, langoustines, horseradish, lemon, gherkins and olives. It can also be home-smoked very successfully.

Tench *(Tinca tinca)*

This fat-bodied relative of the minnow has a coppery-green body covered with small scales and a thick coating of slime. Tench are hardy, fighting fish, which make great sport for anglers. They live in sluggish streams and have a tendency to taste muddy, but they make a good addition to a fish stew. They can also be baked or fried, and should be served with a robustly flavored sauce to enliven the rather bland flesh. They must be scaled and thoroughly cleaned before cooking; scalding them with boiling water helps to remove the scales.

Trout *(family Salmonidae)*

The best-known of all freshwater fish, trout are popular with gourmets and fishermen alike. The two main species are brown trout *(salmo trutta)* and rainbow trout *(salmo gairdneri)*. Rainbow trout are probably the more familiar since they are extensively farmed and are available everywhere. They have silvery-green bodies with dark spots and a pinkish band along the sides. Wild fish have moist white flesh with a sweet flavor; farmed rainbow trout are often fed on a special diet to give the flesh a pink tinge, which is considered to be more appealing.

Brown trout come from cold mountain streams and lakes. They have coppery-brown skin dotted with red or orange and brown spots. Their flesh is a delicate pink and their flavor exquisite, but sadly they are seldom found at stores; to enjoy a fresh brown trout, you should befriend an angler.

Golden trout and coral trout are both farmed hybrid trout, with beautiful, vibrantly coloured skin. Their pinkish flesh is more like that of rainbow trout and tastes very similar.

Habitat Rainbow trout are native to America, but have been introduced to many other parts of the world. Brown trout are natives of Europe; they too have been introduced to America. Golden trout are not found naturally in the wild, but are increasingly farmed for their attractive coloration.

Other names In French, trout is *truite*, in Italian, *trota*, in Spanish, *trucha*.

Buying Trout are available all year round, usually farmed. Unlike many other fish, they are quite robust and freeze well, so frozen trout are perfectly acceptable. For fresh trout, look for a good coating of slime, bright clear eyes and red gills. Trout are almost always sold whole with the

*Left:
Coral trout*

head on. They are very inexpensive, and you should allow one fish per person, unless they are very large.

Cooking Trout are arguably the most versatile of all fish and can be cooked in myriad ways. They are easy to eat, as the flesh falls away from the bone once cooked. The best way to cook a freshly-caught trout is *à la meunière*; dust it with flour, fry in clarified butter until golden brown, and season with lemon juice and parsley. Live trout can be cooked *au bleu*. Other cooking methods include poaching in *court-bouillon*, baking, braising, frying, broiling and grilling. Trout marry well with many flavors, such as bacon, onions, garlic, mushrooms and truffles. In Normandy, they are often baked *en papillote* with apples, cider and cream. They are also excellent for home-smoking and make delicious mousses and terrines. A classic, if clichéd, recipe is trout with almonds (hazelnuts make good alternatives). If you find roes in your trout, these can be puréed, mixed with seasoned bread crumbs and used as a stuffing for the fish.

Alternatives Almost any freshwater fish can be used instead of trout.

Whitefish *(family Salmonidae)*

Members of the salmon family, whitefish are silvery white in color. They resemble trout, but have larger scales and smaller mouths. White fish live in cold, clear lochs and lakes in northern Europe and America. In Britain they are sometimes called vendace or powan. They have a pleasant texture and flavor, somewhere between trout and grayling, but not as fine as either.

Left: Golden trout are spectacular in appearance, with iridescent golden skin.

DRIED AND SALTED FISH

Since prehistoric times, the dehydrating effects of sun and wind have been used as a means of preserving fish almost indefinitely. Even today, in remote communities, long ropes strung with split and salted fish hung out to dry like washing are a common sight. Any fish can be dried in this way; before the days of frozen fish, fishermen would salt and dry whatever they had caught in their nets—cod, haddock, herring, mackerel and even freshwater fish such as eel, pike, salmon and sturgeon.

Dried/Salt cod and Stockfish

The most common commercially available dried fish is cod and its relatives (haddock, ling and pollack). When dried, these look—and feel—like old shoe leather, but once reconstituted in water, the flesh softens and tastes delicious when cooked. Depending on its country of origin, dried cod is known as *baccalà* (Italy), *bacalhau* (Portugal) and stockfish (Scandinavia, northern Europe, the Caribbean and Africa). Stock fish differs from other types of dried cod in that it is not salted before being dried. Whatever the type, dried cod must be soaked for many hours in fresh, cold water—sometimes for up to a couple of weeks—before it becomes palatable. Stockfish needs to be beaten with a rolling pin to tenderize it, and you may find you need a saw to cut it.

Above: Bombay duck

The world is divided between those who believe that the result is worth all this effort and those who detest salt cod in all its forms. The Portuguese boast that they have a different recipe for every day of the year. The Scandinavians and the northern Italians love salt cod, too, while the French pound it into a rich creamy mousse, *brandade de morue*, made with of olive oil and garlic.

Buying Depending on where you buy it, dried and salt cod may be split down the backbone or sold whole. Make sure you buy the best quality fish, or no

Below: Salt cod

amount of soaking will restore its original texture. Thick middle cuts are better than end cuts. Salt cod will keep for months if stored in a dry place.

Preparing Salt cod needs less soaking than stockfish, but it still needs to be left to soften in a bowl of cold water for at least 24 hours. The best way to reconstitute it is to leave the bowl under a running faucet; if this is not practical, change the water every 8–12 hours. Taste the fish before cooking to check that it is not excessively salty; if it is, continue to soak it.

Cooking Dried and salt cod can be poached or baked. Never cook it in boiling water, as it tends to toughen. It is a classic ingredient of Provençal *allioli*, a salad consisting of vegetables and hard-boiled eggs served with garlic mayonnaise. Olive oil complements it well. In Spain and Portugal, salt cod is often cooked with tomatoes, peppers, olives, onions and garlic. It marries well with potatoes and split peas, in a stew or on top of a mound of creamy mashed potatoes. It makes wonderful fish cakes, fritters and mousses.

Bombay duck

Why this dried form of a small transparent fish from the Indian sub-continent should be called Bombay duck, no one knows for sure; it is

Above: Mojama

Above: Shark's fin

Mojama

Popular in Spain, Sicily and other countries with an Arabic influence, *mojama*, *mosciame* or *missama* is made from fillets of tuna that are salted, then dried in the sun for about three weeks. It is eaten as a snack with a glass of chilled fino sherry, or served on slices of baguette that have been rubbed generously with garlic and drizzled with olive oil.

Below, clockwise from bottom left: sevruga, oscietra and beluga caviar

possibly a corruption of the Bombay name for the fish, *bommaloe macchli*. As soon as the fish is caught, it is filleted and hung on cane frames to dry. Bombay duck looks and tastes vaguely like pork crackling. It is served as an appetizer or used as a garnish for curries and rice dishes. Uncooked Bombay duck has an unpleasantly pungent smell that fades a little when it is broiled, but is intensified when it is deep-fried. When broiling Bombay duck, keep the heat low. It is ready when it is crisp and curls at the edges. When cold, serve with drinks or crumble over curries or rice.

Shark's fin

Dried shark's fin is highly prized in China, where it is served at banquets, either braised or as the central ingredient in an extremely expensive soup. The fins from the many species of sharks that inhabit the Indo-Pacific oceans are sun-dried and preserved in lime. In its dried state, shark's fin looks like a very bushy beard, but after long soaking it reconstitutes into a gelatinous, viscous mass with a texture resembling calf's foot jelly. It is highly nutritious and is eaten as a tonic.

SALTED FISH ROE

The best-known and most expensive salted fish roe is caviar, the eggs of the sturgeon. Other salted roes include gray mullet, cod, lumpfish and salmon. In Sweden, bleak roe is compressed into a form of caviar paste called *løjrom* or *kaviar*, which has a pretty orangey-pink color. It tastes rather sweet, and is definitely an acquired taste.

Caviar

Made from sturgeon roe lightly cured with salt and borax, caviar is the most expensive luxury food in the world. It has a unique texture, the tiny eggs bursting on the roof of the mouth to release a salty liquid with an elusive, incomparable flavor. The three main types of caviar take their names from the species of sturgeon from which the eggs come. The rarest and most expensive is beluga, which comes from the largest fish; one beluga can contain over 110 pounds of roe. The dark gray eggs are quite large and well separated. Oscietra is golden brown, with smaller grains and an oily texture, which many prefer to beluga. Sevruga is the cheapest caviar. It comes from the smallest and most prolific fish and has small pale greenish-gray grains with a markedly salty flavor. Arguably the best caviar of all comes from Iran; the finest is marketed as "Imperial caviar" and each tin contains only the eggs from a single fish. The best caviar is "harvested" from fish that are just about to spawn; the eggs are very pale and full of flavor.

Each type of caviar is graded. The finest, malassol, is slightly salted. Second grade caviar is saltier and may be made from a mixture of roes. Inferior quality sevruga roe is pressed into a solid mass (pressed caviar), which squashes the eggs. It has a strong, salty taste and can be oily. It is fine for cooking, however, and has the advantage of being cheaper. The best caviar is always fresh; pasteurization will ensure that it keeps longer, but the quality will be compromised.

Despite its high price, caviar is so sought-after that the world's population of sturgeon is endangered almost to the point of extinction, due to over-fishing, poaching and pollution. Sturgeon were once common in European rivers, but are now found almost exclusively in the Caspian Sea. Recently, however, the fish have been farmed successfully in France, so there may be some hope for the future of caviar.

Buying Never buy caviar that seems suspiciously cheap; it may not have been cured properly, or may have been made with damaged eggs. There is a huge illicit trade in second-rate caviar, which can taste unacceptably oily or salty. At worst, it might even poison you. You get what you pay for, so buy the best you can afford from a reputable dealer. Caviar should be kept in the refrigerator at 32–37°F; any warmer and it will become too oily. Once you have opened a can or jar of caviar, eat the contents within a week.

Above: Black and red lumpfish roe

Serving Caviar should be served chilled, on a bed of ice. Never serve or eat it with a silver spoon, as this will react with the caviar and give it a metallic taste. A proper caviar spoon is made of bone, but a plastic spoon would do in a pinch. Traditionally, caviar is served with *blinis* and sour cream. Chopped hard-boiled egg and onions are also good accompaniments. It is also delicious served with

toast and unsalted butter. Some people believe that a squeeze of lemon enhances the flavor, others think it spoils the taste. Allow about 1 ounce caviar per person as a first course. Or use a few grains to garnish seafood or egg dishes.

Above: Gray mullet roe or bottarga

Right: Trout caviar

Far right: Salmon caviar, which is also known as keta.

Lumpfish roe

Sometimes known as "mock" or Danish caviar, this is the roe of the arctic lumpfish, which is as unpleasant as its name. The tiny eggs are dyed black or orange-red and look pretty as a garnish for canapés. They can be eaten with sour cream and blinis, but bear no resemblance to real caviar. Lumpfish roe is sold in glass jars.

Gray mullet roe/Bottarga/Tarama

Dried gray mullet roe is regarded as a great delicacy and is very nutritious. The orange roe is salted, then dried and pressed. It is usually packed in a sausage shape inside a thin skin, which should be removed before the roe is used. Wrapped in plastic wrap, it will keep for several months. Gray mullet roe is the traditional ingredient of taramasalata, although smoked cod's roe is often used instead. In Mediterranean countries it is also known as bottarga or *poutargue*.

Salmon caviar/Keta

This is made from vibrant orange-pink salmon roe. The eggs are much larger than sturgeon caviar and have a pleasant, mild flavor and an excellent texture. They make a very attractive garnish for fish pâtés and mousses, or can be eaten like caviar with sour cream and blinis. A good squeeze of lemon enhances the flavor. The name *keta* comes from the Russian for chum salmon. Salmon caviar is sold in jars. Trout caviar is also available.

PICKLED FISH

Pickling in vinegar or brine is another effective way of preserving fish. It is particularly well suited to oily fish such as herrings and eels.

Baltic/Bismarck herring

The herrings are split like kippers and marinated in white wine vinegar and spices. The fillets are layered with onion rings and carrot rounds for 24 hours. These are delicious with sour cream.

Maatjes herring

Fat young female herrings (the name means "maiden" or "virgin" in Dutch) are lightly cured in salt, sugar, spices and saltpeter, which turns the flesh

Below: Maatjes herring

Above: Baltic or bismarck herring

brownish-pink. In Holland and Belgium they are eaten with chopped raw onion. The Scandinavian equivalent is *matjes*. These have a stronger flavor and are generally eaten with sour cream and chopped hard-boiled egg.

Pickled herring

Herring fillets are marinated in vinegar and spices, then coated in a sour cream sauce.

Soused herring and Bratheringe

These marinated herrings are simple to prepare at home. In the German version, *bratheringe*, herring fillets are lightly floured and fried until golden, then steeped in a boiled marinade of vinegar, pickling spice and herbs. Soused herring are not fried before being marinated.

Below: Pickled herring

Rollmop Herrings

Like *ceviche*, rollmops are not cooked by heat, but by the action of vinegar. For four servings, halve 8 herring fillets lengthwise and soak them for several hours in heavily-salted water. Make a marinade by mixing about 2½ cups vinegar with 2 bay leaves, ½ teaspoon white peppercorns, 1 tablespoon pickling spice and 1 sliced sweet onion in a saucepan. Bring to a boil, then let sit until cold. Drain and dry the herring fillets. Slice a second sweet onion finely. Roll each herring fillet around a little sliced onion and some of the peppercorns and spices. Secure with a toothpick and pack tightly into a preserving jar. Pour in the marinade and let sit for at least five days before eating.

Below: Rollmop herrings

Rollmops

These consist of herring fillets rolled up, skin-side out, around whole peppercorns and pickling spice, and secured with wooden toothpicks. The rolls are marinated in white wine vinegar with onion slices and, sometimes, gherkins. Serve rollmops with rye bread and butter, or a cucumber salad dressed with a sour cream and dill sauce.

Gravad lax/Gravlax

A wonderfully succulent Swedish specialty, *gravad lax* has achieved great popularity. It is fresh raw salmon fillet cured with dill, sugar, salt and coarse peppercorns. *Gravad lax* is widely available, often sold with dill-flavored mustard sauce, which makes the perfect accompaniment.

Jellied eels

Market stalls in Britain selling this traditional Cockney dish are becoming increasingly rare, but jellied eels are available frozen and in cans. Jellied eels are made by boiling pieces of eel in a

Below: Gravad lax

Below: Jellied eels

marinade of white wine vinegar and herbs, then leaving them in the liquid with chopped parsley until the mixture sets to a light jelly. Serve with thick slices of bread and butter.

Home-cured Gravad Lax

Although almost every supermarket sells ready-cured *gravad lax*, it is very easy to prepare at home. For eight people, you will need 2¼–2½ pounds absolutely fresh middle-cut salmon, boned and cut lengthwise into two fillets. For the curing mix, combine 2 tablespoons coarse sea salt, 2 tablespoons sugar, 1–2 tablespoons coarsely crushed peppercorns (black or white) and a good handful of fresh dill, chopped. Lay one salmon fillet skin-side down in a nonmetallic dish. Cover with a generous layer of the curing mix. Lay the second fillet on top, skin-side up, and sprinkle on the remaining curing mix. Cover with plastic wrap. Place a wooden board slightly larger than the fish on top of the salmon and weight down with heavy cans or weights. Set aside in the refrigerator for at least 72 hours, turning the salmon every 12 hours and basting it with the juices that have oozed out. To serve, slice the *gravad lax* on the diagonal, a little thicker than you would for smoked salmon. Serve with a sweet mustard and dill sauce.

CANNED FISH

This is a very useful staple ingredient. While it never has the subtle texture and flavor of fresh fish, canned fish can be excellent in its own right and is invaluable for salads and sandwiches.

Anchovies

Fillets of this fish are canned in oil (olive oil is best) in small oblong cans or bottled in jars. The salty fillets are a staple ingredient of *salade niçoise* and *tapenade* (olive and anchovy paste), and are used as a topping for pizzas and *crostini*. They can be mashed into butter as a topping for broiled fish, or chopped and mixed into tomato sauces. Anchovies enhance the flavor of many non-fish dishes (roast lamb, for example) without making them taste fishy. Once opened, anchovies perish quickly, so try to use the whole can or jar at once. Any leftovers should be submerged in oil and kept for only a day or two. As an alternative to canned anchovies, try salted anchovies, which are packed in barrels with salt and cured for several months. Rinse well before using.

Pilchards

These fish are large, older sardines. They lack the subtle flavor of their younger siblings, so are usually canned in tomato sauce.

Salmon

Canned salmon is quite different in flavor and texture from fresh fish, but is useful to have on hand. It is richer in calcium than fresh salmon, because

the bones are softened during the canning process and can easily be eaten. Canned salmon was once the mainstay of sandwiches, salads, fish cakes and fish pies, but it has been overshadowed by inexpensive farmed fresh salmon. Canned salmon is available in several grades, from the cheapest pink chum salmon to the best-quality wild red Alaskan fish, which has a better flavor and texture. Canned salmon is good for making mousses, soufflés and fish cakes.

Sardines

These were the first fish to be canned; in 1834, a canning factory opened in Brittany to process the sardines that abounded on the Breton coast. For years, tiny Breton sardines were the best, but these fish have all but disappeared and most sardines canned in France now come from North Africa. Large numbers of sardines are also canned in Spain and Portugal. The finest sardines are fried in olive oil before canning, a time-consuming process that makes them expensive. Most sardines are beheaded and gutted before being packed raw, complete with backbones, in peanut or olive oil. Inferior or damaged fish are packed in tomato or mustard sauce. Sardines in

Above: Canned tuna

Above: Canned anchovies

Left: Sardines, which were the first fish to be canned.

olive oil are the best; the more expensive varieties are left to age for at least a year before being sold to soften the bones and intensify the flavor. The best way to enjoy canned sardines is to serve them whole on toast. They can also be mashed with lemon juice and cayenne pepper to make a pâté, stuffed into hard-boiled eggs or made into sandwiches.

Tuna

In recent years, canned tuna has received bad press because dolphins were often caught in the tuna nets and slaughtered unnecessarily. Nowadays, tuna canners have become more ecologically aware and most tuna is line-caught. The best canned tuna is the pale albacore, which is usually canned in one solid piece. Cheaper varieties such as skipjack and yellowfin are often sold as chunks or flaky broken pieces. Tuna comes packed in olive oil, vegetable oil or water, which is healthier and lighter.

Canned tuna is a versatile ingredient that can be served with pasta, used in sandwiches and salads and made into a pâté or fish loaf. It is used in the classic Italian dish *vitello tonnato*, which comprises loin of veal coated in a thick tuna-flavored mayonnaise.

SMOKED FISH

Another ancient and traditional way of preserving fish is smoking. Today it is used less for preserving and more for imparting a unique flavor. There are two methods of smoking fish, cold and hot smoking, which give very different results. For both methods, the fish must first be salted in dry salt or brine. They are then smoked over different types of wood, which impart its distinctive flavor to the fish. Every smokery produces fish with a different texture and taste.

COLD-SMOKED FISH

A high degree of skill is needed when cold smoking to get the flavor and texture just right. The process is done at a temperature of about 86–95°F, which cures but does not cook the fish. Some cold-smoked fish such as smoked salmon, halibut and trout are eaten raw; others, such as kippers and haddock, are usually cooked, although they can be marinated and eaten just as they are.

Smoked salmon

The best-loved of all smoked fish, smoked salmon is made by brining the fish, then dry curing it in sugar with flavorings such as molasses or whiskey, and smoking it over wood chips (usually oak). Different wood chips give different flavors; some Scottish and Irish salmon is smoked over a fire made from old whiskey barrels, which impart the flavor of the spirit. Depending on the strength of the cure, the type of wood used and the smoking time, smoked salmon can

Below: Smoked halibut

Above: Smoked salmon

vary in color from very pale pink to deep brownish-red. The best smoked salmon has a fairly mild flavor and a moist, succulent texture.

Buying Smoked salmon is usually sold ready-sliced, with the slices separated by sheets of transparent paper. Whole sides are sliced and the slices are reassembled to restore the original shape of the fillet. Avoid buying sliced fish that is not layered with paper, as the slices stick together. The thinner the salmon is sliced the better; thickly-sliced fish can be coarse. Whole sides are sometimes sold unsliced; these are cheaper, but you need an extremely sharp flexible knife and a degree of skill to slice the fish yourself. The most expensive smoked salmon is made from wild fish, but good-quality farmed fish give excellent results, and it can be difficult to distinguish between the two.

Freshly-sliced smoked salmon is best, but vacuum packs are a better value and perfectly acceptable when purchased from a reliable supplier. Frozen smoked salmon is also available and can be used in a pinch. Smoked salmon trimmings are much cheaper than slices and are perfect for making mousses, pâtés and omelets. Lox is a popular heavily-cured salmon with a deep reddish-gold color.

Serving Top-quality smoked salmon should be eaten just as it is, served with thinly sliced brown bread and butter. Cheaper salmon can be served in traditional Jewish style, with cream cheese as a topping for bagels (add some thin rings of raw onion, if desired), or in sandwiches. Smoked salmon makes a delicious salad. Scraps can be stirred into omelets, quiches or flans, mixed into pasta, puréed to make mousses, or mashed into hard-boiled egg yolks and piled back into the whites. If you are slicing smoked salmon yourself, slice thinly across the grain, working from head to tail. You will need a very sharp, flexible knife with a long blade.

Cold-smoked trout

A cheaper alternative to smoked salmon is cold-smoked trout, which looks like salmon, but has a more delicate flavor. It can be eaten in the same way as smoked salmon, with thinly sliced brown bread and butter.

Smoked halibut

Sold thinly sliced like smoked salmon, smoked halibut has translucent white flesh and a very delicate flavor. It makes an excellent addition to a plate of assorted smoked fish, or can be used like smoked haddock. The flavor can be enhanced with a mild, creamy horseradish sauce.

Above: Finnan haddock

can be used in any smoked haddock recipe, but must be boned and skinned after cooking. It is delicious served topped with a poached egg.

Glasgow pales

Similar to finnan haddock, Glasgow pales are lightly brined and smoked, resulting in a very delicate flavor.
Buying If possible, avoid buying dyed smoked haddock whose only dubious merit is that it adds color to fish pies and similar dishes. Undyed smoked fillets are fine for such dishes, but for plain broiled or poached haddock, you cannot beat finnan haddock.
Cooking Smoked haddock is succulent and delicious. It is usually eaten hot, but fillets can be thinly sliced and marinated (a splash of whiskey works wonders) and eaten raw as an appetizer. Smoked haddock can be broiled like kippers or poached in milk or water. Serve it with butter or topped with a poached egg, or *à la florentine* on a bed of creamed spinach. A classic Scottish dish is ham 'n' haddie, in which finnan haddock is fried in ham fat and topped with slices of fried ham.

Smoked haddock is used in another Scottish dish, cullen skink, a substantial chowder. It makes excellent mousse or pâté, and also features in kedgeree and omelet Arnold Bennett, a sumptuous omelet oozing with cheese, cream and smoked haddock.

Smoked sturgeon

This smoked fish has pale pinkish flesh with a rich flavor and a succulent texture. Like smoked salmon, it should be thinly sliced across the grain. As it is a luxury fish, it should be treated like the very best smoked salmon and served in the same way. Eat it with thinly-sliced brown bread and butter.

Below: Smoked sturgeon

Above: Smoked haddock fillets

Smoked haddock

There are various forms of smoked haddock, from fluorescent dyed yellow fillets to pale naturally cured fillets and finnan haddock or "haddie," which are split and look like pale golden kippers. It is now known that the artificial dyes used to color smoked haddock can be carcinogenic; dyed fillets are also often artificially flavored with chemicals that simulate the effect of smoking, so avoid these and enjoy natural pale beige fillets.

Finnan haddock or "haddie"

These distinctively pale, whole split haddock (with the bone left in) are named after the Scottish village of Findon where the special smoking process originated. The process gives the fish a beautiful pale corn color and a subtle smoked flavor. Finnan haddock

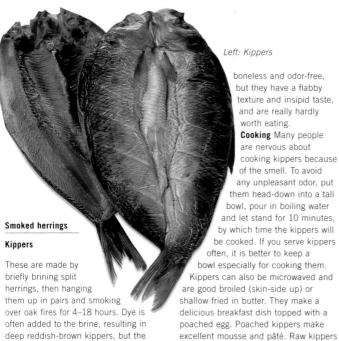

Smoked herrings

Kippers

These are made by briefly brining split herrings, then hanging them up in pairs and smoking over oak fires for 4–18 hours. Dye is often added to the brine, resulting in deep reddish-brown kippers, but the best (notably Manx and Loch Fyne kippers) are undyed. Kippers can be unpopular because they have so many bones, but these are easy to deal with once you know how.

Buying Look for the plumpest kippers you can find; lean kippers can be dry. As a rule of thumb, the darker the fish, the poorer the quality. Always buy undyed kippers if possible. Frozen boil-in-the bag kipper fillets are convenient,

Left: Kippers

boneless and odor-free, but they have a flabby texture and insipid taste, and are really hardly worth eating.

Cooking Many people are nervous about cooking kippers because of the smell. To avoid any unpleasant odor, put them head-down into a tall bowl, pour in boiling water and let stand for 10 minutes, by which time the kippers will be cooked. If you serve kippers often, it is better to keep a bowl especially for cooking them. Kippers can also be microwaved and are good broiled (skin-side up) or shallow fried in butter. They make a delicious breakfast dish topped with a poached egg. Poached kippers make excellent mousse and pâté. Raw kippers can be marinated and served as an appetizer.

Bloaters

Herrings that are left ungutted before being briefly salted, then smoked for 12 hours, are called bloaters. The guts impart a slightly gamey flavor, and the enzymes they contain cause the herring

Below: Bloaters

Boning cooked kippers

1 Lay the kipper on a plate, skin-side up. Run a knife point around the edge to lift up the skin.

2 Run the knife point down the backbone and eat the flesh that lies on top of the fine bones.

to become bloated during smoking. Because they are not gutted, bloaters do not keep as well as other smoked herring and should be eaten within a few days. Always gut them before serving. Despite their unattractive name, they are quite pleasing to look at, with silvery skin and moist flesh.

Other varieties *Harengs saurs* are a specialty of Boulogne; they are even more bloated than English bloaters. The most bloated of all are the Swedish *surströmming*. Like *harengs saurs*, they are traditionally eaten with potatoes.

Cooking Bloaters can be eaten as they are in salads and sandwiches. They can also be mashed into a paste with lemon juice and cayenne pepper or broiled and served with butter. To skin bloaters, pour on boiling water and let sit for 2 minutes, then peel off the skin.

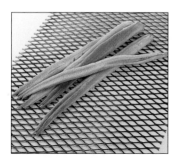

Above: Smoked eel fillets

HOT-SMOKED FISH

Fish that are cured or hot-smoked at a temperature of 176–185°F, which simultaneously cooks and cures them, need no further cooking. Trout, mackerel, eel and herrings can all be hot-smoked. Recently it has become fashionable to hot-smoke salmon, producing a very different flavor and texture from that of salmon that has been cold-smoked.

Arbroath smokies

These hot-smoked haddock have been beheaded and gutted but left whole. They have deep golden skin and soft pale gold flesh with a more delicate

Below: Smoked eel

flavor than cold-smoked haddock. In their native Scotland, they are a favorite breakfast or supper dish. Smokies are sold whole, so ask the fishmonger to split them open for you. Broil and serve with plenty of butter. When mashed with butter and lemon juice, Arbroath smokies make a delicious pâté.

Below: Arbroath smokies are always sold in pairs, tied with string.

Smoked eel

This fish has a very rich, dense texture and can only be eaten in small amounts. The skin, which is easily removed, is black and shiny and the flesh has a pinkish tinge. The eel can be served on its own as an hors d'oeuvre, with horseradish or mustard sauce to cut the richness, or made into a salad or pâté. It is particularly delicious served on a bed of celeriac *rémoulade* (grated celeriac in a mustard-flavored mayonnaise). Smoked eel also makes a good addition to a platter of mixed smoked fish.

When buying smoked eel, make sure that the skin is shiny and has not dried out. For an ample serving for one, you will need about 3½ ounces.

Brisling, Sild and Sprats

Not to everyone's taste, these small, hot-smoked herring with rich oily flesh are usually skinned and filleted and served cold as an appetizer with bread and butter. They can also be brushed with a little melted butter and lightly broiled, then served hot with toast.

Below: Hot-smoked sprats

Above: Smoked trout fillets

Buckling

Above: Buckling

These are large, fat ungutted herrings with a rich flavor. They are best eaten cold with bread and butter, but can be mashed into a paste or broiled and served with scrambled eggs.

Smoked mackerel

This has a rich flavor and a succulent velvety-smooth texture. The fillets are sold loose or pre-packed. They are sometimes coated in a thick layer of crushed peppercorns. Smoked mackerel can be eaten cold in a salad, or with horseradish sauce and lemon. It makes an excellent pâté and can be flaked and added to an omelet or quiche. Try it instead of smoked haddock in a kedgeree. Allow one fillet

per person. To skin smoked mackerel, lay the fish on a board, skin-side up. Starting at the tail end, peel back the skin toward the head. Pull off any fins together with their bones.

Smoked trout

Among the finest of all hot-smoked fish, trout should be plump and moist, with a beautiful golden-pink color. The flesh has a delicate flavor and is less rich than smoked herring or mackerel. The best smoked trout is first brined, then gutted and smoked over

Below: Smoked sea trout

birch with the addition of a little peat for a smokier flavor. Smoked trout is usually sold as skinned fillets, but you may occasionally find them whole, with the head on. Skin them like smoked mackerel. Smoked trout is delicious served on its own with dill or horseradish sauce. It can be made into mousses or pâté and is also good in salads, omelets and flans. Allow one fillet per person as an appetizer; two as a main course.

Above: Smoked mackerel fillets

Below: Smoked mackerel

FISH SAUCES AND PASTES

For centuries, man has produced fish sauces made by fermenting whole fish or various parts, including the entrails, into a savory, salty liquid to flavor and enhance fish dishes. The Romans' favorite condiment was *garum*, a pungent sauce obtained by soaking pieces of oily fish and their guts in brine flavored with herbs. Similar sauces exist today, notably in the Far East. The area around Nice also boasts *pissalat*, a sauce made from fermented anchovies. Don't be confused by the term "sauce," these are flavorings or condiments, not to be served on their own.

Anchovy extract

Salted anchovies are processed into a thick, rich pinkish-brown sauce with an intensely salty flavor. A few drops will enhance the flavor of almost any savory dish, but anchovy extract must be used sparingly, or it will overpower the other ingredients.

Nam pla/Thai fish sauce

Almost unheard of in the West a few years ago, *nam pla* is now an essential ingredient in every adventurous cook's pantry. It is a staple ingredient in all Far Eastern cooking; in Vietnam, it is called *nuoc cham*. The pungent, salty brown liquid is produced by

Right, from left:
Nam pla,
Worcestershire
sauce and
anchovy extract

packing small fish such as anchovies in brine in barrels and letting them ferment in the hot sun for several months. Strangely, the resulting sauce does not taste like fish; it is more like a very intense soy sauce. It can be added to any savory dishes, or mixed with flavorings such as garlic, lime juice and chili to make a dipping sauce, or can be used to add flavor to salad dressings. The color of *nam pla* should be a clear amber; if it is dark brown it will taste too fishy.

Above: Shrimp paste

Shrimp paste

A specialty of Malaysia and Indonesia, shrimp paste is made from salted, fermented shrimps. This powerful smelling paste, called *blachan*, *terasi* or *belacan*, is sold in blocks and is mixed with other ingredients to make a flavoring for stir-fries, soups and other savory dishes.

Worcestershire sauce

Anyone who has tasted this spicy sauce may be surprised to learn that it contains anchovies. Originally produced in India, the precise ingredients of Worcestershire sauce remain a closely-guarded secret, but they include malt and wine vinegar, molasses, tamarind, garlic, onions and spices, as well as anchovies.

Worcestershire sauce gives a lift to any savory dish and can be used sparingly to enliven a marinade for fish or meat. It is also essential for making a Bloody Mary cocktail. The "original and genuine" Worcestershire sauce made by Lea and Perrins is superior to all its imitators.

CRUSTACEANS

All crustaceans belong to the enormous family of decapods, ten-limbed creatures that are believed to be descendants of invertebrates that lived on the earth over 200 million and possibly up to 390 million years ago. One can only marvel at the imagination of the first person who thought of eating a crustacean. These curious-looking creatures with their hard carapaces and spidery limbs hardly look like the most attractive of foods, but the sweet flesh concealed within the shell is delicious.

CRABS AND LOBSTERS

CRABS

There are dozens of varieties of crab, ranging from hefty common crabs that will make a meal for several people, to tiny shore crabs that are good only for making soup. They are great wanderers, traveling hundreds of miles in a year from feeding to spawning grounds. As a result, crabs are often caught in baited pots sited on the sea bed far from the shore. As their bodies grow, crabs outgrow their shells and shed them while they grow a new carapace. At first the new shells are soft. These "soft-shell" crabs are a delicacy and can be eaten shell and all. Female crabs are known as hens. They have sweeter flesh than the males, but are smaller and their claws contain less flesh.

Below: Blue crabs

Above: Common or brown crab

Right: Soft-shell crabs

Other names In French, crab is *crabe*, *tourteau* (common edible crab) or *araignée* (spider crab). In Italian, it is *granchio* or *granseola*, in Spanish, *cangrejo* or *centolla*.

Blue crab *(Callinectes sapidus)*

These crabs have steely-gray bodies and bright, electric blue legs and claws. They are found in American waters and are prized for their white meat.

Soft-shell crabs are blue crabs that have shed their hard carapaces, leaving them deliciously tender, with sweet creamy flesh. They are extremely delicate and do not keep or travel well, so they are generally sold frozen, although you may find fresh soft-shell crabs in the United States in the summer months.

Common edible crab/Brown crab *(Cancer pagarus)*

The bodies of these large brownish-red crabs can measure well over 8 inches. They have big claws that can deliver an extremely nasty pinch, but they contain plenty of tasty meat. Common edible crabs are found on Atlantic coasts and parts of the Mediterranean.
Cooking These are the perfect crabs for boiling to serve cold with mayonnaise. The claws contain plenty of firm meat. After cooking, this can be removed from

Below: Spider crab

Spider crab *(Maia squinado)*

These alarming-looking crabs have spiny shells and long slender legs, which give them the appearance of enormous reddish-pink spiders; hence their alternative name of "sea spider." Those found along the Atlantic coasts measure about 8 inches across, but the giant species, found in the waters around Japan, measures up to 16 inches, with a claw span of almost 9¾ feet—a truly terrifying sight for arachnophobes.

Snow crab *(Chionoetes* spp*)*

Also known as queen crabs, these crabs from the north Pacific have roundish pinkish-brown bodies and exceptionally long legs. The delicious, sweet flesh is difficult to remove from the body, but the claw meat is more accessible. Snow crabmeat is usually sold frozen or canned.

the shell in one piece, marinated in a dressing containing Worcestershire sauce and Tabasco and served as a cocktail snack. The claw meat is also delicious deep-fried. The liver and roe of these crabs are delicious as well.

Dungeness/California crab *(Cancer magister)*

These trapezium-shaped crabs are found all along the Pacific coast, from Mexico to Alaska. They are very similar to common edible crabs and can be cooked in exactly the same way.

King crab *(Paralithodes camtschiatica)*

Looking like gigantic spiny spiders, king crabs are hideous to behold, but very good to eat. Their very size is awe-inspiring; a mature male king crab can weigh up to 26½ pounds and measure 39 inches across. Their triangular bodies are bright red, with a pale creamy underside. Every part tastes good, from the body meat to that from the narrow claws and long, dangly legs.
Buying Only male king crabs are sold; they are much larger and meatier than the females. Cooked legs are available frozen, and king crabmeat is frequently canned. Unlike most crabmeat, canned king crab is of excellent quality and highly prized. The best comes from Alaska, Japan and Russia, where it is sold as Kamchatka crab.

Stone crab *(family Lithodidae)*

Similar in appearance to king crabs, stone crabs live at great depths. They have a superb flavor, but are usually sold frozen or canned rather than fresh.

Below: King crab claws

Above: Swimming crabs

Swimming crab *(family Portunidae)*

The main distinguishing feature of swimming crabs is their extra pair of legs, shaped rather like paddles. Among the many species of swimming crabs are mud or mangrove, shore and velvet crabs. Shore crabs are eaten in Italy in their soft-shelled state; they also make delicious soup. Mud crabs, with their excellent claw meat, are popular in Australia and Southeast Asia.

Cooking Crab can be cooked in a multitude of ways. The sweet, succulent meat is rich and filling, so it needs a light touch when cooking; refreshing flavors suit it better than creamy sauces. Picking it out of the shell is hard work, but the result is well worth the effort. Recipes for crabmeat include deviled crab (where the meat is removed from the shell and cooked with mustard, horseradish, spices and bread crumbs), crab mornay, in which the meat is combined with a Gruyère cheese sauce enriched with sherry and mushrooms, and potted crab. The flesh marries well with clean Asian flavors such as lime juice, cilantro and chili; combined with these, it makes the perfect summer salad. Crabmeat is

perfect for fish cakes such as Maryland or Thai crab cakes. It also makes excellent soup; a classic Scottish dish is *partan bree*, a creamy crab soup made with fish stock, milk and rice.

In the shell, crab can be boiled and served with mayonnaise, steamed with aromatics or baked with ginger and scallions.

Soft-shell crabs are usually lightly coated in flour and deep-fried. A Venetian specialty is *molecchie fritte;* the crabs are soaked in beaten egg before being fried. In China, soft-shell crabs are served with a spicy garnish of chili or ginger. Soft-shell crabs can also be sautéed in butter and sprinkled with toasted almonds, or brushed with melted butter and lemon juice, then tossed lightly in flour before broiling.

Crawfish *(Palinurus vulgaris)*

Crawfish are similar to lobsters, except that they have spiny shells and no claws. They are variously known as spiny lobsters, rock lobsters, langouste and crayfish (but must not be confused with freshwater crayfish). Crawfish are found on the rocky sea bed in many parts of the world. The color of their shells varies according to where they come from: Atlantic crawfish are dark

reddish-brown; those from the Florida coast are brown with pale spots; warm-water varieties can be pink or bluish-green. All turn pink or red when cooked. Crawfish have dense, very white flesh, similar to that of lobster, but with a milder flavor. Those from the Atlantic are the finest and sweetest. Crawfish from warmer waters can tend to be a little coarse.

Other names In France, crawfish are called *langouste,* in Italy they are *aragosta,* in Spain, *langosta.*

Buying Crawfish are generally sold cooked. Females have the better flavor, so look for the egg sac underneath the thorax. Because there is no claw meat, allow one 1 pound crawfish per person. Florida crawfish are often sold frozen as "lobster" tails.

Cooking Cook as lobster. Crawfish benefit from spicy seasonings and are excellent in Asian recipes.

Crayfish *(Astacus astacus)* **and yabby** *(Cherax)*

Crayfish are miniature freshwater lobsters, which grow to a maximum length of 4 inches. The exception is a species found in Tasmania, which can weigh up to 13 pounds. Crayfish have a superb flavor and, whatever their color when alive, turn a glorious deep scarlet when cooked. Over three hundred species are found in well-oxygenated streams throughout Europe, America and Australia, although most of the European species have been wiped out, largely through pollution and disease. Crayfish can be farmed successfully; unfortunately, the most prolific variety are the voracious American signal crayfish; these are prone to a killer disease, which they pass on to wild native crayfish, resulting in near-extinction.

Other names The most commonly available crayfish are the European, the red-claw, the American signal, the red Louisiana swamp, the greenish Turkish crayfish, the Australian yabby and the large marron, which is a deep purplish-gray color. In France, crayfish are called *écrevisse,* in Italy, *gambero di fiume,* in Spain, *cangrejo de rio.*

Buying Fresh crayfish should be bought alive. There is a lot of wastage, so allow 8–12 crayfish per serving. Keep the shells to make stock, soup or sauces. Frozen crayfish are also available. These are fine in casseroles, but are not worth eating on their own.

Cooking Crayfish feature in many luxurious dishes, including bisque (a rich creamy soup), sauces and mousses. They are superb poached in a court-bouillon for about 5 minutes and served cold with mayonnaise or hot with lemony melted butter. Only the tail and claw meat is eaten; the head is often used as a garnish. The cleaned heads and shells can be used to make a shellfish stock or soup.

Below: Crayfish are tiny freshwater lobsters; there are hundreds of species.

Langoustines/Dublin Bay prawns/Scampi
(Nephrops norvegicus)

Smaller relatives of lobsters, langoustines have smooth-shelled narrow bodies with long thin, knobbly claws. They are salmon pink in color. The largest can measure up to 9 inches, but the average length is about 4½ inches. Langoustines were originally found in Norway, hence their Latin name, and they are still sometimes known as Norway lobsters. Nowadays, they are caught all along the Atlantic coast, in the Adriatic and western Mediterranean. The colder the water in which langoustines live, the better the flavor.

Other names The French know them as *langoustine*; the Italians call them *scampo*, while in Spain they are called *cigala* or *langostina*.

Shelling cooked crayfish

1 Hold the crayfish between your finger and thumb and gently twist off the tail.

2 Hold the tail shell between your thumb and index finger, twist and pull off the flat end; the thread-like intestinal tract will come out. Peel the tail.

3 Hold the head and thorax in one hand. Use the other index finger to prise off the whole underside, including the gills and innards, and discard these.

4 Finally, gently twist off the claws from the head.

Left: These freshwater crustaceans, called cherabin in Australia and black tiger or African prawns elsewhere, are sometimes confused with crayfish and scampi, because they have a pair of extremely long, thin claws.

delicate and delicious. They must be cooked very briefly. Roast in oil and garlic in a hot oven for 3–5 minutes; split them and broil or grill for about 2 minutes on each side, or poach in a court-bouillon and serve hot with melted butter. Remember that most langoustines on sale are already cooked, so subject them to as little heat as possible. Whole langoustines are delicious served cold with mayonnaise. They make a wonderful addition to a *plateau de fruits de mer*. Langoustine tails can be baked *au gratin* in a creamy sauce with mushrooms and Gruyère cheese, or served Scottish-style in a whiskey-flavored sauce. They can also be deep-fried and served with lemon wedges, but take care not to overcook them.

Buying Langoustines deteriorate very rapidly once caught, so are often cooked and frozen at sea. Live langoustines are therefore something of a rarity in British fish markets, although you will often find them in Europe. If you are lucky enough to find live langoustines, and can be certain of cooking them soon after purchase, they will be an excellent buy. It is important to check that they are still moving; if they have died, they will have an unpleasant woolly texture. Unlike other crustaceans, langoustines do not change color when cooked, so make sure you know what you are buying. Langoustines are graded by size; larger specimens are better value, as they contain more meat. They are also available frozen, often as scampi tails. If they have been shelled, allow about 4 ounces per person; you will need twice this amount if the langoustines are in the shell.

Cooking Most people must have encountered tasteless, badly cooked scampi at some time in their lives. When langoustines are properly cooked, however, their flavor is

Above: Langoustines, which are also known as Dublin Bay prawns and scampi

Left: Canadian lobsters are air-freighted live to Europe.

If you buy a live lobster, make sure that the pincers are secured with a stout rubber band.

Other names In French, lobster is called *homard*; in Italian, it is *astice*, and in Spanish, *bogavante*.

Canadian/American lobster *(Homarus americanus)*

The hardiest species of lobster, these are found in large numbers in the waters around Canada and the North American Atlantic. They resemble the European lobster, but are greener in color, and the claws are slightly rounder and fleshier. Although they make excellent eating, their flavor does not quite match up to that of the European lobster. The best-known American lobster is the Maine lobster. Canadian and Maine lobsters are air-freighted live to Europe to meet the demand for these crustaceans. Even taking into account the freight costs, they are considerably cheaper than their European counterparts.

Below: Maine lobster resembles the European lobster, but is less expensive.

LOBSTER

These are the ultimate luxury seafood. Their uniquely firm, sweet flesh has a delicious flavor, and many people regard them as the finest crustaceans of all. The best lobsters live in cold waters, scavenging for food on the rocky sea bed. Like crabs, they "molt" every couple of years, casting off their outgrown shells. Their color varies according to their habitat, from steely blue to greenish-brown to reddish-purple; all turn brick red when cooked. Lobsters grow very slowly, only reaching maturity at six years old, by which time they are about 7 inches long. If you are lucky enough to find a 2¼ pound lobster, it will be about ten years old. This explains why lobsters are in such short supply.

Lobsters must be bought live or freshly boiled. The powerful pincers, which the creature uses for catching and crushing its prey, can be dangerous.

European lobster *(Homarus gammarus)*

These lobsters, which come from England, Scotland, Ireland, Norway and Brittany, are regarded as having the finest flavor of all. They have distinctive blue-black coloring, and are sometimes speckled with bright blue. European lobsters are becoming increasingly rare and expensive. If they are caught in reasonable numbers during the summer months, they are often held in vivariums, massive holding tanks built into the sea.

Unfortunately, lobsters do not eat in captivity, so although the vivariums ensure that they are available

Right: Squat lobster is a warm-water variety from Australia and is seldom sold in Europe.

Below: The European lobster, which is becoming rare—and very expensive— is considered the best lobster of all.

throughout the year, the quality deteriorates as the season progresses; by early spring, they tend to be thin and undernourished.

Slipper/Squat lobster *(Scyllarus arctus)*

There are over fifty species of these warm-water lobsters. They have wide, flattened bodies and spindly clawed legs. The best known squat lobsters are the Australian "bugs," and the best known of these are the Balmain and Moreton Bay bugs. The comparatively small tails contain deliciously sweet flesh. Squat lobsters are seldom sold in Europe, but can occasionally be found in France, where they are known as *cigales* (grasshoppers). Italians call them *cicala di mare,* and in Spain they are called *cigarra*.

Cooking lobster

All types of lobster are best cooked very simply to allow the delicate flavor to speak for itself. They can be boiled in salted water or court-bouillon and served hot with melted butter or cold with mayonnaise, plainly broiled or fried in the shell with oil and butter. A plain boiled lobster can be the crowning glory of a *plateau de fruits de mer.*

Classical French cooking has a plethora of rich lobster recipes that reflect the luxurious quality of these crustaceans. These dishes, which are usually served with rice to offset the richness, include Lobster Cardinale, with mushrooms and truffles in a velvety sauce; Lobster Newburg, with a cognac and sherry-flavored cream sauce; Lobster Bretonne, with shrimp and mushrooms in a white wine sauce; and the world-famous Lobster Thermidor, with its unctuous brandy and mustard-flavored sauce. More modern recipes combine lobster with Asian flavors such as ginger and star anise, but these spices should be used in moderation.

Lobster is superb with fresh pasta. Use it as a filling for ravioli or toss it into tagliolini with lemon juice and butter. Cold boiled lobster can be diced and made into a lobster cocktail or added to a salad. When cooking lobster, keep the shells to use in a shellfish stock or soup.

Preparing a cooked lobster
You'll need a large, heavy knife or cleaver and a lobster pick to remove the meat from the legs.

1 Hold the body of the lobster firmly in one hand and twist off the claws one at a time.

2 Hold the lobster the right way up on a cutting board. Insert a large sharp knife at right angles to the seam between the body and head and press down firmly to split the body and tail lengthwise.

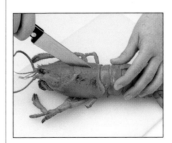

3 Turn the lobster around to face the other way and cut firmly through the head. Separate the lobster into two halves and discard the stomach sac.

4 Twist off the legs and then flatten them lightly with the back of the knife. Use a lobster pick to remove the flesh.

5 To remove the meat from the claws, first break up the claws into sections. Hold the larger section of the claw, curved side down, in one hand and sharply pull off the smaller pincer. Twist off the lower section of the claw at the joint.

6 Gently crack the claw shell with a mallet or the end of a rolling pin and remove the flesh.

7 The lobster can be broiled in the shell with butter, or the flesh can be diced and used in sauces.

SHRIMP

Shrimp are the world's most popular crustaceans and are eaten all over the world. Thousands of species of shrimp are found in all the world's oceans and also in fresh water. When shrimp are very large, they are often called—and sold as—prawns. In the fish trade, any shrimp measuring less than about 2 inches are known as shrimp. Most shrimp have narrow, tapering bodies, curled over at the tail, and long antennae. As is the case with other crustaceans, shrimp that come from colder waters have a better flavor than those that come from warm waters.

Above: Pink shrimp

COLD-WATER SHRIMP

Pink shrimp *(Palaemon serratus)*

These translucent, brownish shrimp can grow up to 4 inches in length. They are found in deep waters in the Atlantic Ocean and Mediterranean Sea, but related species are found throughout the world. The French and Italians consider these shrimp the best of all; they have an exceptionally good flavor and turn a glorious red when cooked.

Below: Mediterranean shrimp

As a result, they command enormously high prices.

Other names Common shrimp are also known as sword shrimp or Algerian shrimp. In France, they are called *crevette rose* or *bouquet*, in Italy, they are *gamberello*, in Spain, *camarón* or *quisquilla*.

Deep-sea shrimp *(Pandalus borealis)*

Sometimes sold as "large shrimp," these cold-water shrimp live at great depths in the North Sea. They are hermaphrodites. All begin life as males, but they become female halfway through their lifespan. Deep-sea shrimp have translucent pink bodies, which turn pale salmon-pink on cooking. They have a delicious, delicate, juicy flavor and are almost always sold cooked.

Other names In France, these large shrimp are called *crevette*; Italians know them as *gambero*, while in Spain they are called *camarón*.

Peeling and deveining shrimp

1 Hold the shrimp in the middle and pull off the head and legs. Peel off the shell, leaving on the end of the tail, if desired.

2 To devein, use a small sharp knife to make a shallow incision down the center of the curved back of the shrimp. Use the knife tip to remove the black vein (intestinal tract) and discard it.

Mediterranean shrimp *(Aristeus antennatus)*

These large shrimp can measure up to 4 inches. The color varies—the heads can be anything from blood-red to deep coral—but once cooked, they turn a brilliant red. The flesh is delicious and very succulent. Mediterranean shrimp are sold cooked and should be served as they are, with mayonnaise and French bread. Allow 3–4 each as an appetizer.

Other names Also known as blue or red shrimp, Mediterranean shrimp are called *crevette rouge* in France; they are called *gambero rosso* in Italy, and *carabinero* in Spain.

Common/Brown shrimp (*Crangon crangon*)

These small shrimps have translucent gray bodies and measure only about 2 inches. They live in soft sand in shallow waters, emerging at night in darker camouflage to hunt for their prey. When cooked, they turn brownish-gray. Their small size makes them difficult to peel, but they can be eaten whole, and their flavor is incomparable, with a wonderful tang of the sea. They are used to make potted shrimp.
Other names The French call these shrimps *crevette grise* or *boucaud*; the Italians know them as *gamberetto grigio*; the Spanish call them *quisquilla*.

Left: Brown shrimp

Below: Tiger shrimp

WARM-WATER SHRIMP

Gulf shrimp (*Hymenopenaeus robustus*)

Warm-water shrimp from the Gulf of Mexico, these are usually bright red, but may sometimes be grayish-pink in color. Gulf shrimp can grow very large, up to 1½ ounces in weight, and have very succulent flesh.

Kuruma/Japanese shrimp (*Penaeus japonicus*)

These large shrimp can grow to a length of 9 inches. They have yellowish tails flecked with black. Kuruma are found throughout the Indo-Pacific region and in the Red Sea; some have migrated through the Suez Canal to the eastern Mediterranean.

Tiger/Jumbo shrimp (*Penaeus monodon*)

These huge shrimp are found throughout the Indo-Pacific. They can grow up to 13 inches in length and are ideal for grilling. In their raw state, they

Below: Gulf shrimp

Butterflied shrimp
Shrimp look very attractive when they are butterflied.

1 The easiest way of doing this is to deepen the incision made to remove the vein, cutting almost but not quite through to the belly.

2 The shrimp is then opened out flat. If the shrimp are large, make the incision through the belly to give a more pronounced shape.

---

are a translucent greenish-gray. Although their flavor is not as good as that of cold-water shrimp, tiger shrimp have succulent, firm flesh. In Europe, they are seldom sold fresh, but they freeze well and are available peeled or in the shell. Peeled tiger shrimp usually have the end of the tail left on so that they can be eaten with the fingers.
Cooking The cardinal rule with any shrimp is not to overcook them. Ready-cooked shrimp should preferably be eaten without further cooking. Serve them simply, with lemon and brown bread and butter, or in a shrimp cocktail or salad. If you must cook them, use them in a dish such as pasta where they need only be heated through. They add extra flavor and texture to other fish dishes, such as fish pies, terrines and flans, and combine well with other shellfish. Small shrimp make an excellent filling for omelets, vol-au-vents or tartlets.

Raw shrimp can be boiled briefly in salt water or court-bouillon and are delicious broiled, grilled or deep-fried in batter. Combined with squid and other fish, deep-fried shrimp are an essential ingredient of an Italian *fritto misto*. Warm-water shrimp can be used for stir-fries, curries or kebabs.

GASTROPODS

Also known as univalves, gastropods are single-shelled creatures belonging to the snail family. Most marine gastropods have the familiar snail shape, with a single spiral shell, but some look more like bivalves, and others have no shell at all. All gastropods have a single, large foot that they extend and contract to crawl along at a "snail's pace." Edible gastropods vary in size from periwinkles to conches measuring up to 12 inches. All can be delicious if properly cooked.

Abalone/Ormer/Sea ear

You could be forgiven for thinking that abalone *(Haliotis tuberculata)* were bivalves, since their ear-shaped shells give them the appearance of large mussels. Like all gastropods, they have a large, muscled foot that they use to cling to rocks and cliffs. This immensely strong foot can withstand strains up to four thousand times the weight of the abalone, which makes it very difficult to prise them from the rocks, and helps to explain why they are so expensive. Another reason for their cost is that they feed exclusively on seaweed; as their habitat becomes polluted, they die, so they are becoming increasingly rare. In some countries abalone have become a protected species. They are highly prized not only for their flesh, but also for their beautiful shells. These are

lined with iridescent mother-of-pearl. There are over a hundred species of abalone living in warm waters throughout the world. Most can grow to about 8 inches in length, but the shell of the red abalone *(Haliotis rufescens)*, found in the American Pacific, grows up to 12 inches. Their firm flesh, which must be tenderized before it can be eaten, has a subtle flavor of iodine.

Other names In the Channel Islands, one of the few places in Europe where abalone are still found, they are known as ormers. In South Africa, they are known as *perlemoen* or Venus' ear. The French call them *ormeau* or *oreilles de St Pierre*, the Italians, *orecchia marina*, the Spanish, *oreja de mar*.

Buying In Europe, there is a closed season for abalone, and they are limited for only a few days in early spring. You are more likely to find fresh abalone in America, Australia and the Far East. These are often sold sliced and tenderized ready for cooking. Abalone is also available canned, frozen and dried.

Preparing and Cooking Before cooking, the intestinal sac and dark membrane and skirt must be removed. To remove the white flesh, run a sharp knife between it and the shell. Abalone flesh

Below: Abalone are large shellfish, which can grow to 12 inches in length.

Above: Limpets

must be beaten vigorously with a wooden mallet to tenderize it. In Japan, it is then sliced thinly and eaten raw as sashimi. If it is cooked, the technique is the same as that for squid—it must either be cooked very briefly, or cooked slowly for a long time. Thin slices can be sautéed quickly in hot butter, or cut into strips and deep-fried in batter or egg and bread crumbs. In China, abalone is braised with dried mushrooms; in France, it is stewed slowly with dry white wine and shallots. In the Channel Islands, ormers are traditionally cooked in a casserole with bacon and potatoes. Abalone makes an excellent chowder.

Conch *(Strombus gigas)*

Pronounced "konk," conch is a large relative of the whelk. It has a distinctive spiral shell. As with all such gastropods, the opening is protected by a hard operculum, or "trap door," which must be removed for access to the flesh inside. Conch are native to Florida, the Pacific coast and the Caribbean. The shells are sought after as ornaments and musical instruments. The pinkish flesh is tasty and chewy, and must be beaten to tenderize it before eating.

Buying In their native countries, conches are available all year round. The best are young specimens, known as "thin-lipped" conches; older conches are described as "thick-lipped." They are generally sold out of the shell.

Cooking After tenderizing, conch meat can be marinated and eaten raw, or cooked in a chowder. Some conches can cause stomach upsets; the risk of this occurring can be reduced if the conch is boiled in two changes of water.

Above: Whelks

Limpets *(Patella vulgata)*

These gastropods have conical shells. They are found throughout the world, clinging tightly to rocks. When the tide goes out, they nestle into holes in the sand, emerging at night to crawl in a 39 inches circle around their hole in search of food. Limpets have quite a good flavor, but the small amount of flesh they contain can be very tough. It takes a great deal of effort to prise them off the rocks, so only the larger varieties, which yield more flesh, are eaten. Limpets are not available commercially so you will have to harvest them yourself.

Cooking Wash the limpets and boil them in sea water or heavily-salted water for 5–7 minutes, or cook the flesh in seafood dishes or soups.

Whelks *(Buccinum undatum)*

Smaller relatives of the conch, whelks have pretty spiral shells measuring up to 4 inches. They have rubbery, pinkish flesh with a good flavor, largely because they are scavengers and will bore through the shell of other shellfish to eat their flesh.

Other names There are many varieties of whelk, including the common, the dog, the spiral and the knobbled or giant American whelk, which can grow to 8 inches in length. In French, they are variously known as *bulot*, *buccin* and *escargot de mer* (sea snail), in Italian, *buccina*, in Spanish, *bocina* or *caracola*.

Buying Whelks should be bought alive; check that the operculum is tightly closed. They are sometimes sold ready-boiled and removed from the shell, but these can be rather dry. You will also find whelks pickled in vinegar, or ready-cooked and bottled in brine.

Cooking The best way to cook whelks is to boil them in sea water or heavily salted water for about 5 minutes. Use a toothpick to prise the flesh out of the shell. The flesh of large whelks can be sautéed after boiling, or deep-fried in batter. It can be used instead of clams in a chowder, or added to cooked shellfish dishes or salads.

Periwinkles *(Littorina littorea)*

These tiny marine snails have thick greenish-brown or black shells, each with a pointed end. Most grow no larger than 1½ inches and contain a morsel of chewy flesh.

Other names In France, they are *bigourneau* or *littorine*, in Italy, *chiocciola di mare*, in Spain, *bigaro*.

Buying Fresh periwinkles should be bought alive; check that the operculum is tightly closed. They are also available cooked and bottled in vinegar.

Cooking Like whelks, periwinkles need only brief cooking. Serve as an appetizer with vinegar or mayonnaise, or as part of a shellfish platter.

Left: Periwinkles

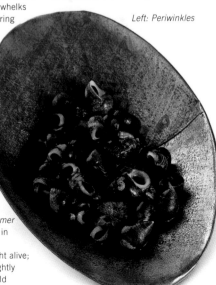

Cooking and picking periwinkles and whelks

1 Bring a large pan of well-salted water to a boil. Drop in the periwinkles or whelks and simmer for about 5 minutes for periwinkles; 10 minutes for whelks. Drain.

2 If the operculum is still covering the opening of the shell, remove it with a toothpick or pin. Insert the toothpick or pin into the shell and pull out the flesh.

MOLLUSKS

The mollusk family is divided into bivalves such as mussels and oysters, which have a hinged external shell, and gastropods such as whelks and periwinkles, which have a single external shell. Cephalopods (squid, cuttlefish and octopus) are yet another group; unlike gastropods and bivalves, they have internal shells.

BIVALVES

CLAMS

There are hundreds of species of clam, ranging from the aptly-named giant clam which can grow to a length of 4¼ feet, to tiny pebble-like Venus and littleneck clams measuring barely 2 inches. Americans are passionate about clams and eat them in all sizes and forms. Their enthusiasm has spread to Europe, where clams are now extensively farmed. Large species, such as the fully mature American quahog (pronounced co-hog), have very thick warty shells; small varieties have smooth shells marked with fine circular striations. Clams have a fine, sweet flavor and firm texture, and are delicious cooked or raw.

Below: Palourde or carpetshell clams have tender flesh that can be eaten raw.

Cherrystone/Littleneck clam *(Mercenaria mercenaria)*

These small clams have an attractive brown and white patterned shell. They are actually quahogs, the popular name deriving from their size. The smallest are the baby littlenecks, with 1½–2-inch shells. The slightly larger cherrystones (about 3 inches), named after Cherrystone Creek in Virginia, are about five years old. Both are often served raw on the half shell; cooked,

Above: Venus clams

they make wonderful pasta sauces. Larger quahogs, which are unsuitable for eating raw, are known as steamer clams. They have quite a strong flavor and are often used for making clam chowder or pasta sauces.
Other names The French call them *palourde*, the Italians, *vongola dura*, the Spanish, *almeja* or *clame*.

Geoduck clam *(Panopea generosa)*

These enormous clams are the largest of all American Pacific shellfish and can weigh up to 8¾ pounds. Half this weight is made up of two long siphons, which can be extended to more than 4¼ feet to take in and expel water. Unlike the soft-shell clam, the geoduck cannot retract these siphons into the shell, and they are often sold separately. Geoducks can bury themselves up to 4 feet deep in sand, and it takes two people to pull them out. The siphons and flesh are sliced before cooking.

Palourde/Carpetshell clam *(Venerupis decussata)*

These small (1½–3-inch) clams have attractive grooved brown shells with a yellow lattice pattern. The flesh is exceptionally tender, so they can be eaten raw, but are also good broiled.

Other names In French they are *palourde*, in Italian, *vongola verace*, in Spanish, *almeja fina*.

Praire/Warty Venus clam *(Venus verrucosa)*

The unattractively named warty Venus is a smallish clam measuring 1–3 inches. The thick shell has concentric stripes, some of which end in warty protuberances. These clams are widely distributed on sandy coasts, from Africa to Europe. They are often eaten raw on the half shell, but are also excellent cooked. The Italians dignify them with the name of "sea truffles."

Below: Cherrystone clams

Other names Sometimes known as baby clams, the word *praire* comes from the French, who also call these mollusks *coque rayé*. In Italy they are *verrucosa* or *tartufo di mare*, in Spain, *almeja vieja*.

Razorshell/Razor clam *(Solen marginatus)*

Resembling an old-fashioned cut-throat razor, these clams have tubular shells that are striped gold and brown. Their flesh is unattractive but tastes delicious. Razorshells are often served raw, but can be cooked like any other clam. They can often be found on sandy beaches at low tide, but as they can burrow into the sand at great speed to conceal themselves, you will need to act fast if you want to catch them.

Other names Razorshells are sometimes known as jack-knife clams. The French call them *couteau*, the Italians, *cannolicchio* or *cappa lunga*; their Spanish name is *navaja* or *longuerión*.

Soft-shell/Long-neck clam *(family Myidae)*

The shells of these wide oval clams gape slightly at the posterior end, giving them their nickname of "gapers." They burrow deep into sand and silt, so have a long tube that acts as a siphon for taking in and expelling water. This siphon can be eaten raw, or made into chowder or creamed dishes. Soft-shell clams are often used in clambakes.

Other names In French they are *mye*, in Italian, *vongola molle*, in Spanish, *almeja de rio*.

Cooking Small clams and razorshells can be eaten raw, steamed or cooked in soups and sauces. Larger clams can be stuffed and baked or broiled like mussels, cut into strips and deep-fried in batter or bread crumbs, or stewed with white wine or onions and tomatoes. Steamed clams can be added to salads or sauces or used as a garnish. Never throw away the juices these clams contain; they are extremely nutritious and delicious, and can be used in drinks such as *clamata*, shellfish stock or soup.

Below: Razor clams are often served raw.

Clambakes

A favorite pastime is the clambake, a beach picnic in which soft-shell or hard-shell clams are steamed over seaweed laid on hot rocks. A pit is dug in the sand, rocks are placed inside and heated, then draped with wet seaweed. The clams are steamed over the seaweed, along with corn, sweet potatoes and, sometimes, lobsters or soft-shell crabs. The process of digging the pit and cooking the clams takes at least 4 hours, so a clambake can provide a whole day's entertainment.

Cockles

Although traditionally thought of as a typically British food, varieties of cockle *(Cardium edule)* are found all over the world. Their two equal heart-shaped shells are 1–1½ inches long and have 26 defined ribs. Inside lies a morsel of delicate flesh and its coral.

Other names In America, cockles are sometimes known as heart clams. In France, they are *coque*, in Italy, *cuore*, in Spain, *berberecho*.

Buying Fresh cockles are sold by volume; 1 pint weighs about 1 pound. Those with paler flesh are said to taste better than those with dark flesh.

Above: Cockles

The color of the shell is an indication of the color of the flesh, so choose cockles with pale shells. Shelled cockles are available frozen and bottled in brine or vinegar.

Cooking Cockles are full of sand, so must be soaked in salted cold water for several hours before eating. They can be eaten raw or boiled and served with vinegar and brown bread and butter. They are excellent steamed, stewed with tomatoes and onions or made into soup. Cockles can be added to risotto, pasta and other seafood dishes or served cold as an hors d'oeuvre or salad.

Below: Large New Zealand greenshell or green-lipped mussels.

Right: Ever-popular, black-shelled mussels

Dog cockle
(Glycymeridae)

With their large, flat striated shells, dog cockles resemble scallops. There are four known species of these tropical and warm-water bivalves— the true dog cockle, the bittersweet cockle, the violet bittersweet and the giant bittersweet. All are perfectly good to eat, but have a coarser texture and flavor than true cockles. They can be cooked in the same way as cockles and mussels.

Other names In French they are *amande*, in Italian, *pié d'asino* (ass's foot), in Spanish, *almendra de mar*.

Mussels *(Mytilus edulis)*

Once regarded as the poor relation of the shellfish family, mussels are now very popular, but still comparatively cheap. These succulent bivalves, with their elongated blue-black shells, have been eaten since earliest times. Unlike most other bivalves, they do not use a muscular foot to anchor themselves to rocks and poles, but do so with a byssus or "beard," a wiry substance produced by a gland at the base of the

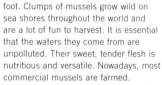

foot. Clumps of mussels grow wild on sea shores throughout the world and are a lot of fun to harvest. It is essential that the waters they come from are unpolluted. Their sweet, tender flesh is nutritious and versatile. Nowadays, most commercial mussels are farmed.

There are many varieties of mussel. The best and most succulent are the blue or European mussels from cold British waters, which can grow to a length of 4 inches, although the average size is nearer 2 inches. They are large, with sweet-flavored flesh, which in the female is a beautiful orange; males have paler, cream-colored flesh. The largest of all are the New Zealand greenshell or green-lipped mussels *(Perna canaliculus)*, which have a distinctive green lip around the internal border of the shell. These can grow to over 9 inches and are very meaty and substantial. They are ideal for stuffing, but their flavor is not as good as that of blue mussels.

Other names In French, it is *moule*, in Italian, *cozza*, in Spanish, *mejillón*.

Buying Most mussels are farmed and are usually cleaned. They are available all year round and are cheap, so buy more than you think you will need to allow for wastage; 2¼ pounds will provide a generous meal for two people. Shelled mussels are available frozen, smoked and bottled in brine or vinegar.

Cooking Mussels are extremely versatile. They can be eaten raw or steamed very simply, as in *moules marinière*. They are also good steamed with Mediterranean or Asian seasonings. Large mussels can be stuffed and baked or broiled with flavored butter, bacon or pesto. They can be wrapped in bacon, threaded onto skewers and broiled; cooked in cream, wine or cider, deep-fried and used in omelets, soufflés, hot or cold soups, curries, pasta sauces, rice dishes such as paella and seafood salads. The national dish of Belgium is *moules frites*, mussels with french fries, served with a glass of beer. For an unusual and piquant hors d'oeuvre, serve cold steamed mussels *à la ravigote*, with a vinaigrette flavored with chopped hard-boiled eggs, fresh herbs and gherkins.

OYSTERS

One of life's great luxuries, oysters evoke passionate feelings—people tend either to love or loathe them. Their unique, salty, iodized flavor and slippery texture may not appeal to everyone, but their reputation as an aphrodisiac

Below: Native oysters are the finest and most expensive of all oysters.

(Casanova was said to eat at least fifty every day) has contributed to their popularity, and they are highly prized all over the world. It was not always so; for centuries, oysters were regarded as food for the poor. Apprentices revolted at having to eat them every day of the week. As they became scarce, however, their popularity increased.

Over 100 different varieties of oyster live in the temperate and warm waters of the world. All have thick, irregular, grayish shells, one flat, the other hollow. The highly nutritious flesh is pinkish-gray with a darker mantle and a slippery texture. Their reproductive life is highly unusual. Some are hermaphrodite; others change sex from male to female in alternate years.

Oysters have been eaten for thousands of years. They were enjoyed by the Celts and Ancient Greeks, but it was the Romans who first discovered the secret of oyster cultivation. By the 19th century, European oyster beds had been so comprehensively over-fished and stocks were so low that Napoleon III ordered that shipments of oysters be brought from abroad. It is good that he did so; in 1868, a ship carrying quantities of Portuguese oysters was forced to take shelter from a storm in

the Gironde estuary. Fearing that his cargo of oysters was going bad, the captain flung them overboard. They bred prolifically, rapidly replenishing the native stocks, and managed to survive a catastrophic epidemic in 1921, which wiped out the native oysters. In 1967, however, they too were totally decimated by the deadly bonamia virus. Oyster cultivation on a massive scale was the only answer; nowadays, oysters are commercially produced throughout the industrialized world.

Oyster cultivation

Centuries of over-fishing and disease have decimated the world's natural stocks of oysters, a sad state of affairs that has been somewhat alleviated by oyster farming. Oysters have been farmed since Roman times, but cultivation has now become a highly lucrative business, despite being labor-intensive and very slow.

Oysters need constant cosseting from the moment of hatching. A single oyster produces up to a hundred million eggs every breeding season, of which only ten oysters will survive long enough to end up on your plate. It takes at least three years to produce an oyster of marketable size; natives take up to seven years and the giant "royals" take ten years to mature. The minuscule spats must first be caught and encouraged to settle on lime-soaked tiles or slates.

After about nine months, they are transferred to oyster parks, where they are enclosed in wire cages and carefully nurtured while they feed on plankton. After being left to grow for two or three years, they are placed in nets and fattened for about a year in shallow beds or *claires*. The final stage of the lengthy process involves placing them in clean beds for several days under stringent hygiene conditions to expel any impurities. Small wonder that they are so expensive!

Left: Gigas oysters

Portuguese cupped oysters are cultivated on a large scale, they are known as *fines de claires* after the fattening beds where they are farmed. Fatter, tastier (and, of course, more expensive) specimens are called *spéciales claires*.

Sydney rock oyster *(Crassostrea commercialis)*

This sex-changing cupped oyster is extremely fertile and is farmed in huge numbers on the coast of New South Wales. It grows quickly and has a good flavor, but has the disadvantage of being difficult to open.

Buying The age-old rule that oysters should not be bought when there is no "r" in the month still holds good in the northern hemisphere, not because they are poisonous, as was once supposed, but because their flesh becomes unpleasantly soft and milky during the summer breeding season from May to August. Smoked oysters are available and you may also find frozen oysters.

Cooking Oysters are best eaten raw with just a squeeze of lemon or a dash of Tabasco. If you prefer to cook them, do so very briefly. They are good poached or steamed and served with a *beurre blanc* or Champagne sauce; stuffed and grilled; deep-fried in cornmeal batter; or as a luxurious addition to steak and kidney pie.

Left: Portuguese cupped oysters

Eastern/Atlantic oyster *(Crassostrea virginica)*

With rounded shells like those of the native oyster, these actually belong to the Portuguese oyster family and have a similar texture and flavor. In America, they are named after their place of origin; the best known is the Blue Point.

Native oyster *(Ostrea edulis)*

Considered the finest of all oysters, Natives are slow-growers, taking three years to reach their full size of 2–4½ inches. Their round shells vary in color from grayish-green to beige, depending on their habitat, and they have a wonderful flavor. Native oysters are named after their place of origin. Among the best known are the French Belon, the English Whitstable, Colchester and Helford, the Irish Galway and the Belgian Ostendes. Native oysters are the most expensive of all oysters.

Other names The French call them *huitre plate* or *belon*, to the Italians they are *ostrica*, while in Spain, they are called *ostra plana*.

Pacific/Gigas oyster *(Crassostrea gigas)*

These large cupped bivalves with their craggy elongated shells are the most widely farmed oysters in the world. They are resistant to disease and can grow to 6 inches in the space of four years, which makes them comparatively economical to produce. Their texture is not as fine as that of natives, but their large size makes them more suitable for cooking than other oysters.

Other names The Pacific oyster is also known as the rock or Japanese oyster. In French, it is *creuse* (hollow), in Italian, *ostrica*, in Spanish *ostión*.

Portuguese cupped oyster *(Crassostrea angulata)*

These scaly grayish-brown oysters are considered finer than gigas, but not as good as natives. Their flesh is rather coarse and they are declining in popularity. In France, where

SCALLOPS

Surely the most attractive of all shellfish, scallops (*Peeten maximus*) have two fan-shaped shells, one flat and the other curved, with grooves radiating out from the hinge to the outside edge. They are found on sandy seabeds in many parts of the world from Iceland to Japan. Unlike many bivalves, they do not burrow into the sand, but "swim" above the sea bed by opening and closing their shells, which gives them the appearance of leaping through the water. There are about three hundred species of scallop throughout the world, with shells ranging in color from beige to brown, salmon pink, yellow and orange. The most common species is the common or great scallop, whose reddish-brown shell grows to a diameter of 2–2½ inches. Scallop shells contain a nugget of sweet, firm white flesh joined to the vibrant orange crescent-shaped roe or "coral," which is a delicacy in its own right.

Scallops are deeply symbolic and have long been associated with beauty. According to the legend depicted by Botticelli in one of his most famous paintings, the goddess Venus was born from a scallop shell; her Greek counterpart, Aphrodite, rode across the sea in a scallop shell pulled by six sea horses. Thanks to a miracle involving St. James, scallop shells became the symbol of Christianity and the emblem of medieval pilgrims visiting the shrine at Santiago de Compostela in Spain.

Other names Sometimes known as "pilgrim shells," scallops are *coquille St. Jacques* in French, *pettine* in Italian, *viera* in Spanish.

Buying Scallops are available almost all year round, but are best in winter when the roes are full and firm. The finest are individually hand-caught by divers; needless to say, they are also the most expensive. If you buy scallops in the shell, keep the shells to use as serving dishes for all sorts of fish recipes. Allow 4–5 large scallops per person as a main course, three times this number if they are small. Scallops are also available

Above: Queen scallops

shelled, which saves the effort of cleaning them. Always try to buy scallops with their delicious coral, although this is not always possible. Avoid frozen scallops, which have little or no taste.

Cooking The beard and all dark colored parts of the scallop must be removed before they are cooked and eaten. If the scallops are large, slice the white flesh in half horizontally. Scallops can be thinly sliced and eaten raw with a squeeze of lemon and a drizzle of olive oil. They need only the briefest cooking time to preserve their uniquely firm yet tender texture. Scallops can be poached for a couple of minutes in court-bouillon and served warm or cold in a salad with a tomato and basil vinaigrette or mayonnaise.

Whole scallops in the shell can be baked; seal the shells with a flour and water paste to trap juices. They are equally delicious wrapped in bacon and broiled; coated in egg and bread crumbs and deep-fried; pan-fried for about 30 seconds on each side; stir-fried with colorful vegetables; or steamed with ginger and soy sauce. They make wonderful patés and mousses. A classic dish is *coquilles St. Jacques*, in which poached scallops and corals are sliced, returned to the half shell and coated with Mornay (cheese) sauce, then broiled or baked until browned. A border of mashed potatoes is often piped round the edge of the shell.

Queen scallop *(Chlamys opercularis)*

These miniature scallops measure only about 1¼ inches across. Their cream-colored shells are marked with attractive brown ridges and contain a small nugget of white flesh and a tiny pointed coral. Queen scallops are considerably cheaper than larger scallops, but have the same sweet flavor. They are often sold out of the shell; allow at least a dozen per person. "Queenies," as they are sometimes known, are commercially farmed. They are popular in Asia and are widely used in Chinese cooking.

Above: King scallops

CEPHALOPODS

Despite their appearance, cephalopods, which include cuttlefish, octopus and squid, are mollusks and are more closely related to snails than to fish. They are highly developed creatures with three-dimensional vision, memory and the ability to swim at high speeds. They can also change color according to the environment. Their name derives from the Greek for "head with feet," which sums up their appearance very accurately. The bulbous head contains the mouth, which has two jaws, much like a parrot's beak. This is surrounded by tentacles covered with suckers, which are used for crawling and for seizing their prey. The sack-shaped body contains a mantle cavity that houses the stomach, gills and sex organs. Although they developed from snail-like creatures, cephalopods no longer have an external shell; instead, most have an internal calcareous shell made from spongy material that they can inflate to make themselves buoyant. The most familiar of these is the cuttlebone, from the cuttlefish. Cuttlebones often wash up on beaches, and are used by bird-owners to provide calcium for their pets. In Roman times, ladies ground up cuttlebones and used the powder on their faces and to clean their teeth and their jewelry.

Most cephalopods also contain an ink sac that emits a blackish fluid designed to repel predators and provide a "smokescreen" for the creature when it is under attack. This fluid, or ink, is delicious and can be used for cooking.

Below: Baby cuttlefish

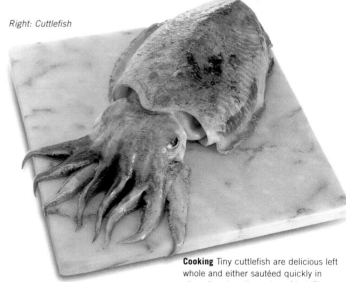

Right: Cuttlefish

Cephalopods are found in almost all the world's oceans. Unlike many sea creatures, they have not yet suffered from overfishing and are still a sustainable food source.

Cuttlefish

The common cuttlefish *(Sepia officinalis)* has a flattened oval head with brownish camouflage stripes on the back and light coloration on the underside. It has eight stubby tentacles and two long tentacles for catching its prey. These are kept rolled up and hidden in openings near its mouth. Cuttlefish are comparatively small, with bodies measuring 10–12 inches. When unfurled, the catching tentacles double its length. As is the case with all cephalopods, the smaller the cuttlefish, the more tender the flesh. The smallest species is the Mediterranean little or dwarf cuttlefish *(sepiola)*, which grows to only 1¼–2½ inches. They are delicious, but time-consuming to prepare, as the tiny cuttlebones must be removed before cooking.

Other names The common cuttlefish is *seiche* in French, *seppia* in Italian, and *sepia* in Spanish. Dwarf cuttlefish are *supion* or *chipiron* in French, *seppiolina* in Italian, and *chipirón* in Spanish.

Cooking Tiny cuttlefish are delicious left whole and either sautéed quickly in olive oil and garlic or deep-fried. They make an excellent addition to rice dishes. Larger specimens can be cooked like squid. A classic Spanish dish is *sepia en su tinta*, cuttlefish cooked in its own ink.

Octopuses *(Octopus vulgaris)*

Unlike cuttlefish and squid, the octopus has no internal shell, nor does it possess tentacles or fins. Octopuses spend their lives lurking in clefts in the rocks on the sea bed, blocking the entrance to their secret holes with shellfish and stones. Their eight equal-size tentacles each have two rows of suckers and can grow to a length of 16¼ feet. The larger an octopus grows, the tougher it becomes, so smaller specimens make the best eating. Octopus ink is contained in the liver and has a much stronger flavor than cuttlefish or squid ink.

Other names Octopus is *poulpe* or *pieuvre* in French; *polpo* in Italian, *pulpo* in Spanish.

Buying It is usually sold ready-prepared and frozen, although you may find whole fresh octopus in Mediterranean fish markets. Look for specimens with two rows of suckers on the tentacles; those with only a single row are curled octopus, which are inferior.

Right: Baby octopus

Cooking Octopus needs long, slow cooking. Before including it in a recipe, it is a good idea to blanch or marinate it. If the octopus has not been prepared already, cut off the tentacles and press out the beak from the head. Discard the head, turn the body inside out and discard the entrails. Rinse it thoroughly, then pound the body and tentacles with a mallet to tenderize them before cutting them into strips. Simmer the octopus in stock or salted water for at least 1 hour, until tender. Octopus can also be stewed with Mediterranean vegetables or robust red wine, or stuffed and baked slowly. Small specimens can be cut into rings and sautéed gently in olive oil. Octopus is best served warm as a salad, dressed with a simple olive oil and lemon vinaigrette. Whole octopus can be cooked slowly in its own juices and ink, but be aware that the ink has a strong flavor that is not to everyone's taste. The Japanese are very fond of octopus and use the boiled tentacles for sushi.

Squid *(Loliginidae)*

These have elongated heads and slender, torpedo-shaped bodies, which end in a kite-shaped fin. Their internal shell is a transparent quill, which looks like a piece of clear acetate. They have ten tentacles, two of which are very long. Squid range from tiny creatures only 3 inches long to the giant squid that weighs several tons and can grow to a length of 55¼ feet. The most common squid is the calamary or long-finned squid *(Loligo vulgaris)*, which is found throughout Europe. It

has smooth, sandy-red spotted skin and weighs up to 4½ pounds. The so-called flying squid does not actually fly, but propels itself out of the water and glides through the air like a guided missile. Squid has firm, lean, white flesh that can be tender and delicious when properly cooked.

Other names In French squid is *encornet* or *calmar*; in Italian it is *calamaro*; in Spanish *calamar* or *puntilla*.

Buying Whole squid are sold fresh or frozen and are available all year round. Make sure they contain their ink sac. Some fishmongers and supermarkets also sell squid ink separately. Squid is also available ready-cleaned, which is very convenient. Whole tentacles and rings are available frozen, sometimes as part of a mixed *fruits de mer*. You can also buy ready-battered squid rings for deep-frying, but these are best avoided. Allow about 7 ounces squid per person.

Cooking The cardinal rule with squid is to cook it either very briefly or for a long time; anything in between and it

Above: Squid

becomes tough and rubbery. The bodies can be stuffed and baked in tomato sauce, or braised with onions and tomatoes. Squid rings can be coated in batter and deep-fried, or boiled briefly and used for a salad. Tiny squid are delicious grilled, sautéed, or coated with egg and bread crumbs and deep-fried. Squid can be added to pasta sauces and rice dishes such as paella. It goes well with such apparently unlikely ingredients as chorizo sausage and black pudding. Squid is frequently used in Asian recipes and lends itself to flavorings such as ginger, chile and lime. The ink can be used to color and flavor homemade pasta and risotto.

Above: Octopus

OTHER EDIBLE SEA CREATURES

The sea is full of wonderful creatures whose strange appearance belies their delicious taste. They may be soft and gelatinous like jellyfish, warty like sea cucumbers or menacingly spiny like sea urchins, but somewhere in the world, they will be regarded as a great delicacy.

Above: Dried jellyfish

Jellyfish *(Scyphoza)*

Jellyfish can strike terror into the hearts of those who have been stung by them. These strange, transparent creatures, with their dangling tentacles, look like open parachutes. They inhabit every ocean of the world, but are eaten almost exclusively in Asia, where they are dried and used to add texture and flavor to many seafood dishes.
Buying and using You will find dried jellyfish at any Asian food store, together with jellyfish preserved in brine. Both types must be soaked in several changes of water before use. In China, slices of dried jellyfish are scalded in boiling water until they curl up, then drained and served in a dressing of soy sauce, sesame oil and rice vinegar. They are also added to shellfish or chicken stir-fries. In Japan, crisply fried strips of jellyfish are served with vinegar, and are sometimes combined with sea urchins.

Sea cucumber *(Holothurioidea)*

It is hard to imagine why anyone would want to eat these repulsive-looking, warty, cucumber-shaped creatures, which rejoice in the alternative unattractive name of sea slugs, but they are considered a great delicacy in Japan and China, where they are reputed to be an aphrodisiac. The plethora of prickles along their backs are actually feet, which enable them to crawl along the sea bed. Sea cucumber is known in Asia as *trepang* or *balatin*. In Japan, it is sliced and eaten raw as sashimi. Sea cucumber is available dried, but requires many hours of soaking to make it palatable. It is used in soup and in several complicated recipes that take so long to prepare that one feels it must have charms that are not apparent to Western palates.

Sea squirt *(Ascidiacea)*

There are over a thousand species of sea squirts, small invertebrates whose bodies are enclosed in thick

Above: Sea cucumber

leathery "tunics." They have two orifices or spouts through which they siphon water in and squirt it out, and attach themselves to the sea bed or rocks and crevices. They are found in the Mediterranean, where they are a popular if esoteric food, particularly in Spain and the south of France, where the local name, *violet*, refers to the sea squirt's resemblance to a large purple fig. Enthusiasts eat them by splitting them in half, then scooping out the soft yellow part inside and eating it raw, despite the strong aroma of iodine. Sea squirts can accumulate

Right: Sea squirt

Opening sea urchins

1 Wearing rubber gloves, hold the sea urchin in the palm of your hand and carefully cut around the soft tissue on the underside, using a special knife or a pair of sharp, pointed scissors.

2 Lift off the top of the sea urchin and remove the mouth and innards, which are inedible. Keep the juices to flavor shellfish sauces, egg dishes or soup.

3 Use a teaspoon to scoop out the bright orange coral.

Right: Prickly sea urchins

toxins, so should never be eaten if they come from polluted waters. **Other names** In French, sea squirt is *violet* or *figue de mer,* in Italian, *ovo di mare.*

Sea urchin *(Echinoidea)*

One of the most unpleasant experiences a traveler can have is to tread on the long, poisonous spines of a sea urchin. To lovers of seafood, however, eating these marine creatures is one of life's great gastronomic pleasures. There are over eight hundred species of sea urchin, found all over the world, but only a few are edible. The most common European variety is the *Paracentrotus lividus,* a greenish or purplish-black hemispherical creature that measures about 3 inches across, and whose shell is covered with long spines, much like those of a hedgehog. The females are slightly larger than the males and are said to taste better. Only the orange or yellow ovaries or gonads (known as the coral) are eaten; these have a pungent taste reminiscent of iodine.

Other names In French, sea urchins are variously known as *oursin, châtaigne de mer* (sea chestnut) and *hérisson de mer* (sea hedgehog); in Italian, they are *riccio di mare,* in Spanish, *erizo de mar.*

Buying Overfishing has made sea urchins rare and expensive. The best

are the purple or green urchins with long spines; short-spined, whitish species have an extremely strong flavor and are best used in cooked dishes. Look for urchins with firm spines and a tightly closed mouth (on the underside). If you find a source of fresh sea urchins, they can be kept in the refrigerator for up to three days.

Preparing The best implement for opening sea urchins is a *coupe oursin.* Failing this, use very sharp scissors. Wearing gloves, cut into the soft tissue around the mouth and lift off the top to reveal the coral. Alternatively, slice off the top like a boiled egg.

Cooking Sea urchins can be eaten raw or used to flavor sauces, pasta, omelets and scrambled eggs. They make wonderful soup, which can be served in small portions in the shell and eaten with a teaspoon. The shells can also be used as containers for other seafood such as langoustines in a sea urchin sauce.

FISH AND SHELLFISH RECIPES

Fish and shellfish are both nutritious and enticing, and when
properly cooked can be some of the most delicious foods
imaginable. Every fish and shellfish has its own unique flavor,
offering something for all tastes. In this collection of
inspirational recipes there is a host of stunning
contemporary creations, as well as time-honored
classic dishes. With the increasingly wide range of
fish and shellfish available at fishmongers and
supermarkets, you can allow yourself the
pleasure of experimenting and enjoying
these wonderful dishes.

SOUPS

From light, spicy broths to hearty stews, fish and shellfish soups are
delightful. Chilled Cucumber and Shrimp Soup is perfect for summer
eating, while Scallop and Jerusalem Artichoke Soup and substantial
Bouillabaisse make wonderful winter warmers, along with
Clam Chowder from New England. For real luxury,
treat yourself and your guests to creamy Lobster Bisque, or travel to
Asia with spicy Malaysian Shrimp Laksa and the
wonderfully fragrant Thai Fish Broth.

CHILLED CUCUMBER AND SHRIMP SOUP

IF YOU'VE NEVER SERVED A CHILLED SOUP BEFORE, THIS IS THE ONE TO TRY. DELICIOUS AND LIGHT, IT'S THE PERFECT WAY TO CELEBRATE SUMMER.

2 Stir in the milk, bring almost to the boiling point, then lower the heat and simmer for 5 minutes. Transfer the soup to a blender or food processor and purée until smooth. Season to taste.

3 Pour the soup into a large bowl and let cool. When cool, stir in the shrimp, chopped herbs and cream. Cover, transfer to the refrigerator and chill for at least 2 hours.

4 To serve, ladle the soup into four individual bowls and top each portion with a dollop of crème fraîche or sour cream, if using, and place a shrimp on the edge of each dish. Sprinkle a little extra chopped dill on the soup and tuck two or three chives under the shrimp on the edge of the bowls to garnish. Serve immediately.

SERVES FOUR

INGREDIENTS
  2 tablespoons butter
  2 shallots, finely chopped
  2 garlic cloves, crushed
  1 cucumber, peeled, seeded
    and diced
  1¼ cups milk
  8 ounces cooked peeled shrimp
  1 tablespoon each finely chopped
    fresh mint, dill, chives and chervil
  1¼ cups whipping cream
  salt and ground white pepper
For the garnish
  2 tablespoons crème fraîche or
    sour cream (optional)
  4 large, cooked shrimp, peeled with
    tail intact
  fresh dill and chives

1 Melt the butter in a saucepan and cook the shallots and garlic over low heat until soft but not colored. Add the cucumber and cook gently, stirring frequently, until tender.

COOK'S TIP
If you prefer hot soup, reheat it gently until hot but not boiling. Do not boil, or the delicate flavor will be spoiled.

VARIATION
If desired, you can use other cooked shellfish instead of the peeled shrimp—try fresh, frozen or canned crabmeat, or cooked, flaked salmon fillet.

SCALLOP AND JERUSALEM ARTICHOKE SOUP

*THE SUBTLE SWEETNESS OF SCALLOPS COMBINES WELL WITH THE FLAVOR OF JERUSALEM ARTICHOKES IN
THIS ATTRACTIVE GOLDEN SOUP. FOR AN EVEN MORE COLORFUL VERSION, SUBSTITUTE PUMPKIN FOR
THE ARTICHOKES AND USE EXTRA STOCK INSTEAD OF THE MILK.*

SERVES SIX

INGREDIENTS

2¼ pounds Jerusalem artichokes
juice of ½ lemon
½ cup butter
1 onion, finely chopped
2½ cups fish stock
1¼ cups milk
generous pinch of
   saffron threads
6 large or 12 small scallops, with
   their corals
⅔ cup whipping cream
salt and ground white pepper
3 tablespoons sliced almonds and
   1 tablespoon finely chopped
   fresh chervil, to garnish

1 Working quickly, scrub and peel the
Jerusalem artichokes, cut them into
¾-inch chunks and drop them
into a bowl of cold water, which has
been acidulated with the lemon juice.
This will prevent the artichokes
from discoloring.

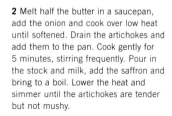

2 Melt half the butter in a saucepan,
add the onion and cook over low heat
until softened. Drain the artichokes and
add them to the pan. Cook gently for
5 minutes, stirring frequently. Pour in
the stock and milk, add the saffron and
bring to a boil. Lower the heat and
simmer until the artichokes are tender
but not mushy.

3 Meanwhile, carefully separate the
scallop corals from the white flesh.
Prick the corals and slice each scallop
in half horizontally. Heat half the
remaining butter in a frying pan, add
the scallops and corals and cook very
briefly (for about 1 minute) on each
side. Dice the scallops and corals,
keeping them separate, and set them
aside until needed.

4 When the artichokes are cooked,
transfer the contents of the pan to a
blender or food processor. Add half the
white scallop meat and purée until very
smooth. Return the soup to the clean
pan, season with salt and white pepper
and keep hot over low heat while you
prepare the garnish.

5 Heat the remaining butter in a frying
pan, add the almonds and toss over
medium heat until golden brown. Add
the diced corals and cook for about
30 seconds. Stir the cream into the
soup and add the remaining diced
white scallop meat. Ladle the soup into
individual bowls and garnish each
serving with the almonds, scallop corals
and a sprinkling of chervil.

MATELOTE

TRADITIONALLY THIS FISHERMEN'S CHUNKY SOUP IS MADE FROM FRESHWATER FISH, INCLUDING EEL. ANY FIRM FISH CAN BE USED, BUT TRY TO INCLUDE AT LEAST SOME EEL, AND USE A ROBUST DRY WHITE OR RED WINE FOR EXTRA FLAVOR.

SERVES SIX

INGREDIENTS
  2¼ pounds mixed fish, including
    1 pound conger eel if possible
  ¼ cup butter
  1 onion, thickly sliced
  2 celery stalks, thickly sliced
  2 carrots, thickly sliced
  1 bottle dry white or red wine
  1 fresh bouquet garni containing
    parsley, bay leaf and chervil
  2 cloves
  6 black peppercorns
  beurre manié for thickening, see
    Cook's Tip
  salt and cayenne pepper
For the garnish
  2 tablespoons butter
  12 baby onions, peeled
  12 button mushrooms
  chopped flat-leaf parsley

1 Cut all the fish into thick slices, removing any obvious bones. Melt the butter in a large saucepan, put in the fish and sliced vegetables and stir over medium heat until lightly browned. Pour in the wine and enough cold water to cover. Add the bouquet garni and spices and season. Bring to a boil, lower the heat and simmer gently for 20–30 minutes, until the fish is tender, skimming the surface occasionally.

2 Meanwhile, prepare the garnish. Heat the butter in a deep frying pan and sauté the baby onions until golden and tender. Add the mushrooms and sauté until golden. Season and keep hot.

3 Strain the soup through a large sieve placed over a clean pan. Discard the herbs and spices in the sieve, then divide the fish among deep soup plates (you can skin the fish if you want to, but this is not essential) and keep hot.

4 Reheat the soup until it boils. Lower the heat and whisk in the *beurre manié* little by little until the soup thickens. Season it and pour on the fish. Garnish each portion with the sautéed baby onions and mushrooms and sprinkle with chopped parsley.

COOK'S TIP
To make the *beurre manié* for thickening, mix 1 tablespoon softened butter with 1 tablespoon all-purpose flour. Add to the boiling soup a pinch at a time, whisking constantly.

FISH SOUP <u>WITH</u> ROUILLE

MAKING THIS SOUP IS SIMPLICITY ITSELF, YET THE FLAVOR SUGGESTS IT IS THE PRODUCT OF PAINSTAKING PREPARATION AND COOKING.

SERVES SIX

INGREDIENTS
   2¼ pounds mixed fish
   2 tablespoons olive oil
   1 onion, chopped
   1 carrot, chopped
   1 leek, chopped
   2 large ripe tomatoes, chopped
   1 red bell pepper, seeded
     and chopped
   2 garlic cloves, peeled
   ⅔ cup tomato paste
   1 large fresh bouquet garni,
     containing 3 parsley sprigs,
     3 celery stalks and 3 bay leaves
   1¼ cups dry white wine
   salt and ground black pepper
For the rouille
   2 garlic cloves, roughly chopped
   1 teaspoon coarse salt
   1 thick slice of white bread, crust
     removed, soaked in water and
     squeezed dry
   1 fresh red chile, seeded and
     roughly chopped
   3 tablespoons olive oil
   salt and cayenne pepper
For the garnish
   12 slices of baguette, toasted
   2 ounces Gruyère cheese,
     finely grated

1 Cut the fish into 3-inch chunks, removing any obvious bones. Heat the oil in a large saucepan, then add the fish and chopped vegetables. Stir until these begin to color.

2 Add all the other soup ingredients, then pour in just enough cold water to cover the mixture. Season well and bring to just below the boiling point, then lower the heat to a bare simmer, cover and cook for 1 hour.

3 Meanwhile, make the rouille. Put the garlic and coarse salt in a mortar and crush into a paste with a pestle. Add the soaked bread and chile and pound until smooth, or purée in a food processor. Whisk in the olive oil, a drop at a time, to make a smooth, shiny sauce that resembles mayonnaise. Season with salt and add a pinch of cayenne if you want a fiery taste. Set the rouille aside.

4 Lift out and discard the bouquet garni from the soup. Purée the soup in batches in a food processor, then strain through a fine sieve placed over a clean pan, pushing the solids through with the back of a ladle.

5 Reheat the soup without letting it boil. Check the seasoning and ladle into individual bowls. Top each serving with two slices of toasted baguette, a spoonful of rouille and some grated Gruyère.

COOK'S TIP
Any firm fish can be used for this recipe. If you use whole fish, include the head, which enhance the flavor of the soup.

LOBSTER BISQUE

BISQUE IS A LUXURIOUS, VELVETY SOUP, WHICH CAN BE MADE WITH ANY CRUSTACEANS.

SERVES SIX

INGREDIENTS
1¼ pounds fresh lobster
6 tablespoons butter
1 onion, chopped
1 carrot, diced
1 celery stalk, diced
3 tablespoons brandy, plus extra for
  serving (optional)
1 cup dry white wine
4 cups fish stock
1 tablespoon tomato paste
scant ½ cup long-grain rice
1 fresh bouquet garni
⅔ cup heavy cream, plus extra
  to garnish
salt, ground white pepper and
  cayenne pepper

1 Cut the lobster into pieces. Melt half the butter in a large saucepan, add the vegetables and cook over low heat until soft. Put in the lobster and stir until the shell on each piece turns red.

2 Pour in the brandy and set it on fire. When the flames die down, add the wine and boil until reduced by half. Pour in the fish stock and simmer for 2–3 minutes. Remove the lobster.

3 Stir in the tomato paste and rice, add the bouquet garni and cook until the rice is tender. Meanwhile, remove the lobster meat from the shell and return the shells to the saucepan. Dice the lobster meat and set it aside.

COOK'S TIP
It is best to buy a live lobster, chilling it in the freezer until it is comatose and then killing it just before cooking. If you can't face the procedure, use a cooked lobster; take care not to overcook the flesh. Stir for only 30–60 seconds.

4 When the rice is cooked, discard all the larger bits of shell. Transfer the mixture to a blender or food processor and process into a purée. Press the purée through a fine sieve placed over the clean pan. Stir the mixture, then heat until almost boiling. Season with salt, pepper and cayenne, then lower the heat and stir in the cream. Dice the remaining butter and whisk it into the bisque. Add the diced lobster meat and serve immediately. If desired, pour a small spoonful of brandy into each soup bowl and swirl in a little extra cream.

BOUILLABAISSE

AUTHENTIC BOUILLABAISSE COMES FROM THE SOUTH OF FRANCE AND INCLUDES RASCASSE (SCORPION FISH) AS AN ESSENTIAL INGREDIENT. IT IS, HOWEVER, PERFECTLY POSSIBLE TO MAKE THIS WONDERFUL MAIN-COURSE SOUP WITHOUT IT. USE AS LARGE A VARIETY OF FISH AS YOU CAN.

SERVES FOUR

INGREDIENTS

3 tablespoons olive oil
2 onions, chopped
2 leeks, white parts only, chopped
4 garlic cloves, chopped
1 pound ripe tomatoes, peeled
  and chopped
12 cups boiling fish stock or water
1 tablespoon tomato paste
large pinch of saffron threads
1 fresh bouquet garni, containing
  2 thyme sprigs, 2 bay leaves and
  2 fennel sprigs
6½ pounds mixed fish, cleaned and
  cut into large chunks
4 potatoes, peeled and thickly sliced
salt, pepper and cayenne pepper
a bowl of rouille (see Fish Soup) and
  a bowl of aïoli (see Provençal Aïoli
  with Salt Cod), to serve
For the garnish
  16 slices of French bread, toasted
    and rubbed with garlic
  2 tablespoons chopped parsley

2 Simmer the soup for 5–8 minutes, removing each type of fish as it becomes cooked. Continue to cook until the potatoes are very tender. Season well with salt, pepper and cayenne.

3 Divide the fish and potatoes among individual soup plates. Strain the soup and ladle it onto the fish. Garnish with toasted French bread and parsley. Serve with rouille and aïoli.

1 Heat the oil in a large saucepan. Add the onions, leeks, garlic and tomatoes. Cook until slightly softened. Stir in the stock or water, tomato paste and saffron. Add the bouquet garni and boil until the oil is amalgamated. Lower the heat; add the fish and potatoes.

COOK'S TIP
Suitable fish for Bouillabaisse include conger eel, monkfish and John Dory, among others.

CLAM CHOWDER

IF FRESH CLAMS ARE HARD TO FIND, USE FROZEN OR CANNED CLAMS FOR THIS CLASSIC RECIPE FROM NEW ENGLAND. LARGE CLAMS SHOULD BE CUT INTO SMALLER CHUNKS. RESERVE A FEW CLAMS IN THEIR SHELLS FOR GARNISH, IF DESIRED. TRADITIONALLY, THE SOUP IS SERVED WITH SALTINES OR OTHER CRACKERS. YOU SHOULD BE ABLE TO FIND THESE AT ANY SUPERMARKET.

SERVES FOUR

INGREDIENTS
3¾ ounces salt pork or thinly sliced
   unsmoked bacon, diced
1 large onion, chopped
2 potatoes, peeled and cut into
   ½-inch cubes
1 bay leaf
1 fresh thyme sprig
1¼ cups milk
14 ounces cooked shelled clams,
   cooking liquid reserved
⅔ cup heavy cream
salt, ground white pepper and
   cayenne pepper
finely chopped fresh parsley, to garnish

1 Put the salt pork or bacon in a saucepan, and heat gently, stirring frequently, until the fat runs and the meat is starting to brown. Add the chopped onion and cook over low heat until softened but not browned.

2 Add the cubed potatoes, the bay leaf and thyme sprig, stir well to coat with fat, then pour in the milk and reserved clam liquid and bring to a boil. Lower the heat and simmer for about 10 minutes, until the potatoes are tender but still firm. Lift out the bay leaf and thyme sprig and discard.

3 Remove the shells from most of the clams. Add all the clams to the pan and season to taste with salt, pepper and cayenne. Simmer gently for 5 more minutes, then stir in the cream. Heat until the soup is very hot, but do not let it boil. Pour into a tureen, garnish with the chopped parsley and serve.

CHINESE CRAB AND CORN SOUP

FROZEN WHITE CRABMEAT WORKS AS WELL AS FRESH IN THIS DELICATELY FLAVORED SOUP.

SERVES FOUR

INGREDIENTS
2½ cups fish or chicken stock
1-inch piece fresh ginger root, peeled
   and very finely sliced
14-ounce can creamed corn
5 ounces cooked white crabmeat
1 tablespoon arrowroot or cornstarch
1 tablespoon rice wine or dry sherry
1–2 tablespoons light soy sauce
1 egg white
salt and ground white pepper
shredded scallions, to garnish

1 Put the stock and ginger in a large saucepan and bring to a boil. Stir in the creamed corn and bring back to a boil.

2 Switch off the heat and add the crabmeat. Put the arrowroot or cornstarch in a cup and stir in the rice wine or sherry to make a smooth paste; stir this into the soup. Cook over low heat for about 3 minutes, until the soup has thickened and is slightly glutinous in consistency. Add light soy sauce, salt and white pepper to taste.

3 In a bowl, whisk the egg white into a stiff foam. Gradually fold it into the soup. Ladle the soup into heated bowls, garnish each portion with scallions and serve.

VARIATION
To make shrimp and corn soup, substitute 5 ounces cooked peeled shrimp for the crabmeat. Chop the peeled shrimp roughly and add to the soup at the beginning of step 2.

COOK'S TIP
This soup is sometimes made with regular corn, but creamed corn gives a better texture. If you can't find it in a can, use thawed frozen creamed corn instead; the results will be just as good.

THAI FISH BROTH

LEMONGRASS, CHILES AND GALANGAL ARE AMONG THE FLAVORINGS USED IN THIS FRAGRANT SOUP.

SERVES TWO TO THREE

INGREDIENTS
4 cups fish or light chicken stock
4 lemongrass stalks
3 limes
2 small fresh hot red chiles, seeded
   and thinly sliced
¾-inch piece fresh galangal, peeled
   and thinly sliced
6 cilantro stems, with leaves
2 kaffir lime leaves, coarsely
   chopped (optional)
12 ounces monkfish fillet, skinned
   and cut into 1-inch pieces
1 tablespoon rice vinegar
3 tablespoons *nam pla* (Thai fish
   sauce)
2 tablespoons chopped cilantro
   leaves, to garnish

1 Pour the stock into a saucepan and bring it to a boil. Meanwhile, slice the bulb end of each lemongrass stalk diagonally into pieces about ⅛ inch thick. Peel off four wide strips of lime zest with a potato peeler, taking care to avoid the white pith underneath, which would make the soup bitter. Squeeze the limes and reserve the juice.

2 Add the sliced lemongrass, lime zest, chiles, galangal and cilantro stems to the stock, with the kaffir lime leaves, if using. Simmer for 1–2 minutes.

VARIATIONS
Shrimp, scallops, squid or sole can be substituted for the monkfish. If you use kaffir lime leaves, you will need the juice of only 2 limes.

3 Add the monkfish, rice vinegar and *nam pla*, with half the reserved lime juice. Simmer for about 3 minutes, until the fish is just cooked. Lift out and discard the cilantro stems, taste the broth and add more lime juice if necessary; the soup should taste quite sour. Sprinkle with the cilantro leaves and serve very hot.

MALAYSIAN SHRIMP LAKSA

THIS SPICY SHRIMP AND NOODLE SOUP TASTES JUST AS GOOD WHEN MADE WITH FRESH CRABMEAT OR ANY FLAKED COOKED FISH. IF YOU ARE SHORT ON TIME OR CAN'T FIND ALL THE SPICY PASTE INGREDIENTS, BUY READY-MADE LAKSA PASTE, WHICH IS AVAILABLE AT ASIAN FOOD STORES.

SERVES TWO TO THREE

INGREDIENTS

4 ounces rice vermicelli or stir-fry
   rice noodles
1 tablespoon vegetable or
   peanut oil
2½ cups fish stock
1⅔ cups thin coconut milk
2 tablespoons *nam pla* (Thai
   fish sauce)
½ lime
16–24 cooked peeled shrimp
salt and cayenne pepper
¼ cup cilantro sprigs and leaves,
   chopped, to garnish

For the spicy paste
2 lemongrass stalks, finely chopped
2 fresh red chiles, seeded
   and chopped
1-inch piece fresh ginger root, peeled
   and sliced
½ teaspoon *blachan* (dried
   shrimp paste)
2 garlic cloves, chopped
½ teaspoon ground turmeric
2 tablespoons tamarind paste

1 Cook the rice vermicelli or noodles in a large saucepan of boiling salted water according to the instructions on the package. Transfer to a large sieve or colander, then rinse under cold water and drain. Keep warm.

2 To make the spicy paste, place all the prepared ingredients in a mortar and pound with a pestle. Alternatively, put the ingredients in a food processor and process until a smooth paste is formed.

3 Heat the vegetable or peanut oil in a large saucepan, add the spicy paste and fry, stirring constantly, for a few moments to release all the flavors, but be careful not to let it burn.

4 Add the fish stock and coconut milk and bring to a boil. Stir in the *nam pla*, then simmer for 5 minutes. Season with salt and cayenne to taste, adding a squeeze of lime. Add the shrimp and heat through for a few seconds.

5 Divide the noodles among two or three soup plates. Pour in the soup, making sure that each portion includes an equal number of shrimp. Garnish with cilantro and serve piping hot.

APPETIZERS

Fish and shellfish make a perfect light start to any meal, whatever the main course. Titillate your tastebuds with refreshing Ceviche or that old favorite, Shrimp Cocktail. Classic Oysters Rockefeller and Gratin of Mussels with Pesto are as succulent as they are sophisticated, while deliciously crisp Deviled Whitebait provides piquancy and crunch. If you prefer fish to shellfish, Red Snapper Dolmades make an unusual appetizer.

CEVICHE

YOU CAN USE ALMOST ANY FIRM-FLESHED FISH FOR THIS SOUTH AMERICAN DISH, PROVIDED THAT IT IS PERFECTLY FRESH. THE FISH IS "COOKED" BY THE ACTION OF THE ACIDIC LIME JUICE. ADJUST THE AMOUNT OF CHILE ACCORDING TO YOUR TASTE.

SERVES SIX

INGREDIENTS
    1½ pounds halibut, turbot, sea bass
      or salmon fillet, skinned
    juice of 3 limes
    1–2 fresh red chiles, seeded and very
      finely chopped
    1 tablespoon olive oil
    salt
For the garnish
    4 large firm tomatoes, peeled, seeded
      and diced
    1 ripe avocado, peeled
      and diced
    1 tablespoon lemon juice
    2 tablespoons olive oil
    2 tablespoons cilantro leaves

1 Cut the fish into strips measuring about 2 × ½ inches. Lay these in a shallow dish and pour on the lime juice, turning the fish strips to coat them all over in the juice. Cover with plastic wrap and let sit for 1 hour.

2 Combine all the garnish ingredients, except the cilantro. Set aside.

3 Season the fish with salt and sprinkle on the chiles. Drizzle on the olive oil. Toss the fish in the mixture, then replace the cover. Let marinate in the refrigerator for 15–30 more minutes.

4 To serve, divide the garnish among six plates. Spoon on the ceviche, sprinkle with cilantro and serve.

MARINATED SMOKED HADDOCK FILLETS

THIS SIMPLE DISH IS ALSO EXCELLENT MADE WITH KIPPER FILLETS; USE WHISKEY INSTEAD OF THE RUM. IF YOU PREFER, OMIT THE SPIRITS AND ADD A TEASPOON OF SUGAR TO THE MARINADE.

SERVES SIX

INGREDIENTS

1 pound undyed smoked haddock
   fillet, skinned
1 onion, very thinly sliced
   into rings
1–2 teaspoons Dijon mustard
2 tablespoons lemon juice
6 tablespoons olive oil
3 tablespoons dark rum
12 small new potatoes, scrubbed
2 tablespoons chopped fresh dill,
   plus 6 dill sprigs to garnish
ground black pepper

COOK'S TIP

Try to get a large, thick haddock fillet. If all you can find are small pieces, you can still make the dish, but serve the pieces whole instead of slicing them.

1 Cut the fish fillet in half lengthwise. Arrange the pieces in a single layer in a shallow nonmetallic dish. Sprinkle the onion rings evenly on top.

2 Whisk together the mustard, lemon juice and some pepper. Add the oil gradually, whisking. Pour two-thirds of the dressing on the fish. Cover the dish with plastic wrap and let the fish marinate for 2 hours in a cool place. Sprinkle on the rum and marinate for 1 hour more.

3 Cook the potatoes in boiling salted water until tender. Drain, cut in half and transfer to a bowl. Cool until warm, then toss in the remaining dressing. Stir in the dill, cover and set aside.

4 Slice the haddock thinly, as for smoked salmon, or leave whole. Arrange on individual plates and spoon on some marinade and onion rings. Pile the potato halves on one side of each plate and garnish each portion with dill. Serve chilled or at room temperature.

MOULES PROVENÇALES

EATING THESE DELECTABLE MUSSELS IS A MESSY AFFAIR, WHICH IS PART OF THEIR CHARM. PASS PLENTY OF CRUSTY FRENCH BREAD FOR MOPPING UP THE JUICES, AND DON'T FORGET FINGERBOWLS OF WARM WATER AND A PLATE FOR DISCARDED SHELLS.

SERVES FOUR

INGREDIENTS

2 tablespoons olive oil
7 ounces bacon, cubed
1 onion, finely chopped
3 garlic cloves, finely chopped
1 bay leaf
1 tablespoon chopped fresh mixed
  Provençal herbs, thyme, marjoram,
  basil, oregano and savory
1–2 tablespoons sun-dried tomatoes
  in oil, chopped
4 large, very ripe tomatoes, peeled,
  seeded and chopped
½ cup pitted black
  olives, chopped
7 tablespoons dry white wine
5–5¼ pounds live mussels, scrubbed
  and bearded
salt and ground black pepper
4 tablespoons coarsely chopped
  fresh parsley, to garnish

1 Heat the oil in a large saucepan. Fry the bacon until golden and crisp. Remove with a slotted spoon; set aside. Add the onion and garlic to the pan and cook gently until softened. Add the herbs, with both types of tomatoes. Cook gently for 5 minutes, stirring frequently. Stir in the olives and season.

2 Put the wine and mussels in another pan. Cover and shake over high heat for 5 minutes, until the mussels open. Discard any that remain closed.

3 Strain the cooking liquid into the saucepan containing the tomato sauce and boil until reduced by about one-third. Add the mussels and stir to coat them thoroughly with the sauce. Take out the bay leaf.

4 Divide the mussels and sauce among four heated dishes. Sprinkle on the fried bacon and chopped parsley and serve piping hot.

OYSTERS ROCKEFELLER

THIS IS THE PERFECT DISH FOR THOSE WHO PREFER THEIR OYSTERS LIGHTLY COOKED. AS A CHEAPER ALTERNATIVE, FOR THOSE WHO ARE NOT "AS RICH AS ROCKEFELLER," GIVE MUSSELS OR CLAMS THE SAME TREATMENT; THEY WILL ALSO TASTE DELICIOUS.

SERVES SIX

INGREDIENTS
  3 cups coarse salt, plus extra to serve
  24 oysters, opened
  ½ cup butter
  2 shallots, finely chopped
  1¼ pounds spinach leaves,
    finely chopped
  ¼ cup chopped fresh parsley
  ¼ cup chopped celery leaves
  6 tablespoons fresh white
    bread crumbs
  Tabasco sauce or cayenne pepper
  2–4 teaspoons Pernod or Ricard
  salt and ground black pepper
  lemon wedges, to serve

COOK'S TIP
If you prefer a smoother stuffing, process it into a paste in a food processor or blender.

1 Preheat the oven to 425°F. Make a bed of coarse salt on two large baking sheets. Set the oysters in the half-shell in the bed of salt to keep them steady. Set aside.

2 Melt the butter in a frying pan. Add the finely chopped shallots and cook them over low heat for 2–3 minutes, until they are softened. Stir in the spinach and let it wilt.

3 Add the parsley, celery leaves and bread crumbs to the pan and sauté gently for 5 minutes. Season with salt, pepper and Tabasco or cayenne.

4 Divide the stuffing among the oysters. Drizzle a few drops of Pernod or Ricard on each oyster, then bake for about 5 minutes, until bubbling and golden brown. Serve on a heated platter on a shallow salt bed with lemon wedges.

AROMATIC JUMBO SHRIMP

*THERE IS NO ELEGANT WAY TO EAT THESE AROMATIC SHRIMP—JUST HOLD THEM BY THE TAILS, PULL
THEM OFF THE STICKS WITH YOUR FINGERS AND POP THEM INTO YOUR MOUTH.*

SERVES FOUR

INGREDIENTS
   16 jumbo shrimp or scampi tails
   ½ teaspoon chili powder
   1 teaspoon fennel seeds
   5 Szechuan or black peppercorns
   1 star anise, broken into segments
   1 cinnamon stick, broken into pieces
   2 tablespoons peanut or
      sunflower oil
   2 garlic cloves, chopped
   ¾-inch piece fresh ginger root,
      peeled and finely chopped
   1 shallot, chopped
   2 tablespoons water
   2 tablespoons rice vinegar
   2 tablespoons brown sugar
   salt and ground black pepper
   lime slices and chopped scallion,
      to garnish

1 Thread the shrimp or scampi tails
in pairs on eight wooden toothpicks.
Set aside. Heat a frying pan, put in all
the chili powder, fennel seeds,
Szechuan or black peppercorns,
star anise and cinnamon stick and
dry-fry for 1–2 minutes to release the
flavors. Let cool, then coarsely grind
the spices in a grinder or transfer into
a mortar and crush with a pestle.

2 Heat the peanut or sunflower oil in a
shallow pan, add the garlic, ginger and
chopped shallot, and then sauté gently
until very lightly colored. Add the
crushed spices and seasoning and
cook the mixture gently for 2 minutes.
Pour in the water and simmer, stirring,
for 5 minutes.

3 Add the rice vinegar and brown sugar,
stir until dissolved, then add the shrimp
or scampi tails. Cook for 3–5 minutes,
until the seafood has turned pink, but is
still very juicy. Serve hot, garnished with
lime slices and scallion.

COOK'S TIP
If you buy whole shrimp, remove the
heads before cooking them.

SHRIMP AND VEGETABLE CROSTINI

USE BOTTLED CARCIOFINI *(TINY ARTICHOKE HEARTS PRESERVED IN OLIVE OIL) FOR THIS SIMPLE
APPETIZER, THAT CAN BE PREPARED VERY QUICKLY.*

SERVES FOUR

INGREDIENTS
   1 pound whole cooked shrimp,
      in the shell
   4 thick slices of ciabatta, cut
      diagonally across
   3 garlic cloves, peeled and
      2 halved lengthwise
   ¼ cup olive oil
   2 cups button mushrooms, trimmed
   12 drained bottled *carciofini*
   ¼ cup chopped flat-leaf parsley
   salt and ground black pepper

COOK'S TIP
Don't be tempted to use thawed frozen
shrimp, especially those that have been
peeled; freshly cooked shrimp in their
shells are infinitely better.

1 Peel the shrimp and remove the
heads. Rub the ciabatta slices on both
sides with the cut sides of the halved
garlic cloves, drizzle with a little of the
olive oil and toast or broil until lightly
browned. Keep hot.

2 Finely chop the remaining garlic. Heat
the remaining oil in a saucepan and
gently sauté the garlic until golden, but
do not let it brown.

3 Add the mushrooms and stir to
coat with oil. Season and sauté for
2–3 minutes. Gently stir in the drained
carciofini, then add the chopped flat-
leaf parsley.

4 Season again, then stir in the shrimp
and sauté briefly to warm through. Pile
the shrimp mixture onto the ciabatta,
pour on any remaining cooking juices
and serve immediately.

SCALLOPS <u>WITH</u> SAMPHIRE <u>AND</u> LIME

SAMPHIRE HAS A WONDERFUL TASTE AND AROMA OF THE SEA. IT IS THE PERFECT COMPLEMENT TO
SCALLOPS AND HELPS TO CREATE A VERY ATTRACTIVE APPETIZER.

SERVES FOUR

INGREDIENTS
  8 ounces fresh samphire
  12 large or 24 queen scallops, out of
  the shell
  1¼ cups dry white wine
  juice of 2 limes
  1 tablespoon peanut or
  vegetable oil
  ½ cucumber, peeled, seeded
  and diced
  ground black pepper
  chopped fresh parsley, to garnish

1 Wash the fresh samphire in several
changes of cold water. Drain, then trim
off any woody ends. Bring a saucepan
of water to a boil, then drop in the
samphire and cook for 3–5 minutes,
until tender but still crisp. Drain, refresh
under cold water and drain again.

2 If the scallops are large, cut them in
half horizontally. Detach the corals. In a
shallow pan, bring the wine to a boil
and cook until it is reduced by about
one-third. Lower the heat and add the
lime juice to the pan.

3 Add the scallops and corals and
poach gently for 3–4 minutes, until the
scallops are just cooked, but still
opaque. Using a slotted spoon, lift out
the scallops and corals and set aside.

COOK'S TIP
Samphire grows wild in estuaries and
salt marshes in Europe and North
America. High-quality fishmongers
sometimes stock it.

4 Leave the cooking liquid to cool until
tepid, then whisk in the peanut or
vegetable oil. Add the samphire,
cucumber, scallops and corals and toss
lightly to mix. Grind over some black
pepper, cover and let sit at room
temperature for about 1 hour to let the
flavors develop. Divide the mixture
among four individual dishes, and then
garnish with chopped fresh parsley.
Serve the dish at room temperature.

GRATIN OF MUSSELS WITH PESTO

This is the perfect appetizer for serving when time is short, as both the pesto and the mussels can be prepared in advance, and the dish assembled and broiled at the last minute.

SERVES FOUR

INGREDIENTS

36 large live mussels, scrubbed
  and bearded
7 tablespoons dry white wine
¼ cup finely chopped fresh
  flat-leaf parsley
1 garlic clove, finely chopped
2 tablespoons fresh white
  bread crumbs
¼ cup olive oil
chopped fresh basil, to garnish
crusty bread, to serve

For the pesto

2 fat garlic cloves, chopped
½ teaspoon coarse salt
3 cups basil leaves
⅓ cup pine nuts, chopped
⅔ cup freshly grated
  Parmesan cheese
½ cup extra virgin olive oil

1 Put the mussels in a saucepan with the wine, clamp on the lid and shake over high heat for 3–4 minutes, until the mussels have opened. Discard any that remain closed.

2 As soon as the mussels are cool enough to handle, strain the cooking liquid and keep it for another recipe. Discard the empty half-shells. Arrange the mussels in their half-shells in a single layer in four individual gratin dishes. Cover and set aside.

COOK'S TIP

Homemade pesto is best but when basil is out of season—or you are in a hurry— a jar may be used instead.

3 To make the pesto, put the chopped garlic and salt in a mortar and pound into a purée with a pestle. Then add the basil leaves and chopped pine nuts and crush into a thick paste. Work in the Parmesan cheese, and gradually drip in enough olive oil to make a smooth and creamy paste. Alternatively, use a food processor.

4 Spoon pesto on the mussels placed in gratin dishes. Mix the parsley, garlic and bread crumbs. Sprinkle on the mussels. Drizzle with the oil.

5 Preheat the broiler to high. Stand the dishes on a baking sheet and broil for 3 minutes. Garnish with chopped basil and serve with crusty bread.

SHRIMP COCKTAIL

*THERE IS NO BETTER APPETIZER THAN A GOOD, FRESH SHRIMP COCKTAIL—AND NOTHING WORSE THAN
ONE IN WHICH SOGGY SHRIMP SWIM IN A THIN, VINEGARY SAUCE EMBEDDED IN LIMP LETTUCE. THIS
RECIPE SHOWS JUST HOW GOOD A SHRIMP COCKTAIL CAN BE.*

SERVES SIX

INGREDIENTS
¼ cup heavy cream,
  lightly whipped
¼ cup mayonnaise,
  preferably homemade
¼ cup ketchup
1–2 teaspoons Worcestershire sauce
juice of 1 lemon
½ Romaine lettuce or other very
  crisp lettuce
1 pound cooked peeled shrimp
salt, ground black pepper
  and paprika
6 large whole cooked shrimp in the
  shell, to garnish (optional)
thinly sliced brown bread with butter
  and lemon wedges, to serve

1 Place the lightly whipped cream,
mayonnaise and ketchup in a small
bowl and whisk lightly to combine. Add
Worcestershire sauce to taste, then
whisk in enough of the lemon juice to
make a really tangy sauce.

COOK'S TIP
Partly peeled shrimp make a pretty
garnish. To prepare, carefully peel the
body shell from the shrimp and leave the
tail "fan" for decoration.

2 Finely shred the lettuce and fill six
individual glasses one-third full.

3 Stir the shrimp into the sauce, then
check the seasoning and spoon the
shrimp mixture generously on the
lettuce. If desired, drape a whole
cooked shrimp over the edge of each
glass and sprinkle each of the cocktails
with ground black pepper and/or
paprika. Serve immediately, with thinly
sliced brown bread with butter and
lemon wedges.

CRAB SALAD WITH ARUGULA

*IF THE DRESSED CRABS ARE REALLY SMALL, PILE THE SALAD BACK INTO THE SHELLS FOR AN
ATTRACTIVE ALTERNATIVE PRESENTATION.*

SERVES FOUR

INGREDIENTS
white and brown meat from 4 small
  fresh dressed crabs, about 1 pound
1 small red bell pepper, seeded and
  finely chopped
1 small red onion, finely chopped
2 tablespoons drained capers
2 tablespoons chopped cilantro
grated zest and juice of 2 lemons
Tabasco sauce
salt and ground black pepper
lemon zest strips, to garnish
For the arugula salad
  1½ ounces arugula leaves
  2 tablespoons sunflower oil
  1 tablespoon fresh lime juice

1 Put the white and brown crabmeat,
red pepper, onion, capers and cilantro
in a bowl. Add the lemon zest and juice
and toss gently to combine. Season
with a few drops of Tabasco sauce,
according to taste, and a little salt
and pepper.

2 Wash the arugula leaves and pat dry
on paper towels. Divide among four
plates. Combine the oil and lime juice in
a small bowl. Dress the arugula leaves,
then pile the crab salad on top and
serve garnished with lemon zest strips.

RED SNAPPER DOLMADES

IF YOU CANNOT FIND PREPARED GRAPE LEAVES, USE BLANCHED CABBAGE OR LARGE SPINACH LEAVES INSTEAD. FLOUNDER OR LEMON SOLE CAN BE SUBSTITUTED FOR THE RED SNAPPER.

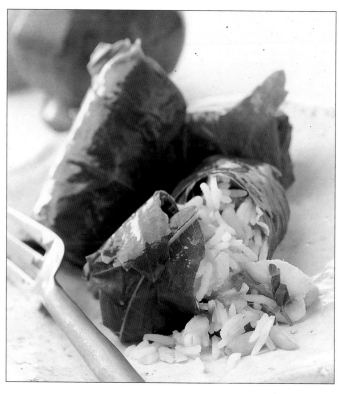

2 Remove the skin from the fish fillets and flake the flesh into a bowl. Gently stir in the cooked rice, pine nuts, the chopped parsley, and lemon zest and juice. Season the filling to taste with salt and ground black pepper.

3 Spoon 2–3 tablespoons of the filling into the middle of each grape leaf. Roll up each filled leaf, tucking in the ends to make a secure package. Arrange the dolmades in an ovenproof dish, with the seams underneath. Then pour in the reserved cooking liquid and place the dolmades in the preheated oven for about 5 minutes, until they are heated through thoroughly.

SERVES FOUR

INGREDIENTS
 8 ounces red snapper fillets, scaled
 3 tablespoons dry white wine
 1 cup cooked long-grain rice
 ⅓ cup pine nuts
 3 tablespoons chopped fresh parsley
 grated zest and juice of ½ lemon
 8 grape leaves in brine, rinsed
  and dried
 salt and ground black pepper
For the orange butter sauce
 grated zest and juice of 2 oranges
 2 shallots, very finely chopped
 2 tablespoons chilled butter, diced

1 Preheat the oven to 400°F. Put the red snapper fillets in a shallow pan and season with salt and pepper. Pour in the wine, bring to a boil, then lower the heat and poach the fish gently for about 3 minutes, until it is just cooked. Strain, reserving the cooking liquid.

4 Meanwhile, make the sauce. Mix the orange zest and juice and the shallots in a small saucepan and boil vigorously for a few minutes, until the mixture is reduced and syrupy.

5 Strain the sauce into a clean pan, discarding the shallots. Beat in the butter, one piece at a time. Reheat gently, but do not let the sauce boil. Drizzle the sauce on the hot dolmades and serve immediately.

SALMON AND SCALLOP BROCHETTES

WITH THEIR DELICATE COLORS AND SUPERB FLAVOR, THESE SKEWERS MAKE THE PERFECT OPENER FOR A SOPHISTICATED MEAL.

SERVES FOUR

INGREDIENTS

8 lemongrass stalks
8 ounces salmon fillet, skinned
8 large scallops, with their corals
   if possible
8 baby onions, peeled
   and blanched
½ yellow bell pepper, cut into
   8 squares
2 tablespoons butter
juice of ½ lemon
salt, ground white pepper
   and paprika
For the sauce
2 tablespoons dry vermouth
¼ cup butter
1 teaspoon chopped fresh tarragon

1 Preheat the broiler to medium-high. Cut off the top 3–4 inches of each lemongrass stalk. Reserve the bulb ends for another dish. Cut the salmon fillet into twelve ¾-inch cubes. Thread the salmon, scallops, corals if available, onions and pepper squares onto the lemongrass and arrange the brochettes in a broiler pan.

2 Melt the butter in a small pan, add the lemon juice and a pinch of paprika and then brush all over the brochettes. Broil the skewers for 2–3 minutes on each side, turning and basting the brochettes every minute, until the fish and scallops are just cooked, but are still very juicy. Transfer to a platter and keep hot while you make the tarragon butter sauce.

3 Pour the dry vermouth and all the leftover cooking juices from the brochettes into a small pan and boil quite fiercely to reduce by half. Add the butter and melt, always stirring. Stir in the chopped fresh tarragon and add salt and ground white pepper to taste. Pour the tarragon butter sauce onto the brochettes and serve.

SOFT-SHELL CRABS <u>WITH</u> CHILE <u>AND</u> SALT

IF FRESH SOFT-SHELL CRABS ARE UNAVAILABLE, YOU CAN BUY FROZEN ONES AT ASIAN SUPERMARKETS. ALLOW TWO SMALL CRABS PER SERVING, OR ONE IF THEY ARE LARGE. ADJUST THE AMOUNT OF CHILE ACCORDING TO YOUR TASTE.

SERVES FOUR

INGREDIENTS
8 small soft-shell crabs, thawed
   if frozen
½ cup all-purpose flour
¼ cup peanut or
   vegetable oil
2 large fresh red chiles, or 1 green
   and 1 red, seeded and thinly sliced
4 scallions or a small bunch of garlic
   chives, chopped
coarse sea salt and ground
   black pepper
To serve
shredded lettuce, daikon and carrot
light soy sauce

COOK'S TIP
The shredded vegetables make a colorful bed for the crabs. If you can't locate any daikon, use celeriac instead.

1 Pat the crabs dry with paper towels. Season the flour with pepper and coat the crabs lightly with the mixture.

2 Heat the oil in a shallow pan until very hot, then put in the crabs (you may need to do this in two batches). Fry for 2–3 minutes on each side, until the crabs are golden brown but still juicy in the middle. Drain the cooked crabs on paper towels and keep hot.

3 Add the sliced chiles and scallions or garlic chives to the oil remaining in the pan and cook gently for about 2 minutes. Sprinkle on a generous pinch of salt, then spread the mixture onto the crabs.

4 Combine the shredded lettuce, daikon and carrot. Arrange on plates, top each portion with two crabs and serve, with light soy sauce for dipping.

DEVILED WHITEBAIT

SERVE THESE DELICIOUSLY CRISP LITTLE FISH WITH LEMON WEDGES AND THINLY SLICED BROWN BREAD AND BUTTER, AND EAT THEM WITH YOUR FINGERS.

SERVES FOUR

INGREDIENTS
oil for deep-frying
⅔ cup milk
1 cup all-purpose flour
1 pound whitebait
salt, freshly ground black pepper and
   cayenne pepper

1 Heat the oil in a large saucepan or deep-fryer. Put the milk in a shallow bowl and spoon the flour into a paper bag. Season the flour with salt, pepper and a little cayenne.

COOK'S TIP
Most whitebait are sold frozen. Thaw them before use and dry them thoroughly on paper towels.

2 Dip a handful of the whitebait into the bowl of milk, drain them well, then put them into the paper bag. Shake gently to coat them evenly in the seasoned flour. Repeat until all the fish have been coated. This is the easiest method of flouring whitebait, but don't add too many at once, or they will stick together.

3 Heat the oil for deep-frying to 375°F or until a cube of stale bread, dropped into the oil, browns in 20 seconds. Add a batch of whitebait, preferably in a chip basket, and fry for 2–3 minutes, until crisp and golden brown. Drain and keep hot while you fry the rest. Sprinkle with more cayenne and serve very hot.

MOUSSES, PÂTÉS
AND TERRINES

Soft-textured fish and shellfish can be puréed to produce attractive light-
textured mousses such as Smoked Fish and Asparagus Mousse. Hot Crab
Soufflés make a substantial appetizer or light lunch or supper dish for a chilly
day, and chunky Haddock and Smoked Salmon Terrine is ideal when the weather
warms up. Celebrate summer with cold creamy Sea Trout Mousse. For the simplest of
dishes, Smoked Mackerel Pâté takes only moments to prepare and is perennially popular.

SEA TROUT MOUSSE

THIS DELICIOUSLY CREAMY MOUSSE MAKES A LITTLE BIT OF SEA TROUT GO A LONG WAY. IT IS EQUALLY GOOD MADE WITH SALMON IF SEA TROUT IS UNAVAILABLE.

SERVES SIX

INGREDIENTS
9 ounces sea trout fillet
½ cup fish stock
2 gelatin leaves, or 1 tablespoon
   powdered gelatin
juice of ½ lemon
2 tablespoons dry sherry or
   dry vermouth
2 tablespoons freshly grated
   Parmesan
1¼ cups whipping cream
2 egg whites
1 tablespoon sunflower oil
salt and ground white pepper
For the garnish
   2-inch piece of cucumber, with peel,
      thinly sliced and halved
   fresh dill or chervil

3 When the trout is cool enough to handle, remove the skin and flake the flesh. Pour the stock into a food processor or blender. Process briefly, then gradually add the flaked trout, lemon juice, sherry or vermouth and Parmesan through the feeder tube, continuing to process the mixture until it is smooth. Scrape into a large bowl and let cool completely.

4 Lightly whip the cream in a bowl; fold it into the cold trout mixture. Season to taste, then cover with plastic wrap and chill until the mousse is just beginning to set. It should have the consistency of mayonnaise.

5 In a greasefree bowl, beat the egg whites with a pinch of salt until softly peaking. Using a large metal spoon, stir one-third into the trout mixture to slacken it, then fold in the rest.

6 Lightly grease six ramekins with the sunflower oil. Divide the mousse among the ramekins and level the surface. Place in the refrigerator for 2–3 hours, until set. Just before serving, arrange a few slices of cucumber and a small herb sprig on each mousse and add a little chopped dill or chervil.

1 Put the sea trout in a shallow pan. Pour in the fish stock and heat to the simmering point. Poach the fish for 3–4 minutes, until it is lightly cooked. Strain the stock into a pitcher and let the trout cool slightly.

2 Add the gelatin to the hot stock and stir until it has completely dissolved. Set aside until required.

COOK'S TIP
Serve the mousse with Melba toast, if desired. Toast thin slices of bread on both sides under the broiler, then cut off the crusts and carefully slice each piece of toast in half horizontally. Return to the broiler pan, untoasted sides up, and broil again. The thin slices will swiftly brown and curl, so watch them closely.

QUENELLES OF SOLE

TRADITIONALLY, THESE LIGHT FISH "DUMPLINGS" ARE MADE WITH PIKE, BUT THEY ARE EVEN BETTER MADE WITH SOLE OR OTHER WHITE FISH. IF YOU ARE FEELING EXTRAVAGANT, SERVE THEM WITH A CREAMY SHELLFISH SAUCE STUDDED WITH CRAYFISH TAILS OR SHRIMP.

SERVES SIX

INGREDIENTS
1 pound sole fillets, skinned and cut
   into large pieces
4 egg whites
2½ cups heavy cream
salt, ground white pepper and
   grated nutmeg
For the sauce
1 small shallot, finely chopped
¼ cup dry vermouth, such as
   Noilly Prat
½ cup fish stock
⅔ cup heavy cream
¼ cup butter, chilled
   and diced
chopped fresh parsley, to garnish

1 Check the sole for stray bones, then put the pieces in a blender or food processor. Add a generous pinch of salt and a grinding of pepper. Switch on and, with the motor running, add the egg whites one at a time through the feeder tube to make a smooth purée. Press the purée through a metal sieve placed over a bowl. Stand the bowl of purée in a larger bowl and surround it with plenty of crushed ice or ice cubes.

2 Whip the cream until very thick and floppy, but not stiff. Gradually fold it into the fish mousse, making sure each spoonful has been completely absorbed before adding the next. Season with salt and pepper, then stir in nutmeg to taste. Cover the bowl of mousse and transfer it, still in its bowl of ice, to the refrigerator. Chill for several hours.

3 To make the sauce, combine the shallot, vermouth and fish stock in a small saucepan. Bring to a boil and cook until reduced by half. Add the cream and boil again until the sauce has the consistency of light cream. Strain, return to the pan and whisk in the butter, one piece at a time, until the sauce is very creamy. Season and keep hot, but do not let it boil.

4 Bring a wide shallow pan of lightly salted water to a boil, then reduce the heat so that the water surface barely trembles. Using two tablespoons dipped in hot water, shape the fish mousse into ovals. As each quenelle is shaped, slip it into the simmering water.

5 Poach the quenelles in batches for 8–10 minutes, until they feel just firm to the touch but are still slightly creamy inside. As each is cooked, lift it out on a slotted spoon, drain on paper towels and keep hot. When all the quenelles are cooked, arrange them on heated plates. Pour the sauce around them. Serve garnished with parsley.

COOK'S TIP
Keep the heat low when poaching; quenelles disintegrate in boiling water.

SMOKED MACKEREL PÂTÉ

SOME OF THE MOST DELICIOUS DISHES ARE ALSO THE SIMPLEST TO MAKE. SERVE THIS POPULAR PÂTÉ WITH WARMED MELBA TOAST AS AN APPETIZER, OR FOR A LIGHT LUNCH WITH WHOLE-WHEAT TOAST.

SERVES SIX

INGREDIENTS

  4 smoked mackerel fillets, skinned
  1 cup cream cheese
  1–2 garlic cloves, finely chopped
  juice of 1 lemon
  2 tablespoons chopped fresh chervil,
    parsley or chives
  1 tablespoon Worcestershire sauce
  salt and cayenne pepper
  fresh chives, to garnish
  warmed Melba toast, to serve

VARIATION
Use peppered mackerel fillets for a more piquant flavor. This pâté can be made with smoked haddock or kipper fillets.

1 Break up the mackerel and put it in a food processor. Add the cream cheese, garlic, lemon juice and herbs.

2 Process the mixture until it is fairly smooth but still has a slightly chunky texture, then add Worcestershire sauce, salt and cayenne pepper to taste. Spoon the pâté into a dish, cover with plastic wrap and chill. Garnish with chives and serve with Melba toast.

BRANDADE OF SALT COD

THERE ARE ALMOST AS MANY VERSIONS OF THIS CREAMY SALT COD PURÉE AS THERE ARE REGIONS IN FRANCE. SOME CONTAIN MASHED POTATOES, OTHERS TRUFFLES. THIS COMPARATIVELY LIGHT RECIPE INCLUDES GARLIC, BUT YOU CAN OMIT IT AND SERVE THE BRANDADE ON TOASTED SLICES OF FRENCH BREAD RUBBED WITH GARLIC, IF DESIRED.

SERVES SIX

INGREDIENTS

  7 ounces salt cod
  1 cup extra virgin
    olive oil
  4 garlic cloves, crushed
  1 cup heavy or whipping cream
  freshly ground white pepper
  shredded scallions, to garnish
  herbed crispbread, to serve

COOK'S TIP
You can purée the fish mixture in a mortar with a pestle. This gives a better texture, but is notoriously hard work.

1 Soak the fish in cold water for 24 hours, changing the water often. Drain. Cut into pieces, place in a shallow pan and pour in cold water to cover. Heat the water until simmering, then poach the fish for 8 minutes, until just cooked. Drain, then remove the skin and bones.

2 Combine the olive oil and garlic in a small saucepan and heat to just below the boiling point. In another saucepan, heat the cream until it starts to simmer.

3 Put the cod into a food processor, process it briefly, then gradually add alternate amounts of the garlic-flavored olive oil and cream, while continuing to process the mixture. The aim is to create a purée with the consistency of mashed potatoes.

4 Add pepper to taste, then scoop the brandade into a serving bowl. Garnish with shredded scallions and serve warm with herbed crispbread.

HOT CRAB SOUFFLÉS

THESE DELICIOUS LITTLE SOUFFLÉS MUST BE SERVED AS SOON AS THEY ARE READY, SO SEAT YOUR GUESTS AT THE TABLE BEFORE TAKING THE SOUFFLÉS OUT OF THE OVEN.

SERVES SIX

INGREDIENTS
  ¼ cup butter
  3 tablespoons fine whole-wheat
    bread crumbs
  4 scallions, finely chopped
  1 tablespoon Malaysian or mild
    Madras curry powder
  2 tablespoons all-purpose flour
  7 tablespoons coconut milk or milk
  ⅔ cup whipping cream
  4 egg yolks
  8 ounces white crabmeat
  mild green Tabasco sauce
  6 egg whites
  salt and ground black pepper

VARIATION
Lobster or salmon can be used instead of crab in these soufflés.

1 Use some of the butter to grease six ramekins or a 7-cup soufflé dish. Sprinkle in the fine whole-wheat bread crumbs, roll the dishes or dish around to coat the bottom and sides completely, then pour out the excess bread crumbs. Preheat the oven to 400°F.

2 Melt the remaining butter in a saucepan, add the scallions and Malaysian or mild Madras curry powder and cook over low heat for about 1 minute, until softened. Stir in the flour and cook for 1 more minute .

3 Gradually add the coconut milk or milk and cream, stirring constantly. Cook until smooth and thick. Off the heat, stir in the egg yolks, then the crab. Season with salt, black pepper and Tabasco sauce.

4 In a greasefree bowl, beat the egg whites stiffly with a pinch of salt. Using a metal spoon, stir one-third into the mixture to slacken it; fold in the rest. Spoon into the dishes or dish.

5 Bake until well-risen and golden brown, and just firm to the touch. Individual soufflés will be ready in about 8 minutes; a large soufflé will take 15–20 minutes. Serve immediately.

SMOKED FISH AND ASPARAGUS MOUSSE

THIS ELEGANT MOUSSE LOOKS VERY SPECIAL WITH ITS STUDDING OF ASPARAGUS AND SMOKED SALMON.
SERVE WITH A MUSTARD AND DILL DRESSING.

SERVES EIGHT

INGREDIENTS

1 tablespoon powdered gelatin
juice of 1 lemon
7 tablespoons fish stock
¼ cup butter, plus extra
  for greasing
2 shallots, finely chopped
8 ounces smoked trout fillets
7 tablespoons sour cream
1 cup low-fat cream cheese or
  cottage cheese
1 egg white
12 spinach leaves, blanched
12 fresh asparagus spears,
  lightly cooked
4 ounces smoked salmon, cut into
  long strips
salt
shredded beets and beet greens,
  to garnish

4 Grease a 4-cup loaf pan or terrine with butter, then line it with the spinach leaves. Carefully spread half the trout mousse on the spinach-covered base, arrange the asparagus spears on top, then cover with the remaining trout mousse.

5 Arrange the smoked salmon strips lengthwise on the mousse and fold over the overhanging spinach leaves. Cover with plastic wrap and chill for 4 hours, until set. To serve, remove the plastic wrap, turn out onto a serving dish and garnish.

1 Sprinkle the gelatin on the lemon juice and let sit until spongy. In a small saucepan, heat the fish stock, then add the soaked gelatin and stir to dissolve completely. Set aside. Melt the butter in a small pan, add the shallots and cook gently until softened but not colored.

2 Break up the smoked trout fillets and put them in a food processor with the shallots, sour cream, stock mixture and cream or cottage cheese. Process until smooth, then spoon into a bowl.

3 In a clean bowl, beat the egg white with a pinch of salt into soft peaks. Fold into the fish. Cover the bowl; chill for 30 minutes or until starting to set.

STRIPED FISH TERRINE

SERVE THIS ATTRACTIVE TERRINE COLD OR JUST WARM, WITH HOLLANDAISE SAUCE, IF DESIRED.
IT IS IDEAL AS AN APPETIZER OR LIGHT LUNCH DISH.

SERVES EIGHT

INGREDIENTS

1 tablespoon sunflower oil
1 pound salmon fillet, skinned
1 pound sole fillets, skinned
3 egg whites
7 tablespoons heavy cream
1 tablespoon fresh chives,
 finely snipped
juice of 1 lemon
scant 1 cup fresh or frozen
 peas, cooked
1 teaspoon chopped fresh mint leaves
salt, ground white pepper and
 grated nutmeg
thinly sliced cucumber, watercress
 and chives, to garnish

3 In a greasefree bowl, beat the egg whites with a pinch of salt until they form soft peaks. Purée the remaining sole in a food processor. Spoon into a mixing bowl, season, then fold in two-thirds of the egg whites, followed by two-thirds of the cream. Put half the mixture into a second bowl; stir in the chives. Add nutmeg to the first bowl.

4 Purée the remaining salmon, scrape it into a bowl; add the lemon juice. Fold in the remaining whites, then cream.

6 Add the salmon mixture, then finish with the plain sole mixture. Cover with the overhanging fish fillets and make a lid of oiled foil. Stand the terrine in a roasting pan and pour in enough boiling water to come halfway up the sides.

7 Bake for 15–20 minutes, until the top fillets are just cooked and the mousse feels springy. Remove the foil, lay a wire rack on top of the terrine and invert both rack and terrine onto a lipped baking sheet to catch the cooking juices that drain out. Keep these to make fish stock or soup.

8 Let the terrine stand for about 15 minutes, then turn the terrine over again. Invert it onto a serving dish and lift off the pan carefully. Serve warm, or chill in the refrigerator first and serve cold. Garnish with thinly sliced cucumber, watercress and chives before serving.

1 Grease a 4-cup loaf pan or terrine with the oil. Slice the salmon thinly; cut it and the sole into long strips, 1 inch wide. Preheat the oven to 400°F.

2 Line the terrine neatly with alternate slices of salmon and sole, letting the ends overhang the edge. You should be left with about a third of the salmon and half the sole.

5 Purée the peas with the mint. Season the mixture and spread it on the bottom of the terrine, smoothing the surface with a spatula. Spread over the sole with chives mixture and spread evenly.

COOK'S TIPS
• Put the salmon in the freezer about an hour before slicing it. If it is almost frozen, it will be much easier to slice.
• You can line the pan or terrine with aluminum foil after greasing and before adding the salmon and sole strips. This makes it easier to turn out the terrine but is not strictly necessary.

HADDOCK AND SMOKED SALMON TERRINE

THIS SUBSTANTIAL TERRINE MAKES A SUPERB DISH FOR A SUMMER BUFFET, ACCOMPANIED BY DILL MAYONNAISE OR A FRESH MANGO SALSA.

SERVES TEN TO TWELVE AS AN APPETIZER,
SIX TO EIGHT AS A MAIN COURSE

INGREDIENTS
   2 tablespoons sunflower oil,
     for greasing
   12 ounces oak-smoked salmon
   2 pounds haddock fillets, skinned
   2 eggs, lightly beaten
   7 tablespoons crème fraîche
   2 tablespoons drained capers
   1 tablespoon drained soft green or
     pink peppercorns
   salt and ground white pepper
   crème fraîche, peppercorns and
     fresh dill and arugula, to garnish

3 Combine the eggs, crème fraîche, capers and green or pink peppercorns in a bowl. Season with salt and pepper; stir in the small pieces of haddock. Spoon the mixture into the mold until it is one-third full. Smooth the surface with a spatula.

6 Stand the terrine in a roasting pan and pour in boiling water to come halfway up the sides. Place in the oven and cook for 45 minutes–1 hour, until the filling is just set.

1 Preheat the oven to 400°F. Grease a 4-cup loaf pan or terrine with the oil. Use some of the salmon to line the pan or terrine; let some of the ends overhang the mold. Reserve the remaining smoked salmon until needed.

4 Wrap the long haddock fillets in the reserved smoked salmon. Lay them on top of the layer of the fish mixture in the pan or terrine.

7 Take the terrine out of the roasting pan, but do not remove the foil cover. Place two or three large heavy pans on the foil to weight it and chill until cold, about 24 hours.

8 About an hour before serving, remove the terrine from the refrigerator, lift off the weights and remove the foil. Carefully invert the terrine onto a serving plate and lift off the pan or terrine.

9 Cut the terrine into thick slices using a sharp knife and serve, garnished with crème fraîche, peppercorns and fronds of dill and arugula leaves.

2 Cut two long slices of haddock the length of the pan or terrine and set aside. Cut the rest of the haddock into small pieces. Season all the haddock with salt and pepper.

5 Fill the pan or terrine with the rest of the fish mixture, smooth the surface and fold the overhanging pieces of smoked salmon on top. Cover tightly with a double thickness of aluminum foil. Tap the terrine to settle the contents.

VARIATION
Use any thick white fish fillets for this terrine: try halibut or Arctic bass.

SMOKED HADDOCK AND AVOCADO MOUSSE

THE FRESH-TASTING SALSA COMPLEMENTS THE SMOOTH CREAMINESS OF THE MOUSSE.

SERVES SIX

INGREDIENTS
- 8 ounces undyed smoked haddock
  fillets, skinned
- ½ onion, cut into thick rings
- 2 tablespoons butter
- 1 bay leaf
- ⅔ cup milk
- 1 ripe avocado
- 2 gelatin leaves, or 1 tablespoon
  powdered gelatin
- 2 tablespoons dry white wine
- 7 tablespoons heavy cream
- 1 egg white
- salt, ground white pepper and
  grated nutmeg

For the salsa
- 3 tomatoes, peeled, seeded
  and diced
- 1 avocado
- 1 small red onion, finely chopped
- 1–2 garlic cloves, finely chopped
- 1 large fresh green chile, seeded and
  finely chopped
- 3 tablespoons extra virgin olive oil
- juice of 1 lime
- 12 lime slices, to garnish

1 Arrange the fish in a single layer in a large shallow pan and lay the onion rings on top. Dot with butter, season with pepper, add the bay leaf and pour in the milk. Poach gently over low heat for 5 minutes or until the fish flakes easily when tested with the tip of a sharp knife. Remove the fish using a slotted spoon and let cool.

VARIATION
Undyed smoked cod can be used instead of the smoked haddock.

2 Using a slotted spoon, lift out and discard the bay leaf and onion. Set the pan over high heat and boil the milk until it has reduced by about two-thirds. Flake the fish into a food processor and strain in the reduced milk. Purée until smooth.

3 Spoon the fish mixture into a bowl. Peel the avocado and cut the flesh into ¼-inch dice. Fold into the fish purée.

4 In a small pan, soak the gelatin leaves in a little cold water until softened. If using powdered gelatin, sprinkle it on 2 tablespoons cold water and let sit until spongy. Add the wine to the softened gelatin and heat gently until completely dissolved, stirring constantly. Pour onto the fish mixture and mix well.

5 Lightly whip the cream in a bowl. In a second, greasefree bowl, beat the egg white with a pinch of salt until stiff. Fold the cream, then the egg white into the fish mixture. Season with salt and pepper and add a little nutmeg.

6 Pour the mixture into six ramekins or molds, cover with plastic wrap and place in the refrigerator for 1 hour, until set.

7 Meanwhile, make the salsa. Put the diced tomatoes in a bowl. Peel and dice the avocado and add it to the tomatoes with the onion, garlic and chile. Add the olive oil and lime juice, with salt and pepper to taste. Chill until needed.

8 To release the mousse, dip the molds into hot water for a couple of seconds, invert onto individual plates and give each mold a sharp tap. Put a spoonful of salsa on each plate and a little on the top of each mousse. Make a cut to the center of each slice of lime and twist a couple of slices onto each plate. Serve with the remaining salsa.

SALADS

What could be nicer on a warm day than a refreshing seafood salad? Take a fresh look at fish as a salad ingredient. Meaty tuna, swordfish, skate and hake make ideal main-course medleys, while lighter offerings such as Insalata di Mare and Asparagus and Langoustine Salad are perfect for summertime alfresco lunches. If you're looking for something out of the ordinary, Warm Monkfish Salad with pine nuts is an unusual and delicious dish, and Red Snapper with Raspberry Dressing is an unexpected delight.

FRESH TUNA SALAD NIÇOISE

FRESH TUNA TRANSFORMS THIS CLASSIC COLORFUL SALAD FROM THE SOUTH OF FRANCE INTO SOMETHING REALLY SPECIAL.

SERVES FOUR

INGREDIENTS

- 4 tuna steaks, about 5 ounces each
- 2 tablespoons olive oil
- 8 ounces fine green beans, trimmed
- 1 small head Romaine lettuce
- 4 new potatoes, boiled
- 4 ripe tomatoes, or 12 cherry tomatoes
- 2 red bell peppers, seeded and cut into thin strips
- 4 hard-boiled eggs, sliced
- 8 drained anchovy fillets in oil, halved lengthwise
- 16 large black olives
- salt and ground black pepper
- 12 fresh basil leaves, to garnish

For the dressing

- 1 tablespoon red wine vinegar
- 6 tablespoons olive oil
- 1 fat garlic clove, crushed

1 Brush the tuna on both sides with a little olive oil and season with salt and pepper. Heat a ridged pan or the broiler until very hot, then broil the tuna steaks for 1–2 minutes on each side; the flesh should still be pink and juicy in the middle. Set aside.

2 Cook the beans in a pan of lightly salted boiling water for 4–5 minutes or until crisp-tender. Drain, refresh under cold water and drain again.

3 Separate the lettuce leaves and wash and dry them. Arrange them on four individual serving plates. Slice the potatoes and tomatoes, if large (leave cherry tomatoes whole) and divide them among the plates. Arrange the fine green beans and red pepper strips on them.

4 Shell the hard-boiled eggs, and cut them into thick slices. Place two half eggs on each plate with an anchovy fillet draped over. Put four olives on each plate.

5 To make the dressing, whisk together the vinegar, olive-oil and garlic and season to taste. Drizzle on the salads, arrange the tuna steaks on top, sprinkle on the basil and serve.

COOK'S TIP

To intensify the flavor of the peppers and improve their texture, broil them until the skins are charred, then put them in a bowl and cover with several layers of paper towels. Let sit for 10–15 minutes, then rub off the skins.

INSALATA DI MARE

YOU CAN VARY THE SEAFOOD IN THIS ITALIAN SALAD ACCORDING TO WHAT IS AVAILABLE, BUT TRY TO INCLUDE AT LEAST TWO KINDS OF SHELLFISH AND SOME SQUID. THE SALAD IS GOOD WARM OR COLD.

SERVES SIX AS AN APPETIZER,
FOUR AS A MAIN COURSE

INGREDIENTS
  1 pound live mussels, scrubbed
    and bearded
  1 pound small clams, scrubbed
  7 tablespoons dry white wine
  8 ounces squid, cleaned
  4 large scallops, with their corals
  2 tablespoons olive oil
  2 garlic cloves, finely chopped
  1 small dried red chile, crumbled
  8 ounces whole cooked shrimp, in
    the shell
  6–8 large endive leaves
  6–8 radicchio leaves
  1 tablespoon chopped flat-leaf
    parsley, to garnish
For the dressing
  1 teaspoon Dijon mustard
  2 tablespoons white wine or
    cider vinegar
  1 teaspoon lemon juice
  ½ cup extra virgin
    olive oil
  salt and ground black pepper

1 Put the mussels and clams in a large saucepan with the white wine. Cover and cook over high heat, shaking the pan occasionally, for about 4 minutes, until they have opened. Discard any that remain closed. Use a slotted spoon to transfer the shellfish to a bowl, then strain and reserve the cooking liquid and set it aside.

2 Cut the squid into thin rings; chop the tentacles. Leave small squid whole. Halve the scallops horizontally.

3 Heat the oil in a frying pan, add the garlic, chile, squid, scallops and corals, and sauté for about 2 minutes, until just cooked and tender. Lift the squid and scallops out of the pan; reserve the oil.

4 When the shellfish are cool enough to handle, shell them, keeping a dozen of each in the shell. Peel all but 6–8 of the shrimp. Pour the shellfish cooking liquid into a small pan, set over high heat and reduce by half. Mix all the shelled and unshelled mussels and clams with the squid and scallops, then add the shrimp.

5 To make the dressing, whisk the mustard with the vinegar and lemon juice and season to taste. Add the olive oil, whisk vigorously, then whisk in the reserved cooking liquid and the oil from the frying pan. Pour the dressing on the seafood mixture and toss lightly to coat well.

6 Arrange the endive and radicchio leaves around the edge of a large serving dish and pile the mixed seafood salad in the center. Sprinkle with the chopped flat-leaf parsley and serve immediately or chill first.

SCALLOP AND GREEN BEAN SALAD

IF YOU PREFER, USE LIGHTLY COOKED SNOWPEAS INSTEAD OF THE GREEN BEANS.

SERVES FOUR

INGREDIENTS
   4 ounces fine green beans, trimmed
   2 good handfuls of frisée lettuce
   leaves, finely shredded
   1 tablespoon butter
   1 tablespoon hazelnut oil
   20 shelled scallops, with corals
   if possible
   2 scallions, very thinly sliced
   salt and ground black pepper
   4 fresh chervil sprigs, to garnish
For the dressing
   2 teaspoons sherry vinegar
   2 tablespoons hazelnut oil
   1 tablespoon finely chopped fresh
   mint leaves

1 Cook the beans in a pan of lightly salted boiling water for about 5 minutes, until crisp-tender. Drain, refresh under cold water, drain again and set aside.

2 Wash and dry the salad leaves; put in a bowl. Mix the dressing, season, pour onto the salad and toss. Divide the salad among four serving plates.

3 Heat the butter and hazelnut oil in a frying pan until sizzling, then add the scallops and their corals and sauté for about 1 minute, tossing the scallops in the fat until they have just turned opaque. Stir in the beans and scallions. Spoon the vegetables onto the salad and pile the scallops and corals into a tower. Garnish and serve.

RED SNAPPER WITH RASPBERRY DRESSING

THE COMBINATION OF RED SNAPPER AND RASPBERRY VINEGAR IS DELICIOUS IN THIS SALAD.
STICK TO THE "RED" THEME BY INCLUDING GREENS SUCH AS RED OAKLEAF LETTUCE AND BABY
RED-STEMMED SWISSCHARD.

SERVES FOUR

INGREDIENTS
   8 red snapper fillets, scaled
   1 tablespoon olive oil
   1 tablespoon raspberry vinegar
   6 ounces mixed dark green and
   red salad greens, such as lamb's
   lettuce, radicchio, oakleaf lettuce
   and arugula
   salt and ground black pepper
For the raspberry dressing
   1 cup raspberries, puréed and sieved
   2 tablespoons raspberry vinegar
   ¼ cup extra virgin olive oil
   ¼–½ teaspoon sugar

COOK'S TIP
To make the raspberry purée, process the fruit in a blender or food processor, then press it through a sieve placed over a bowl to remove the seeds.

1 Lay the red snapper fillets in a shallow dish. Whisk together the olive oil and raspberry vinegar, add a pinch of salt and drizzle the mixture on the fish. Cover and let marinate for 1 hour.

2 Meanwhile, whisk together the dressing ingredients and season to taste.

3 Wash and dry the salad greens, put them in a bowl, pour on most of the dressing and toss lightly.

4 Heat a ridged pan or frying pan until very hot, put in the red snapper fillets and fry for 2–3 minutes on each side, until just cooked. Cut the fillets diagonally in half to make rough diamond shapes.

5 Arrange a tall heap of salad in the middle of each serving plate. Prop up four red snapper fillet halves on the salad on each plate with the reserved dressing spooned around. Serve.

PIQUANT SHRIMP SALAD

THE THAI-INSPIRED DRESSING ADDS A SUPERB FLAVOR TO THE NOODLES AND SHRIMP. THIS DELICIOUS SALAD CAN BE SERVED WARM OR COLD, AND WILL SERVE SIX AS AN APPETIZER.

SERVES FOUR

INGREDIENTS

7 ounces rice vermicelli or stir-fry
   rice noodles
8 ears baby corn, halved
5 ounces snowpeas
1 tablespoon stir-fry oil
2 garlic cloves, finely chopped
1-inch piece fresh ginger root, peeled
   and finely chopped
1 fresh red or green chile, seeded
   and finely chopped
1 pound peeled jumbo shrimp
4 scallions, very thinly sliced
1 tablespoon sesame seeds, toasted
1 lemongrass stalk, thinly shredded,
   to garnish

For the dressing
1 tablespoon snipped chives
1 tablespoon *nam pla* (Thai fish sauce)
1 teaspoon soy sauce
3 tablespoons peanut oil
1 teaspoon sesame oil
2 tablespoons rice vinegar

1 Put the rice vermicelli or noodles in a wide heatproof bowl, pour in boiling water and let sit for 5 minutes. Drain, refresh under cold water and drain again. Put back in the bowl and set aside until needed.

2 Boil or steam the corn and snowpeas for about 3 minutes; they should still be crisp. Refresh under cold water and drain. Now make the dressing. Mix all the ingredients in a screw-top jar, close tightly and shake well to combine.

3 Heat the oil in a large frying pan or wok. Add the garlic, ginger and red or green chile and cook for 1 minute. Add the jumbo shrimp and stir-fry for about 3 minutes, until they have just turned pink. Stir in the scallions, corn, snowpeas and sesame seeds, and toss lightly to mix.

4 Transfer the contents of the pan or wok onto the rice vermicelli or noodles. Pour the dressing on top and toss well. Serve, garnished with lemongrass, or chill for an hour before serving.

HAKE AND POTATO SALAD

*HAKE IS A "MEATY" FISH THAT IS EXCELLENT SERVED COLD IN A SALAD. HERE, THE FLAVOR IS
ENHANCED WITH A PIQUANT DRESSING.*

SERVES FOUR

INGREDIENTS
    1 pound hake fillets
    ²/₃ cup court-bouillon or fish stock
    1 onion, thinly sliced
    1 bay leaf
    1 pound cooked baby new potatoes,
      halved unless tiny
    1 red bell pepper, seeded and diced
    1 cup petits pois, cooked
    2 scallions, thinly sliced
    ½ cucumber, unpeeled and diced
    4 large red lettuce leaves (lollo rosso
      or oakleaf lettuce)
    salt and ground black pepper
For the dressing
    ²/₃ cup plain yogurt
    2 tablespoons olive oil
    juice of ½ lemon
    1–2 tablespoons capers
To garnish
    2 hard-boiled eggs, finely chopped
    1 tablespoon finely chopped fresh
      flat-leaf parsley
    1 tablespoon finely snipped chives

1 Put the hake in a shallow pan with
the court-bouillon or stock, onion slices
and bay leaf. Bring to a boil over
medium heat. Lower the heat and
poach the fish gently for about
10 minutes, until it flakes easily when
tested with the tip of a sharp knife.
Let it cool, then remove the skin and
bones, and separate the flesh into
large flakes.

2 Put the baby new potatoes in a
bowl with the red pepper, petits pois,
scallions and cucumber. Gently stir in
the flaked hake and season with salt
and pepper.

3 Make the dressing by stirring all the
ingredients together in a bowl or
pitcher. Season and spoon or pour on
the salad. Toss gently but thoroughly.

4 Place a lettuce leaf on each plate and
spoon the salad onto it. Mix the finely
chopped hard-boiled eggs for the
garnish with the parsley and chives.
Sprinkle the mixture on each salad.

VARIATION
This is equally good made with halibut,
monkfish or cod. For a change, try it with
a dressing of homemade mayonnaise
mixed with capers.

WARM SWORDFISH AND ARUGULA SALAD

SWORDFISH IS ROBUST ENOUGH TO HANDLE THE SHARP FLAVORS OF ARUGULA AND PECORINO CHEESE. IF YOU CAN'T FIND PECORINO, USE A GOOD PARMESAN INSTEAD. YOU COULD SUBSTITUTE MARLIN OR SHARK FOR THE SWORDFISH, IF DESIRED.

SERVES FOUR

INGREDIENTS
  4 swordfish steaks, about
    6 ounces each
  5 tablespoons extra virgin olive oil,
    plus extra for serving
  juice of 1 lemon
  2 tablespoons finely chopped
    fresh parsley
  4 ounces arugula leaves, stalks
    snipped off
  4 ounces Pecorino cheese
  salt and ground black pepper

1 Lay the swordfish steaks in a shallow dish. Mix 4 tablespoons of the olive oil with the lemon juice. Pour onto the fish. Season, sprinkle on the parsley and turn the fish to coat, cover with plastic wrap and let marinate for 10 minutes.

2 Heat a ridged pan or the broiler until very hot. Take the fish out of the marinade and pat it dry with paper towels. Broil for 2–3 minutes on each side, until the swordfish is just cooked through, but still juicy.

3 Meanwhile, put the arugula leaves in a bowl and season with a little salt and plenty of pepper. Add the remaining 1 tablespoon olive oil and toss well. Shave the Pecorino on top.

4 Place the swordfish steaks on four individual plates and arrange a little pile of salad on each steak. Serve extra olive oil separately so it may be drizzled on the swordfish.

VARIATION
Tuna or shark steaks would be equally good in this recipe.

PROVENÇAL AIOLI <u>WITH</u> SALT COD

THIS SUBSTANTIAL SALAD CONSTITUTES A MEAL ON ITS OWN AND IS ONE OF THE NICEST DISHES FOR
SUMMER ENTERTAINING. VARY THE VEGETABLES ACCORDING TO WHAT IS IN SEASON; IF YOU PREFER
RAW VEGETABLES, INCLUDE RADISHES, YELLOW BELL PEPPER AND CELERY FOR COLOR CONTRAST.

SERVES SIX

INGREDIENTS
    2¼ pounds salt cod, soaked
        overnight in water to cover
    1 fresh bouquet garni
    18 small new potatoes, scrubbed
    1 large fresh mint sprig, torn
    8 ounces green beans, trimmed
    8 ounces broccoli florets
    6 hard-boiled eggs
    12 baby carrots, with leaves if
        possible, scrubbed
    1 large red bell pepper, seeded and
        cut into strips
    2 fennel bulbs, cut into strips
    18 red or yellow cherry tomatoes
    6 large whole cooked shrimp or
        langoustines, in the shell, to
        garnish (optional)
For the aïoli
    2½ cups homemade mayonnaise
    2 fat garlic cloves, (or more if you
        are feeling brave), crushed
    cayenne pepper

1 Drain the cod and put it in a shallow
pan. Pour in enough water to barely
cover the fish and add the bouquet
garni. Bring to a boil, then cover and
poach very gently for about 10 minutes,
until the fish flakes easily when tested
with the tip of a sharp knife. Drain and
set aside until needed.

2 Cook the potatoes with the mint in a
pan of lightly salted boiling water until
just tender. Drain and set aside. Cook
the beans and broccoli in separate
pans of lightly salted boiling water for
3–5 minutes. They should still be very
crisp. Refresh under cold water and
drain again, then set aside.

3 Remove the skin from the cod and
break the flesh into large flakes. Shell
and halve the eggs lengthwise.

4 Pile the cod in the middle of a large
serving platter and arrange the eggs
and all the vegetables around the edges
or randomly. Garnish with the shrimp or
langoustines if you are using them.

5 To make the aïoli, put the homemade
mayonnaise in a bowl and stir in the
crushed garlic and cayenne pepper to
taste. Serve in individual bowls or one
large bowl.

SMOKED EEL AND ENDIVE SALAD

SMOKED EEL HAS BECOME INCREASINGLY POPULAR RECENTLY AND IS SEEN ON SOME OF THE MOST SOPHISTICATED TABLES. IT TASTES GREAT IN A SALAD WITH A REFRESHING CITRUS DRESSING.

SERVES FOUR

INGREDIENTS
  1 pound smoked eel fillets, skinned
  2 large heads of endive, separated
  4 radicchio leaves
  flat-leaf parsley leaves, to garnish
For the citrus dressing
  1 lemon
  1 orange
  1 teaspoon sugar
  1 teaspoon Dijon mustard
  6 tablespoons sunflower oil
  1 tablespoon chopped fresh parsley
  salt and ground black pepper

VARIATION
This salad can also be made with other hot-smoked fish, such as trout or mackerel.

1 Cut the eel fillets diagonally into 8 pieces. Make the dressing. Using a zester, carefully remove the zest in strips from the lemon and the orange. Squeeze the juice of both fruit. Set the lemon juice aside and pour the orange juice in a small pan. Stir in the zests and sugar. Bring to a boil and reduce by half. Let cool.

2 Whisk the Dijon mustard, reserved lemon juice and the sunflower oil together in a bowl. Add the orange juice mixture, then stir in the chopped fresh parsley. Season to taste with salt and ground black pepper and whisk again.

3 Arrange the endive leaves in a circle on individual plates, with the pointed ends radiating outward like the spokes of a wheel. Take the radicchio leaves and arrange them on the plates, between the endive leaves.

4 Drizzle a little of the dressing on the leaves and place four pieces of eel in a star-shape in the middle. Garnish with the parsley leaves and serve. Pass the remaining dressing.

SKATE WITH BITTER GREENS

SKATE HAS A DELICIOUSLY SWEET FLAVOR THAT CONTRASTS WELL WITH THE BITTERNESS OF GREENS SUCH AS ESCAROLE, ARUGULA, FRISÉE AND RADICCHIO. SERVE WITH TOASTED FRENCH BREAD.

SERVES FOUR

INGREDIENTS
  1¾ pounds skate wings
  1 tablespoon white wine vinegar
  4 black peppercorns
  1 fresh thyme sprig
  6-ounce bag of ready-prepared bitter
    salad greens, such as frisée,
    arugula, radicchio and escarole
  1 orange
  2 tomatoes, peeled, seeded
    and diced
For the dressing
  1 tablespoon white wine vinegar
  3 tablespoons olive oil
  2 shallots, finely chopped
  salt and ground black pepper

1 Put the skate wings into a large shallow pan, cover with cold water and add the vinegar, peppercorns and thyme. Bring to a boil, then poach the fish gently for 8–10 minutes, until the flesh comes away easily from the bones.

2 Meanwhile, make the dressing. Whisk the vinegar, olive oil and shallots together in a bowl. Season to taste. Transfer the greens to a bowl, pour over the dressing and toss well.

3 Using a zester, remove the outer zest from the orange, then peel it, removing all the pith. Slice into thin rounds.

4 When the skate is cooked, flake the flesh and mix it into the salad. Add the orange zest shreds, the orange slices and tomatoes, toss gently and serve.

COOK'S TIP
When peeling the orange, take care not to include any of the bitter white pith.

WARM MONKFISH SALAD

MONKFISH HAS A MATCHLESS FLAVOR AND BENEFITS FROM BEING COOKED SIMPLY. TEAMING IT WITH WILTED BABY SPINACH AND TOASTED PINE NUTS IS INSPIRATIONAL.

3 Make the dressing by whisking all the ingredients together until smooth and creamy. Pour the dressing into a small saucepan, season to taste with salt and pepper and heat gently.

4 Heat the oil and butter in a ridged pan or frying pan until sizzling. Add the fish; sauté for 20–30 seconds on each side.

SERVES FOUR

INGREDIENTS
2 monkfish fillets, about
   12 ounces each
1/3 cup pine nuts
1 tablespoon olive oil
1 tablespoon butter
8 ounces baby spinach leaves,
   washed and stems removed
salt and ground black pepper
For the dressing
   1 teaspoon Dijon mustard
   1 teaspoon sherry vinegar
   1/4 cup olive oil
   1 garlic clove, crushed

VARIATION
Substitute other greens for the spinach.

1 Holding the knife at a slight angle, cut each monkfish fillet into 12 diagonal slices. Season lightly and set aside.

2 Heat an empty frying pan, put in the pine nuts and shake them for a few minutes, until golden brown. Do not burn. Transfer to a plate; set aside.

5 Put the spinach leaves in a large bowl and pour on the warm dressing. Sprinkle on the toasted pine nuts, reserving a few, and toss together well. Divide the dressed spinach leaves among four serving plates and arrange the monkfish slices on top. Sprinkle the reserved pine nuts on top and serve.

ASPARAGUS AND LANGOUSTINE SALAD

FOR A REALLY EXTRAVAGANT TREAT, YOU COULD MAKE THIS ATTRACTIVE SALAD WITH MEDALLIONS OF LOBSTER. FOR A CHEAPER VERSION, USE LARGE SHRIMP, ALLOWING SIX PER SERVING.

SERVES FOUR

INGREDIENTS
16 langoustines
16 fresh asparagus spears, trimmed
2 carrots
2 tablespoons olive oil
1 garlic clove, peeled
1 tablespoon chopped fresh tarragon
4 fresh tarragon sprigs and some
   chopped, to garnish
For the dressing
2 tablespoons tarragon vinegar
½ cup olive oil
salt and ground black pepper

1 Shell the langoustines and keep the discarded parts for stock. Set aside.

2 Steam the asparagus over boiling salted water until just tender but still a little crisp. Refresh under cold water, drain and place in a shallow dish.

3 Peel the carrots and cut into fine julienne shreds. Cook in a pan of lightly salted boiling water for about 3 minutes, until tender but still crunchy. Drain, refresh under cold water, drain again. Place in the dish with the asparagus.

4 Make the dressing. In a pitcher, whisk the tarragon vinegar with the oil. Season to taste. Pour onto the asparagus and carrots and let marinate.

5 Heat the oil with the garlic in a frying pan until very hot. Add the langoustines and sauté quickly until just heated through. Discard the garlic.

6 Cut the asparagus spears in half and arrange on four individual plates with the carrots. Drizzle on the dressing left in the dish and top each portion with four langoustine tails. Top with the tarragon sprigs and sprinkle the chopped tarragon on top. Serve immediately.

COOK'S TIP
Most of the langoustines we buy have been cooked at sea. This is necessary because the flesh deteriorates rapidly after death. Bear this in mind when you cook the shellfish. Because they have already been cooked, they will only need to be lightly sautéed until heated through. If you are lucky enough to buy live langoustines, kill them quickly by immersing them in boiling water, then sauté until cooked through.

EVERYDAY
MAIN COURSES

Healthy everyday eating becomes a treat when you serve interesting, affordable fish dishes.

Quick to prepare, low in fat and packed with nutrients, fish makes the perfect

family meal. From simple-to-cook old favorites such as Fish Pie and

Salmon Fish Cakes to Trout with Tamarind and Chili Sauce, and Green

Fish Curry, there's a dish to suit everyone, even those who profess not to

like fish. You will be surprised how little time it takes to make these

delicious everyday meals.

SALMON FISH CAKES

THE SECRET OF A GOOD FISH CAKE IS TO MAKE IT WITH FRESHLY PREPARED FISH AND POTATOES, HOMEMADE BREAD CRUMBS AND PLENTY OF SEASONING.

SERVES FOUR

INGREDIENTS

1 pound cooked salmon fillet
1 pound freshly cooked potatoes, mashed
2 tablespoons butter, melted
2 teaspoons whole-grain mustard
1 tablespoon each chopped fresh dill and chopped fresh parsley
grated zest and juice of ½ lemon
1 tablespoon all-purpose flour
1 egg, lightly beaten
1¼ cups dried bread crumbs
¼ cup sunflower oil
salt and ground black pepper
arugula leaves and chives, to garnish
lemon wedges, to serve

1 Flake the cooked salmon, discarding any skin and bones. Put it in a bowl with the mashed potatoes, melted butter and whole-grain mustard, and mix well. Stir in the dill and parsley and lemon zest and juice. Season to taste with salt and pepper.

2 Divide the mixture into 8 portions and shape each into a ball, then flatten into a thick disc. Dip the fish cakes first in flour, then in egg and finally in bread crumbs, making sure that they are evenly coated.

3 Heat the oil in a frying pan until it is very hot. Fry the fish cakes in batches until golden brown and crisp all over. As each batch is ready, drain on paper towels and keep hot. Garnish with arugula leaves and chives and serve with lemon wedges.

COOK'S TIP

Almost any fresh white or hot-smoked fish is suitable; smoked cod and haddock are particularly good.

CRAB CAKES

UNLIKE FISH CAKES, CRAB CAKES ARE BOUND WITH EGG AND MAYONNAISE OR TARTAR SAUCE INSTEAD OF POTATOES, WHICH MAKES THEM LIGHT IN TEXTURE. IF YOU PREFER, THEY CAN BE BROILED INSTEAD OF FRIED; BRUSH WITH A LITTLE OIL FIRST.

SERVES FOUR

INGREDIENTS
  1 pound mixed brown and white
    crabmeat
  2 tablespoons mayonnaise or
    tartar sauce
  ½–1 teaspoon mustard powder
  1 egg, lightly beaten
  Tabasco sauce
  3 tablespoons chopped fresh parsley
  4 scallions, finely chopped (optional)
  ½–¾ cup dried bread crumbs,
    preferably homemade
  sunflower oil, for frying
  salt, ground black pepper and
    cayenne pepper
  chopped scallions, to garnish
  red onion marmalade, to serve

1 Put the crabmeat in a bowl and stir in the mayonnaise or tartar sauce, with the mustard and egg. Season with Tabasco, salt, pepper and cayenne.

2 Stir in the parsley, scallions, if using, and ½ cup of the bread crumbs. The mixture should be just firm enough to hold together; depending on how much brown crabmeat there is, you may need to add some more bread crumbs.

3 Divide the mixture into 8 portions, roll each into a ball and flatten slightly to make a thick flat disc. Spread out the crab cakes on a platter and put in the refrigerator for 30 minutes before frying.

4 Pour the oil into a shallow pan to a depth of about ¼ inch. Fry the crab cakes in two batches until golden brown all over. Drain on paper towels and keep hot. Serve with a scallion garnish and red onion marmalade.

SARDINE FRITTATA

IT MAY SEEM ODD TO COOK SARDINES IN AN OMELET, BUT THEY ARE SURPRISINGLY DELICIOUS THIS WAY. FROZEN SARDINES ARE FINE FOR THIS DISH. SERVE THE FRITTATA WITH CRISP SAUTÉED POTATOES AND THINLY SLICED CUCUMBER CRESCENTS.

SERVES FOUR

INGREDIENTS
4 fat sardines, cleaned, filleted and
  with heads removed, thawed
  if frozen
juice of 1 lemon
3 tablespoons olive oil
6 large eggs
2 tablespoons chopped fresh parsley
2 tablespoons snipped fresh chives
1 garlic clove, chopped
salt, ground black pepper
  and paprika

1 Open out the sardines and sprinkle the fish with lemon juice, a little salt and paprika. Heat 1 tablespoon olive oil in a frying pan and fry the sardines for 1–2 minutes on each side to seal them. Drain on paper towels, trim off the tails and set aside until required.

2 Separate the eggs. In a bowl, whisk the yolks lightly with the parsley, chives and a little salt and pepper. Beat the whites in a separate bowl with a pinch of salt until fairly stiff. Preheat the broiler to medium-high.

3 Heat the remaining olive oil in a large frying pan, add the garlic and cook over low heat until just golden. Gently combine the egg yolks and whites and ladle half the mixture into the pan. Cook gently until just beginning to set on bottom, then lay the sardines on the frittata and sprinkle lightly with paprika. Pour in the remaining egg mixture and cook gently until the frittata has browned underneath and is beginning to set on top.

4 Put the pan under the broiler and cook until the top of the frittata is golden. Cut into wedges and serve immediately.

COOK'S TIP
It is important to use a frying pan with a handle that can safely be used under the broiler. If your frying pan has a wooden handle, protect it with aluminum foil.

FISH PIE

FISH PIE CAN BE VARIED TO SUIT YOUR TASTE AND BUDGET. THIS IS A SIMPLE VERSION, BUT YOU COULD ADD SHRIMP OR HARD-BOILED EGGS, OR MIX THE POTATO TOPPING WITH SCALLIONS.

SERVES FOUR

INGREDIENTS
    1 pound cod or haddock fillets
    8 ounces smoked cod fillets
    1¼ cups milk
    ½ lemon, sliced
    1 bay leaf
    1 fresh thyme sprig
    4–5 black peppercorns
    ¼ cup butter
    ¼ cup all-purpose flour
    2 tablespoons chopped fresh parsley
    1 teaspoon anchovy paste
    2 cups shiitake or chestnut
      mushrooms, sliced
    salt, ground black pepper and
      cayenne pepper
For the topping
    1 pound potatoes, cooked and
      mashed with milk
    ¼ cup butter
    2 tomatoes, sliced
    ¼ cup grated Cheddar cheese
      (optional)

1 Put the fish skin-side down in a shallow pan. Add the milk, lemon slices, bay leaf, thyme and peppercorns. Bring to a boil, then lower the heat and poach gently for about 5 minutes, until just cooked. Strain off and reserve the milk. Remove the fish skin and flake the flesh, discarding any bones.

2 Melt half the butter in a small saucepan, stir in the flour and cook gently for 1 minute. Add the milk and boil, whisking, until smooth and creamy. Stir in the parsley and anchovy paste and season to taste.

3 Heat the remaining butter in a frying pan, add the sliced mushrooms and sauté until tender. Season and add to the flaked fish. Mix the sauce into the fish and stir gently to combine. Transfer the mixture to an ovenproof casserole.

4 Preheat the oven to 400°F. Beat the mashed potatoes with the butter until very smooth and creamy. Season, then spread the topping evenly on the fish. Fork up the surface and arrange the sliced tomatoes around the edge. Sprinkle the exposed topping with the grated cheese, if using.

5 Bake for 20–25 minutes, until the topping is lightly browned. If you prefer, finish the browning under a hot broiler.

VARIATION
Instead of using plain mashed potatoes, try a mixture of mashed potatoes and mashed rutabagas or sweet potatoes.

SALMON AND SHRIMP FLAN

THIS FLAN IS UNUSUAL BECAUSE IT IS MADE WITH RAW SALMON, WHICH MEANS THAT THE FISH STAYS MOIST. COOKING IT THIS WAY MAKES FOR SUCCULENT RESULTS. THIS VERSATILE DISH MAY BE SERVED HOT WITH VEGETABLES OR COOL WITH MIXED GREENS AND TOMATO WEDGES.

SERVES SIX

INGREDIENTS

12 ounces shortcrust pastry, thawed
   if frozen
8 ounces salmon fillet, skinned
8 ounces cooked peeled shrimp
2 eggs, plus 2 egg yolks
⅔ cup whipping cream
scant 1 cup milk
1 tablespoon chopped fresh dill
salt, ground black pepper
   and paprika
lime slices, tomato wedges and sprigs
   of dill, to garnish

VARIATION

For a more economical version of this
flan, omit the shrimp and use some
extra salmon instead, or use a mixture
of salmon and white fish.

1 Roll out the pastry on a floured work surface and use it to line an 8-inch flan dish or pan. Prick the dough all over and mark the edges with the tines of the fork. Chill in the refrigerator for about 30 minutes. Meanwhile, preheat the oven to 350°F. Bake the pastry for about 30 minutes, until golden brown. Reduce the oven temperature to 325°F.

2 Cut the salmon into ¾-inch cubes. Arrange the salmon and shrimp evenly in the pastry. Dust with paprika.

3 In a bowl, beat together the eggs and yolks, cream, milk and dill and season to taste. Pour onto the salmon and shrimp. Bake for about 30 minutes, until the filling is just set. Serve hot or at room temperature, garnished with lime slices, tomato wedges and dill.

COCONUT BAKED SNAPPER

ADDING A COUPLE OF FRESH RED CHILES TO THE MARINADE GIVES THIS DISH A REALLY SPICY FLAVOR. SERVE THE BAKED SNAPPER WITH PLAIN BOILED RICE.

SERVES FOUR

INGREDIENTS

1 snapper, about 2¼ pounds, scaled
   and cleaned
1⅔ cups coconut milk
7 tablespoons dry white wine
juice of 1 lime
3 tablespoons light soy sauce
1–2 fresh red chiles, seeded and
   finely sliced (optional)
¼ cup chopped fresh parsley
3 tablespoons chopped cilantro
salt and ground black pepper

COOK'S TIP

Any type of snapper or trout can be used
for this recipe. If desired, use one small
fish per person, but be aware that small
snapper can be very bony.

1 Lay the snapper in an ovenproof shallow dish and season with a little salt and plenty of pepper. Combine the coconut milk, wine, lime juice, soy sauce and chiles, if using. Stir in the herbs and pour onto the fish. Cover with plastic wrap and marinate in the refrigerator for about 4 hours, turning the fish over halfway through.

2 Preheat the oven to 375°F. Take the fish out of the marinade and wrap loosely in aluminum foil, spooning on the marinade before sealing the parcel. Support the fish on a clean dish and bake for 30–40 minutes, until the flesh comes away easily from the bone.

FRIED FLOUNDER <u>WITH</u> TOMATO SAUCE

THIS SIMPLE DISH IS PERENNIALLY POPULAR WITH CHILDREN. IT WORKS EQUALLY WELL WITH LEMON SOLE OR DABS (THESE DO NOT NEED SKINNING), OR FILLETS OF HADDOCK AND WHITING.

SERVES FOUR

INGREDIENTS

¼ cup all-purpose flour
2 eggs, beaten
¾ cup dried bread crumbs,
  preferably homemade
4 small flounder, black skin removed
1 tablespoon butter
1 tablespoon sunflower oil
salt and ground black pepper
1 lemon, quartered, to serve
fresh basil leaves, to garnish

For the tomato sauce

2 tablespoons olive oil
1 red onion, finely chopped
1 garlic clove, finely chopped
14-ounce can chopped tomatoes
1 tablespoon tomato paste
1 tablespoon torn fresh basil leaves

1 First, make the tomato sauce. Heat the olive oil in a large saucepan, add the finely chopped onion and garlic and cook gently for about 5 minutes, until softened and pale golden. Stir in the chopped tomatoes and tomato paste and simmer for 20–30 minutes, stirring occasionally. Season with salt and pepper and stir in the basil.

2 Spread out the flour in a shallow dish, pour the beaten eggs into another and spread out the bread crumbs in a third. Season the flounder with salt and pepper.

3 Hold a fish in your left hand and dip it first in flour, then in egg and finally in the bread crumbs, patting the crumbs on with your dry right hand.

4 Heat the butter and oil in a frying pan until foaming. Fry the fish one at a time in the hot fat for about 5 minutes on each side, until golden brown and cooked through, but still juicy in the middle. Drain on paper towels and keep hot while you fry the rest. Serve with lemon wedges and the tomato sauce, garnished with basil leaves.

COD CARAMBA

THIS COLORFUL MEXICAN DISH, WITH ITS CONTRASTING CRUNCHY TOPPING AND TENDER FISH FILLING, CAN BE MADE WITH OTHER ECONOMICAL WHITE FISHES, SUCH AS HADDOCK.

SERVES FOUR TO SIX

INGREDIENTS
  1 pound cod fillets
  8 ounces smoked cod fillets
  1¼ cups fish stock
  ¼ cup butter
  1 onion, sliced
  2 garlic cloves, crushed
  1 green and 1 red bell pepper,
    seeded and diced
  2 zucchini, diced
  ⅔ cup drained canned or thawed
    frozen corn kernels
  2 tomatoes, peeled and chopped
  juice of 1 lime
  Tabasco sauce
  salt, ground black pepper and
    cayenne pepper
For the topping
  3 ounces tortilla chips
  ½ cup grated
    Cheddar cheese
  cilantro sprigs, to garnish
  lime wedges, to serve

1 Lay the fish in a shallow pan and pour in the fish stock. Bring to a boil, lower the heat, cover and poach for about 8 minutes, until the flesh flakes easily when tested with the tip of a sharp knife. Let cool slightly, then remove the skin and separate the flesh into large flakes. Keep hot.

2 Melt the butter in a saucepan, add the onion and garlic and cook over low heat until soft. Add the peppers, stir and cook for 2 minutes. Stir in the zucchini and cook for 3 more minutes, until all the vegetables are tender.

3 Stir in the corn and tomatoes, then add lime juice and Tabasco to taste. Season with salt, black pepper and cayenne. Cook for a couple of minutes to heat the corn and tomatoes, then stir in the fish and transfer to a dish that can safely be used under the broiler.

4 Preheat the broiler. Make the topping by crushing the tortilla chips, then mixing in the cheese. Add cayenne pepper to taste and sprinkle on the fish. Place the dish under the broiler until the topping is crisp and brown. Garnish with cilantro sprigs and lime wedges.

HERRING ᴵᴺ OATMEAL ᵂᴵᵀᴴ BACON

THIS TRADITIONAL SCOTTISH DISH IS CHEAP AND NUTRITIOUS. FOR EASE OF EATING, BONE THE HERRING BEFORE COATING THEM IN THE OATMEAL. IF YOU DON'T LIKE HERRING, USE TROUT OR MACKEREL INSTEAD. FOR EXTRA COLOR AND FLAVOR, SERVE WITH BROILED TOMATOES.

SERVES FOUR

INGREDIENTS
1–1¼ cups oatmeal
2 teaspoons mustard powder
4 herring, about 8 ounces each,
   cleaned, boned, heads and
   tails removed
2 tablespoons sunflower oil
8 strips bacon
salt and ground black pepper
lemon wedges, to serve

COOK'S TIPS
• Use tongs to turn the herring so as
   not to dislodge the oatmeal.
• Cook the herring two at a time.
• Don't overcrowd the frying pan.

1 In a shallow dish, combine the oatmeal and mustard powder with salt and pepper. Press the herring into the mixture one at a time to coat them thickly on both sides. Shake off the excess oatmeal mixture and set the herring aside.

2 Heat the oil in a large frying pan and fry the bacon until crisp. Drain on paper towels and keep hot.

3 Put the herring in the pan and fry for 3–4 minutes on each side, until crisp and golden brown. Serve the herrings with the bacon and lemon wedges.

SKATE ᵂᴵᵀᴴ BLACK BUTTER

SKATE CAN BE QUITE INEXPENSIVE, AND THIS CLASSIC DISH IS PERFECT FOR A FAMILY SUPPER. SERVE WITH STEAMED LEEKS AND PLAIN BOILED POTATOES.

SERVES FOUR

INGREDIENTS
4 skate wings, about
   8 ounces each
¼ cup red wine vinegar
   or malt vinegar
2 tablespoons drained capers in
   vinegar, chopped if large
2 tablespoons chopped fresh parsley
⅔ cup butter
salt and ground black pepper

COOK'S TIP
Despite the title of the recipe, the butter should be a rich golden brown. It should never be allowed to blacken, or it will taste unpleasantly bitter.

1 Put the skate wings in a large, shallow pan, cover with cold water and add a pinch of salt and 1 tablespoon of the red wine or malt vinegar.

2 Bring to a boil, skim the surface, then lower the heat and simmer gently for 10–12 minutes, until the skate flesh comes away from the bone easily. Carefully drain the skate and peel off the skin.

3 Transfer the skate to a warmed serving dish, season with salt and pepper and sprinkle on the capers and parsley. Keep hot.

4 In a small saucepan, heat the butter until it foams and turns a rich nutty brown. Pour it on the skate. Pour the remaining vinegar into the pan and boil until reduced by about two-thirds. Drizzle on the skate and serve.

TROUT <u>WITH</u> TAMARIND <u>AND</u> CHILI SAUCE

TROUT IS A VERY ECONOMICAL FISH BUT CAN TASTE RATHER BLAND. THIS SPICY THAI-INSPIRED SAUCE REALLY GIVES IT ZING. IF YOU LIKE YOUR FOOD VERY SPICY, ADD AN EXTRA CHILE.

SERVES FOUR

INGREDIENTS

   4 trout, 12 ounces each, cleaned
   6 scallions, sliced
   ¼ cup soy sauce
   1 tablespoon stir-fry oil
   2 tablespoons chopped cilantro
For the sauce
   2 ounces tamarind pulp
   7 tablespoons boiling water
   2 shallots, roughly chopped
   1 fresh red chile, seeded
      and chopped
   ½-inch piece fresh ginger root,
      peeled and chopped
   1 teaspoon brown sugar
   3 tablespoons *nam pla* (Thai fish
      sauce)

1 Slash the trout diagonally four or five times on each side with a sharp knife and place in a shallow dish.

2 Fill the cavities with scallions and douse each fish with soy sauce. Carefully turn the fish over to coat both sides with the sauce. Sprinkle on any remaining scallions and set aside until required.

3 Make the sauce. Put the tamarind pulp in a small bowl and pour on the boiling water. Mash with a fork until soft. Transfer to a food processor or blender, add the shallots, fresh chile, ginger, sugar and *nam pla* and process into a coarse pulp.

4 Heat the stir-fry oil in a large frying pan or wok and fry the trout, one at a time if necessary, for about 5 minutes on each side, until the skin is crisp and browned and the flesh cooked. Put on warmed plates and spoon on some sauce. Sprinkle with the cilantro and serve with the remaining sauce.

GREEN FISH CURRY

ANY FIRM-FLESHED FISH CAN BE USED FOR THIS DELICIOUS CURRY, WHICH GETS ITS RICH COLOR FROM A MIXTURE OF FRESH HERBS; TRY EXOTICS SUCH AS MAHI MAHI, HOKI OR SWORDFISH. SERVE IT WITH BASMATI OR THAI FRAGRANT RICE AND LIME WEDGES.

SERVES FOUR

INGREDIENTS

4 garlic cloves, roughly chopped
2-inch piece fresh ginger root, peeled
   and roughly chopped
2 fresh green chiles, seeded and
   roughly chopped
grated zest and juice of 1 lime
1–2 teaspoons shrimp
   paste (optional)
1 teaspoon coriander seeds
1 teaspoon five-spice powder
5 tablespoons sesame oil
2 red onions, finely chopped
2 pounds hoki fillets, skinned
1⅔ cups coconut milk
3 tablespoons *nam pla* (Thai
   fish sauce)
2 ounces cilantro leaves
2 ounces fresh mint leaves
2 ounces fresh basil leaves
6 scallions, chopped
⅔ cup sunflower or peanut oil
sliced fresh green chile and finely
   chopped cilantro, to garnish
cooked Basmati or Thai fragrant rice
   and lime wedges, to serve

1 First, make the curry paste. Combine the garlic, ginger, green chiles, the lime juice and shrimp paste (if using) in a food processor. Add the coriander seeds and five-spice powder, with half the sesame oil. Process into a fine paste, then set aside until required.

2 Heat a wok or large shallow pan, and pour in the remaining sesame oil. When it is hot, stir-fry the red onions over high heat for 2 minutes. Add the fish and stir-fry for 1–2 minutes to brown the fillets on all sides.

3 Lift out the red onions and fish and put them on a plate. Add the curry paste to the wok or pan and fry for 1 minute, stirring. Return the hoki fillets and red onions to the wok or pan, pour in the coconut milk and bring to a boil. Lower the heat, add the *nam pla* (fish sauce) and simmer for 5–7 minutes, until the fish is cooked through.

4 Meanwhile, process the herbs, scallions, lime zest and oil in a food processor into a coarse paste. Stir into the fish curry. Garnish with chile and cilantro and serve with rice and lime wedges.

KEDGEREE

THIS CLASSIC DISH ORIGINATED IN INDIA. IT IS BEST MADE WITH BASMATI RICE, WHICH GOES WELL WITH THE MILD CURRY FLAVOR, BUT LONG-GRAIN RICE WILL DO. FOR A COLORFUL GARNISH, ADD SOME FINELY SLICED RED ONION AND A LITTLE RED ONION MARMALADE.

SERVES FOUR

INGREDIENTS

1 pound undyed smoked
   haddock fillet
3 cups milk
2 bay leaves
½ lemon, sliced
¼ cup butter
1 onion, chopped
½ teaspoon ground turmeric
1 teaspoon mild Madras curry powder
2 green cardamom pods
1¾ cups basmati or long-grain rice,
   washed and drained
4 hard-boiled eggs (not *too* hard),
   roughly chopped
⅔ cup light cream or plain yogurt
   (optional)
2 tablespoons chopped fresh parsley
salt and ground black pepper

1 Put the haddock in a shallow pan and add the milk, bay leaves and lemon slices. Poach gently for 8–10 minutes, until the haddock flakes easily when tested with the tip of a sharp knife. Strain the milk into a pitcher, discarding the bay leaves and lemon slices. Remove the skin from the flesh of the haddock, and flake the flesh into large pieces. Keep hot until needed.

2 Melt the butter in the pan, add the onion and cook over low heat for about 3 minutes, until softened. Stir in the turmeric, the curry powder and cardamom pods and fry for 1 minute.

3 Add the rice, stirring to coat it well with the butter. Pour in the reserved milk, stir and bring to a boil. Lower the heat and simmer the rice for 10–12 minutes, until all the milk has been absorbed and the rice is tender. Season to taste, going easy on the salt.

4 Gently stir in the fish and hard-boiled eggs, with the cream or yogurt, if using. Sprinkle with the parsley and serve.

VARIATION
Use smoked and poached fresh salmon for a delicious change from haddock.

GRILLED MACKEREL <u>WITH</u> SPICY DHAL

OILY FISH LIKE MACKEREL ARE CHEAP AND NUTRITIOUS. THEY ARE BEST SERVED WITH A TART OR SOUR ACCOMPANIMENT, LIKE THESE TAMARIND-FLAVORED LENTILS. SERVE WITH CHOPPED FRESH TOMATOES, ONION SALAD AND FLATBREAD.

<u>SERVES FOUR</u>

INGREDIENTS

1 cup red lentils, or yellow split peas
(soaked overnight)
4 cups water
2 tablespoons sunflower oil
½ teaspoon each mustard seeds,
cumin seeds, fennel seeds, and
fenugreek or cardamom seeds
1 teaspoon ground turmeric
3–4 dried red chiles, crumbled
2 tablespoons tamarind paste
1 teaspoon brown sugar
2 tablespoons chopped cilantro
4 mackerel or 8 large sardines
salt and ground black pepper
fresh red chile slices and finely
chopped cilantro, to garnish
flatbread and tomatoes, to serve

1 Rinse the lentils or split peas, drain them thoroughly and put them in a saucepan. Pour in the water and bring to a boil. Lower the heat, partially cover the pan and simmer the pulses for 30–40 minutes, stirring occasionally, until they are tender and mushy.

2 Heat the oil in a wok or shallow pan. Add the mustard seeds, then cover and cook for a few seconds, until they pop. Remove the lid, add the rest of the seeds, with the turmeric and chiles and fry for a few more seconds.

3 Stir in the pulses, with salt to taste. Mix well; stir in the tamarind paste and sugar. Bring to a boil, then simmer for 10 minutes, until thick. Stir in the chopped cilantro.

4 Meanwhile, clean the fish then heat a ridged pan or the broiler until very hot. Make six diagonal slashes on either side of each fish and remove the head if desired. Season inside and out, then broil for 5–7 minutes on each side, until the skin is crisp. Serve with the dhal, flatbread and tomatoes, garnished with red chile and chopped cilantro.

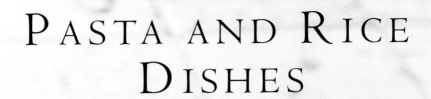

PASTA AND RICE
DISHES

Fish and shellfish make perfect partners for pasta and rice, their lightness and freshness balancing the heaviness of the starch. From simple Pappardelle, Sardine and Fennel Casserole to the ultra-luxurious Lobster Ravioli, there are pasta dishes to suit every occasion and palate. Risotto appears in two guises—dramatically colored and flavored with squid ink, and in a simple version that uses the ready-prepared seafood that most supermarkets now stock.

SEAFOOD LASAGNE

THIS DISH CAN BE AS SIMPLE OR AS ELEGANT AS YOU WANT. FOR A DINNER PARTY, DRESS IT UP WITH SCALLOPS, MUSSELS OR SHRIMP AND A REALLY GENEROUS PINCH OF SAFFRON IN THE SAUCE; FOR A FAMILY SUPPER, USE SIMPLE FISH SUCH AS COD AND SMOKED HADDOCK. THE LASAGNE CAN BE PREPARED IN ADVANCE AND BAKED AT THE LAST MOMENT.

SERVES EIGHT

INGREDIENTS
12 ounces monkfish
12 ounces salmon fillet
12 ounces undyed smoked haddock
4 cups milk
generous 2 cups fish stock
2 bay leaves or a good pinch of
 saffron threads
1 small onion, peeled and halved
6 tablespoons butter, plus extra
 for greasing
3 tablespoons all-purpose flour
2 cups mushrooms, sliced
8–11 ounces no-precook or
 fresh lasagne
¼ cup freshly grated
 Parmesan cheese
salt, ground black pepper, grated
 nutmeg and paprika
arugula leaves, to garnish
For the tomato sauce
2 tablespoons olive oil
1 red onion, finely chopped
1 garlic clove, finely chopped
14-ounce can chopped tomatoes
1 tablespoon tomato paste
1 tablespoon torn fresh basil leaves

1 Make the tomato sauce. Heat the oil in a saucepan and sauté the onion and garlic over low heat for 5 minutes, until softened and golden. Stir in the tomatoes and tomato paste and simmer for 20–30 minutes, stirring occasionally. Season and stir in the basil.

2 Put all the fish in a shallow flameproof dish or pan with the milk, stock, bay leaves or saffron and onion. Bring to a boil over medium heat; poach for 5 minutes, until almost cooked. Let cool.

3 When the fish is almost cold, strain it, reserving the liquid. Remove the skin and any bones and flake the fish.

4 Preheat the oven to 350°F. Melt the butter in a pan, stir in the flour; cook for 2 minutes, stirring. Gradually add the poaching liquid and bring to a boil, stirring. Add the mushrooms, cook for 2–3 minutes; season with salt, pepper and nutmeg.

5 Lightly grease a shallow ovenproof dish. Spoon a thin layer of the mushroom sauce on the bottom of the dish and spread it with a spatula. Stir the fish into the remaining mushroom sauce in the pan.

6 Make a layer of lasagne, then a layer of fish and sauce. Add another layer of lasagne, then spread on all the tomato sauce. Continue to layer the lasagne and fish, finishing with a layer of fish.

7 Sprinkle on the grated Parmesan cheese. Bake for 30–45 minutes, until bubbling and golden. Before serving, sprinkle with paprika and garnish with arugula leaves.

COOK'S TIP
It is preferable to use fresh lasagne, if available. Cook the sheets in a large saucepan of lightly salted boiling water for 3 minutes. Do not overcrowd the pan or the sheets will stick together.

SPAGHETTI AL CARTOCCIO

IN THIS RECIPE, THE COOKING IS FINISHED IN A PAPER PARCEL. WHEN THE PARCEL IS OPENED, THE MOST WONDERFUL AROMA WAFTS OUT. TO SERVE AS AN APPETIZER, BAKE IN TWO LARGER PARCELS.

SERVES FOUR AS A MAIN COURSE,
SIX AS AN APPETIZER

INGREDIENTS
  1¼ pounds live mussels, scrubbed
    and bearded
  1¼ pounds small clams, scrubbed
  7 tablespoons dry white wine
  ¼ cup olive oil
  2 fat garlic cloves, chopped
  2 dried red chiles, crumbled
  7 ounces squid, cut into rings
  7 ounces peeled shrimp
  14 ounces spaghetti
  2 tablespoons chopped fresh parsley
  1 teaspoon chopped fresh oregano or
    ½ teaspoon dried
  salt and ground black pepper
For the tomato sauce
  2 tablespoons olive oil
  1 red onion, finely chopped
  1 garlic clove, finely chopped
  14-ounce can chopped tomatoes
  1 tablespoon tomato paste
  1 tablespoon torn fresh basil leaves

1 Make the tomato sauce. Heat the oil in a saucepan and sauté the onion and garlic over low heat for 5 minutes. Stir in the tomatoes and tomato paste and simmer for 20–30 minutes, stirring occasionally. Season and add the basil.

2 Put the shellfish and wine in a large saucepan and bring to a boil. Put on the lid and shake the pan until all the shells have opened. Discard any that remain closed. Remove most of the molluscs from the shells, leaving about a dozen of each in the shell. Strain the juices and set them aside.

3 Heat the olive oil in a frying pan, add the garlic and sauté until lightly colored. Add the chiles, then put in the squid and shrimp and sauté for 2–3 minutes, until the squid is opaque and the shrimp have turned pink. Add the shellfish and their reserved juices, then stir in the tomato sauce. Set aside.

4 Preheat the oven to 475°F or the broiler to hot. Cook the spaghetti in a saucepan of lightly salted boiling water for about 12 minutes or until it is just tender. Drain very thoroughly, then return to the clean pan and stir in the seafood sauce, tossing to coat all the strands of spaghetti. Stir in the parsley and oregano, with some seasoning.

5 Cut out four 10-inch square pieces of waxed paper. Put a quarter of the spaghetti mixture into the middle of one piece and fold up the edges, pleating them to make a secure bag. Seal the sides first, then blow gently into the top to fill the bag with air. Fold over the top to seal. Make another three parcels with the other sheets of paper and the rest of the spaghetti mixture.

6 Place the parcels on a baking sheet and cook in the hot oven or under the broiler until the paper is browned and slightly charred at the edges. Transfer the parcels to serving plates and open them at the table so that you can enjoy the wonderful aromas.

PAPPARDELLE, SARDINE <u>AND</u> FENNEL CASSEROLE

PAPPARDELLE ARE WIDE, FLAT NOODLES. THEY ARE PERFECT FOR THIS SICILIAN RECIPE. IF YOU CAN'T FIND THEM, ANY WIDE PASTA, SUCH AS MACCHERONCINI OR BUCATINI, WILL DO INSTEAD. THE DISH IS ALSO DELICIOUS MADE WITH FRESH ANCHOVIES.

SERVES SIX

INGREDIENTS

2 fennel bulbs, trimmed
a large pinch of saffron threads
12 sardines, backbones and
    heads removed
¼ cup olive oil
2 shallots, finely chopped
2 garlic cloves, finely chopped
2 fresh red chiles, seeded and
    finely chopped
4 drained canned anchovy fillets, or
    8–12 pitted black olives, chopped
2 tablespoons capers
1 cup pine nuts
1 pound pappardelle
butter, for greasing
2 tablespoons grated Pecorino cheese
salt and ground black pepper

1 Preheat the oven to 400°F. Cut the fennel bulbs in half and cook them in a pan of lightly salted boiling water with the saffron threads for about 10 minutes, until tender. Drain, reserving the cooking liquid, and cut into small dice. Then, finely chop the sardines, season with salt and ground black pepper and set aside until required.

2 Heat the olive oil in a saucepan, add the shallots and garlic and cook until lightly colored. Add the chiles and sardines; fry for 3 minutes. Stir in the fennel and cook gently for 3 minutes. If the mixture seems dry, add a little of the reserved fennel water.

3 Add the anchovies or olives and cook for 1 minute; stir in the capers and pine nuts, and season. Simmer for 3 more minutes, then turn off the heat.

4 Meanwhile, pour the reserved fennel liquid into a saucepan and add enough water to cook the pasta. Stir in a little salt, bring to a boil and add the pappardelle. Cook dried pasta for about 12 minutes, fresh pasta until it rises to the surface of the water. When the pasta is just tender, drain it.

5 Grease a shallow ovenproof dish and put in a layer of pasta, then make a layer of the sardine mixture. Continue until all the pasta and sardine mixture has been used, finishing with the fish. Sprinkle on the Pecorino; bake for 15 minutes, until bubbling and golden brown.

LOBSTER RAVIOLI

IT IS ESSENTIAL TO USE HOMEMADE PASTA TO OBTAIN THE DELICACY AND THINNESS THAT THIS SUPERB FILLING DESERVES. BEFORE YOU START THE RECIPE, MAKE A WELL-FLAVORED FISH STOCK, INCLUDING THE LOBSTER SHELL AND HEAD.

SERVES SIX AS AN APPETIZER,
FOUR AS A MAIN COURSE

INGREDIENTS
  1 lobster, about 1 pound, cooked and
    taken out of the shell
  2 soft white bread slices, about
    2 ounces, crusts removed
  scant 1 cup fish stock, made with
    the lobster shell
  1 egg
  1 cup heavy cream
  1 tablespoon snipped fresh chives,
    plus extra to garnish
  1 tablespoon finely chopped
    fresh chervil
  salt and ground white pepper
  fresh chives, to garnish
For the pasta dough
  2 cups all-purpose flour
  2 eggs, plus 2 egg yolks
For the mushroom sauce
  a large pinch of saffron threads
  2 tablespoons butter
  2 shallots, finely chopped
  3 cups white button mushrooms,
    finely chopped
  juice of ½ lemon
  scant 1 cup heavy cream

1 Make the pasta dough. Sift the flour with a good pinch of salt. Put into a food processor with the eggs and extra yolks; process until the mixture resembles coarse bread crumbs. Turn out onto a floured surface; knead to make a smooth, dryish dough. Wrap in plastic wrap and let rest in the refrigerator for an hour.

2 Meanwhile, make the lobster filling. Cut the lobster meat into large chunks and place in a bowl. Tear the white bread into small pieces and soak them in 3 tablespoons of the fish stock. Place in a food processor with half the egg and 2–3 tablespoons of heavy cream and process until smooth. Stir the mixture into the lobster meat, then add the fresh chives and chervil and season to taste with salt and ground white pepper.

3 Roll out the ravioli dough to a thickness of ⅛ inch, preferably using a pasta machine. The process can be done by hand with a rolling pin but is quite hard work. Divide the dough into four rectangles and dust each rectangle lightly with flour.

4 Spoon six equal heaps of filling onto one sheet of pasta, leaving about 1¼ inches between each pile of filling. Lightly beat the remaining egg with a tablespoon of water and brush it on the pasta between the piles of filling. Cover with a second sheet of pasta. Repeat with the other two sheets of pasta and remaining filling.

5 Using your fingertips, press the top layer of dough down well between the piles of filling, making sure each is well sealed. Cut between the heaps with a 3-inch fluted pastry cutter or a pasta wheel to make twelve ravioli.

6 Place the ravioli in a single layer on a baking sheet, cover with plastic wrap or a damp cloth, and put in the refrigerator while you make the sauces.

7 Make the mushroom sauce. Soak the saffron in 1 tablespoon warm water. Melt the butter in a saucepan and cook the shallots over low heat until they are soft but not colored.

8 Add the chopped mushrooms and lemon juice and continue to cook over low heat until almost all the liquid has evaporated. Stir in the saffron, with its soaking water, and the cream, then cook gently, stirring occasionally, until the sauce has thickened. Keep warm while you cook the ravioli.

9 In another saucepan, bring the remaining fish stock to a boil, stir in the rest of the cream and cook to make a slightly thickened sauce. Season to taste and keep warm. Bring a large saucepan of salted water to a rolling boil. Gently drop in the ravioli (left) and cook for 3–4 minutes, until the pasta is just tender.

10 Place two ravioli (three for a main course) onto the center of individual warmed plates, spoon on a little of the mushroom sauce and pour a ribbon of fish sauce around the edge. Serve immediately, garnished with chopped and whole fresh chives.

LINGUINE ALLE VONGOLE

*USE THE SMALLEST CLAMS YOU CAN FIND FOR THIS RECIPE. YOU WILL HAVE GREAT FUN SLURPING
THEM OUT OF THEIR SHELLS. IF YOU CAN'T FIND LINGUINE, USE THIN SPAGHETTI.*

SERVES FOUR AS A MAIN COURSE,
SIX AS AN APPETIZER

INGREDIENTS
1½ pounds small clams
3 tablespoons olive oil
2 fat garlic cloves, finely chopped
1 tablespoon anchovy paste, or
  4 drained canned anchovy fillets,
  finely chopped
14-ounce can chopped tomatoes
2 tablespoons finely chopped fresh
  flat-leaf parsley
1 pound linguine
salt and ground black pepper

1 Wash and scrub the clams, then put
them in a large saucepan. Cover the
pan and place it over high heat for
3–4 minutes, shaking the pan
occasionally, until all the clams have
opened. Discard any that remain
closed. Strain the clams, reserving the
juices. Shell the clams, if desired.

2 Heat the oil in a saucepan, add the
garlic and sauté gently for 2 minutes,
until lightly colored. Stir in the
anchovy paste or chopped fillets, then
the tomatoes and the reserved clam
juices. Add the parsley, bring to a
boil, then lower the heat and simmer,
uncovered, for 20 minutes, until the
sauce is well reduced and full of flavor.
Season to taste.

3 Cook the linguine in plenty of lightly
salted boiling water until just tender.
Drain the pasta, then put it back in
the pan. Add the clams to the tomato
and anchovy sauce, combine well
then pour the sauce on the linguine
and toss until the pasta is well coated.
Serve immediately.

BLACK FETTUCINE WITH SEAFOOD

*THE DRAMATIC BLACK PASTA MAKES A WONDERFUL CONTRASTING BACKGROUND FOR THE PINK, WHITE
AND GOLDEN SEAFOOD. USE WHATEVER SHELLFISH ARE AVAILABLE; TINY CUTTLEFISH, SMALL SQUID,
CLAMS OR RAZORSHELL CLAMS ARE DELICIOUS IN THIS DISH.*

SERVES FOUR AS A MAIN COURSE,
SIX AS AN APPETIZER

INGREDIENTS
1¾ pounds live mussels, scrubbed
  and bearded
3 tablespoons olive oil
7 tablespoons dry white wine
2 fat garlic cloves, chopped
5 ounces large scallops
7 ounces shrimp, partially shelled
14 ounces black fettucine,
  preferably fresh
salt and ground black pepper
2 tablespoons chopped fresh
  flat-leaf parsley, to garnish

COOK'S TIP
If you can't find black pasta, use green
spinach tagliatelle or fettucine instead.

1 Put the mussels in a saucepan with
1 tablespoon of the oil. Add the wine,
set over high heat, cover and steam for
about 3 minutes, shaking the pan
occasionally, until all the mussels have
opened. Discard any shellfish that
remain closed. Let cool in the
saucepan, then lift out and shell some
of the mussels. Strain the cooking liquid
and set it aside until required.

2 Heat the remaining oil in a large,
deep frying pan. Add the chopped
garlic and sauté for 1 minute, without
letting it brown. Add the scallops and
cook for 1–2 minutes, tossing them
about until they turn opaque. Add the
shrimp and cook for 1 more minute,
then remove the seafood with a slotted
spoon to a bowl and set it aside. Keep
the frying pan handy; it will be needed
for the sauce.

3 Meanwhile, cook the pasta in a large
saucepan of lightly salted boiling water
according to the package instructions
until just tender; fresh pasta will take
only about 2 minutes. Drain.

4 Pour the reserved mussel liquid into
the frying pan and bring it to a boil.
Lower the heat and season. Return the
seafood to the pan, heat for a few
seconds, then stir in the pasta. Toss well,
sprinkle the parsley on top and serve.

STIR-FRIED NOODLES IN SEAFOOD SAUCE

SERVE THIS CHINESE-STYLE PASTA DISH WITH FRESH ASPARAGUS AS AN APPETIZER OR AS A LIGHT AND HEALTHY MAIN COURSE.

SERVES SIX TO EIGHT AS AN APPETIZER,
FOUR AS A MAIN COURSE

INGREDIENTS

    8 ounces Chinese egg noodles
    8 scallions, trimmed
    8 asparagus spears, plus extra
      steamed asparagus spears, to
      serve (optional)
    2 tablespoons stir-fry oil
    2-inch piece fresh ginger root, peeled
      and cut into very fine matchsticks
    3 garlic cloves, chopped
    ¼ cup oyster sauce
    1 pound cooked crabmeat (all white,
      or two-thirds white and
      one-third brown)
    2 tablespoons rice wine vinegar
    1–2 tablespoons light
      soy sauce

1 Put the noodles in a large pan or wok, cover with lightly salted boiling water, place a lid on top and cook for 3–4 minutes or for the time suggested on the package. Drain and set aside.

2 Cut off the green scallion tops and slice them thinly. Set aside. Cut the white parts into ¾-inch lengths and quarter them lengthwise. Cut the asparagus spears on the diagonal into ¾-inch pieces.

3 Heat the stir-fry oil in a saucepan or wok until very hot, then add the ginger, garlic and white scallion batons. Stir-fry over high heat for 1 minute. Add the oyster sauce, crabmeat, rice wine vinegar and soy sauce to taste. Stir-fry for about 2 minutes, until the crab and sauce are hot. Add the noodles and toss until heated through. At the last moment, toss in the scallion tops and serve with a few extra asparagus spears, if desired.

SEAFOOD PAELLA

THERE ARE AS MANY VERSIONS OF PAELLA AS THERE ARE REGIONS OF SPAIN. THOSE FROM NEAR THE COAST CONTAIN A LOT OF SEAFOOD, WHILE INLAND VERSIONS ADD CHICKEN OR PORK. HERE THE ONLY MEAT IS THE CHORIZO, ESSENTIAL FOR AN AUTHENTIC FLAVOR.

SERVES FOUR

INGREDIENTS
3 tablespoons olive oil
1 Spanish onion, chopped
2 fat garlic cloves, chopped
5 ounces chorizo sausage, sliced
11 ounces small squid, cleaned
1 red bell pepper, cut into strips
4 tomatoes, peeled, seeded and
    diced, or 7-ounce can tomatoes
generous 2 cups chicken stock
7 tablespoons dry white wine
1 cup short-grain Spanish rice or
    risotto rice
a large pinch of saffron threads
1 cup fresh or frozen peas
12 large cooked shrimp, in the shell,
    or 8 langoustines
1 pound fresh mussels, scrubbed
1 pound medium clams, scrubbed
salt and ground black pepper

1 Heat the olive oil in a paella pan or wok, add the onion and garlic and sauté until translucent. Add the chorizo and fry until lightly golden.

2 If the squid are very small, leave them whole, otherwise cut the bodies into rings and the tentacles into pieces. Add the squid to the pan and sauté over high heat for 2 minutes.

3 Stir in the pepper strips and tomatoes and simmer gently for 5 minutes, until the pepper strips are tender. Pour in the stock and wine, stir well and bring to a boil.

4 Stir in the rice and saffron threads and season well with salt and pepper. Spread the contents of the pan evenly. Bring the liquid back to a boil, then lower the heat and simmer gently for about 10 minutes.

5 Add the peas, shrimp or langoustines, mussels and clams, stirring them gently into the rice.

6 Cook the paella gently for another 15–20 minutes, until the rice is tender and all the mussels and clams have opened. If any remain closed, discard them. If the paella seems dry, add a little more hot chicken stock. Gently stir everything together and serve piping hot.

RISOTTO NERO

IF YOU HAPPEN TO HAVE SOME SQUID OR CUTTLEFISH COMPLETE WITH INK SAC, RETRIEVE THE INK YOURSELF TO MAKE THIS BLACK RISOTTO. OTHERWISE, YOU CAN BUY SQUID OR CUTTLEFISH INK AT FISHMONGERS AND SOME SUPERMARKETS.

SERVES FOUR

INGREDIENTS

1 pound small cuttlefish or squid,
  with their ink, or 12 ounces
  cuttlefish and 4 packages cuttlefish
  or squid ink
5 cups light fish stock
¼ cup butter
2 tablespoons olive oil
3 shallots, finely chopped
1¾ cups risotto rice
7 tablespoons dry white wine
2 tablespoons chopped fresh
  flat-leaf parsley
salt and ground black pepper

1 If the cuttlefish or squid contain ink, squeeze it out into a small bowl and set it aside. Cut the bodies into thin rings and chop the tentacles. Set aside.

2 Add the ink to the fish stock. Bring to a boil and lower the heat so that the liquid is at a gentle simmer. Heat half the butter and all the olive oil in a large saucepan. Add the chopped shallots and cook for about 3 minutes, until they are soft and translucent.

COOK'S TIP
If you prefer, make the risotto without the cuttlefish or squid and serve it with other fish or shellfish.

3 Add the cuttlefish or squid and cook very gently for 5–7 minutes, until tender. Add the rice and stir well to coat all the grains with fat. Pour in the wine and simmer until most of it has been absorbed by the rice. Add a ladleful of the hot stock and cook, stirring continuously, until it has been absorbed.

4 Continue cooking and stirring for 20–25 minutes, adding the remaining stock a ladleful at a time after the previous amount has been absorbed.

5 Season to taste, then stir in the parsley. Beat in the remaining butter to make the risotto shiny. Spoon the risotto into four warmed dishes and serve.

SEAFOOD RISOTTO

MOST SUPERMARKETS NOW STOCK PACKS OF READY-PREPARED MIXED SEAFOOD SUCH AS SHRIMP, SQUID AND MUSSELS, WHICH ARE IDEAL FOR MAKING THIS QUICK AND EASY RISOTTO.

SERVES FOUR

INGREDIENTS
4 cups fish or shellfish stock
¼ cup butter
2 shallots, chopped
2 garlic cloves, chopped
1¾ cups risotto rice
⅔ cup dry white wine
½ teaspoon powdered saffron, or a
   pinch of saffron threads
14 ounces mixed prepared seafood
2 tablespoons freshly grated
   Parmesan cheese
2 tablespoons chopped fresh
   flat-leaf parsley, to garnish
salt and ground black pepper

1 Pour the fish or shellfish stock into a large saucepan. Bring it to a boil, then reduce the heat and keep it at a gentle simmer. The water needs to be hot when it is added to the rice.

2 Melt the butter in a heavy saucepan, add the shallots and garlic and cook over low heat until soft but not colored. Add the rice, stir well to coat the grains with butter, then pour in the wine. Cook over medium heat, stirring occasionally, until the wine has been absorbed by the rice.

COOK'S TIP
It is essential to use risotto rice for this dish. You can buy arborio or carnaroli risotto rice at an Italian food store, or a large supermarket.

3 Add a ladleful of hot stock and the saffron, and cook, stirring continuously, until the liquid has been absorbed. Add the seafood and stir well. Continue to add stock a ladleful at a time, waiting until each amount has been absorbed before adding more. Stir the mixture for about 20 minutes, until the rice is swollen and creamy, but still with a little bite in the middle.

VARIATION
Use peeled shrimp, or cubes of fish such as cod or salmon instead of the mixed prepared seafood.

4 Vigorously mix in the freshly grated Parmesan cheese and season to taste, then sprinkle on the chopped parsley and serve immediately.

LIGHT AND HEALTHY DISHES

What could be healthier than a meal based on simply cooked fish and shellfish?

We should all include fish in our diet at least twice a week, particularly the oily fish

that are so beneficial to health. Here are vibrant, attractive dishes certain to inspire, such as

Roast Cod with Pancetta and Lima Beans, Moroccan Spiced Mackerel, and Hoki

Stir-Fry. All are quick to prepare and so full of fresh, natural flavors that

healthy eating becomes pure pleasure.

STEAMED LETTUCE-WRAPPED SOLE

IF YOU CAN AFFORD IT, USE DOVER SOLE FILLETS FOR THIS RECIPE; IF NOT, LEMON SOLE, TROUT, FLOUNDER AND BRILL ARE ALL EXCELLENT COOKED THIS WAY.

SERVES FOUR

INGREDIENTS

2 large sole fillets, skinned
1 tablespoon sesame seeds
1 tablespoon sunflower or
   peanut oil
2 teaspoons sesame oil
1-inch piece fresh ginger root, peeled
   and grated
3 garlic cloves, finely chopped
1 tablespoon soy sauce or *nam pla*
   (Thai fish sauce)
juice of 1 lemon
2 scallions, thinly sliced
8 large soft lettuce leaves
12 large fresh mussels, scrubbed
   and bearded

1 Cut the sole fillets in half lengthwise. Season, and set aside. Prepare a

2 Heat a heavy frying pan until hot. Toast the sesame seeds lightly but do not let them burn. Set aside in a bowl until required.

3 Heat the oils in the frying pan over medium heat. Add the ginger and garlic and cook until lightly colored; stir in the soy sauce or *nam pla*, lemon juice and scallions. Off the heat, stir in the toasted sesame seeds.

4 Lay the pieces of fish on baking parchment, skinned-side up; spread each evenly with the ginger mixture. Roll up each piece, starting at the tail end. Place on a baking sheet.

5 Plunge the lettuce leaves into the boiling water you have prepared for the steamer and immediately lift them out with tongs or a slotted spoon. Lay them out flat on paper towels and gently pat them dry. Wrap each sole parcel in two lettuce leaves, making sure that the filling is well covered to keep it in place.

6 Arrange the fish parcels in a steamer basket, cover and steam over simmering water for 8 minutes. Add the mussels and steam for 2–4 minutes, until opened. Discard any that remain closed. Put the parcels on individual warmed plates, halve and garnish with mussels. Serve immediately.

SMOKED HADDOCK WITH MUSTARD CABBAGE

THIS SIMPLE DISH TAKES LESS THAN TWENTY MINUTES TO MAKE AND IS QUITE DELICIOUS. SERVE IT WITH NEW POTATOES.

2 Meanwhile put the haddock in a large shallow pan with the milk, onion and bay leaves. Add the lemon slices and peppercorns. Bring to the simmering point, cover and poach until the fish flakes easily when tested with the tip of a knife. This will take 8–10 minutes, depending on the thickness of the fillets. Take the pan off the heat and set aside until needed. Preheat the broiler.

3 Cut the tomatoes in half horizontally, season them with salt and pepper and broil until lightly browned. Drain the cabbage, refresh under cold water and drain again.

4 Melt the butter in a shallow pan or wok, add the cabbage and toss over the heat for 2 minutes. Mix in the mustard and season to taste, then transfer the cabbage into a warmed serving dish.

SERVES FOUR

INGREDIENTS

  1 Savoy or pointu cabbage
  1½ pounds undyed smoked
    haddock fillet
  1¼ cups milk
  ½ onion, peeled and sliced into rings
  2 bay leaves
  ½ lemon, sliced
  4 white peppercorns
  4 ripe tomatoes
  ¼ cup butter
  2 tablespoons whole-grain mustard
  juice of 1 lemon
  salt and ground black pepper
  2 tablespoons chopped fresh parsley,
    to garnish

1 Cut the cabbage in half, remove the central core and thick ribs, then shred the cabbage. Cook in a pan of lightly salted boiling water, or steam over boiling water for about 10 minutes, until just tender. Leave in the pan or steamer until needed.

5 Drain the haddock. Skin and cut the fish into four pieces. Place on top of the cabbage with some onion rings and grilled tomato halves. Pour on the lemon juice, then sprinkle with chopped parsley and serve.

BAKED SEA BASS WITH FENNEL

SEA BASS HAS A WONDERFUL FLAVOR, BUT CHEAPER ALTERNATIVES, SUCH AS SNAPPER, CAN BE USED.
SERVE WITH CRISPLY COOKED GREEN BEANS TOSSED IN OLIVE OIL AND GARLIC.

SERVES FOUR

INGREDIENTS
4 fennel bulbs, trimmed
4 tomatoes, peeled and diced
8 drained canned anchovy fillets,
  halved lengthwise
a large pinch of saffron threads,
  soaked in 2 tablespoons hot water
2/3 cup chicken or fish stock
2 red or yellow bell peppers, seeded
  and each cut into 12 strips
4 garlic cloves, chopped
1 tablespoon chopped fresh marjoram
3 tablespoons olive oil
1 sea bass, about 4–4½ pounds,
  scaled and cleaned
salt and ground black pepper
chopped parsley, to garnish

1 Preheat the oven to 400°F. Quarter the fennel bulbs lengthwise. Cook in lightly salted boiling water for 5 minutes, until barely tender. Drain and arrange in a shallow ovenproof dish. Season with pepper; set aside.

2 Spoon the diced tomatoes and anchovy strips on top of the fennel. Stir the saffron and its soaking water into the stock and pour the mixture onto the tomatoes. Lay the strips of pepper alongside the fennel and sprinkle with the garlic and marjoram. Drizzle 2 tablespoons of the olive oil overthe peppers and season with salt and pepper.

VARIATION
If desired, use large pieces of thick-cut halibut or turbot for this dish.

3 Bake the vegetables for 15 minutes. Season the prepared sea bass inside and out and lay it on top of the fennel and pepper mixture. Drizzle the remaining olive oil on the fish and bake for 30–40 more minutes, until the sea bass flesh comes away easily from the bone when tested with the point of a knife. Serve immediately, garnished with parsley.

MOROCCAN SPICED MACKEREL

MACKEREL IS EXTREMELY GOOD FOR YOU, BUT SOME PEOPLE FIND ITS HEALTHY OILINESS TOO MUCH
TO TAKE. THE MOROCCAN SPICES IN THIS RECIPE COUNTERACT THE RICHNESS OF THE FISH.

SERVES FOUR

INGREDIENTS
2/3 cup sunflower oil
1 tablespoon paprika
1–2 teaspoons harissa or
  chili powder
2 teaspoons ground cumin
2 teaspoons ground coriander
2 garlic cloves, crushed
juice of 2 lemons
2 tablespoons chopped fresh
  mint leaves
2 tablespoons chopped cilantro
4 mackerel, cleaned
salt and ground black pepper
lemon wedges, to serve
mint sprigs, to garnish

1 In a bowl, whisk together the oil, spices, garlic and lemon juice. Season, then stir in the mint and cilantro to make a spicy marinade.

2 Make two or three diagonal slashes on either side of each mackerel so that they may absorb the marinade. Pour the marinade into a shallow nonmetallic dish that is large enough to hold the fish in a single layer.

3 Put in the mackerel and turn them over in the marinade, spooning it into the slashes. Cover the dish with plastic wrap and place in the refrigerator for at least 3 hours or more if desired.

4 When you are ready to cook the mackerel, preheat the broiler to medium-high. Transfer the fish to a rack set over a broiling pan and broil for 5–7 minutes on each side until just cooked, turning the fish once and basting them several times with the marinade. Serve hot or cold with lemon wedges, garnished with mint. Herb-flavored couscous or rice make good accompaniments.

COOK'S TIP
These spicy mackerel can be cooked on a grill. Make sure the coals are very hot before you begin cooking. Arrange the fish on a large hinged rack to make turning easier, and grill for 5–7 minutes, turning once.

VARIATION
Trout, bonito and bluefish are also good cooked this way.

ASIAN FISH EN PAPILLOTE

THE AROMATIC SMELL THAT WAFTS OUT OF THESE FISH PARCELS AS YOU OPEN THEM IS DELICIOUSLY TEMPTING. IF YOU DON'T LIKE ASIAN FLAVORS, USE WHITE WINE, HERBS AND THINLY SLICED VEGETABLES, OR MEDITERRANEAN INGREDIENTS SUCH AS TOMATOES, BASIL AND OLIVES.

SERVES FOUR

INGREDIENTS
  2 carrots
  2 zucchini
  6 scallions
  1-inch piece fresh
    ginger, peeled
  1 lime
  2 garlic cloves, thinly sliced
  2 tablespoons teriyaki marinade or
    nam pla (Thai fish sauce)
  1–2 teaspoons clear sesame oil
  4 salmon fillets, about
    7 ounces each
  ground black pepper
  rice, to serve

VARIATION
Thick fillets of hake, halibut, hoki and fresh or undyed smoked haddock and cod can all be used for this dish.

1 Cut the carrots, zucchini and scallions into matchsticks and set them aside. Cut the ginger into matchsticks and put these in a small bowl. Using a zester, pare the lime thinly. Add the pared zest to the ginger, with the garlic. Squeeze the lime juice.

2 Place the teriyaki marinade or *nam pla* into a bowl and stir in the lime juice and sesame oil.

3 Preheat the oven to 425°F. Cut out four rounds of baking parchment, each with a diameter of 16 inches. Season the salmon with pepper. Lay a fillet on one side of each baking parchment round, about 1¼-inch off center. Sprinkle a quarter of the ginger mixture on each and pile a quarter of the vegetable matchsticks on top. Spoon a quarter of the teriyaki or *nam pla* mixture on top.

4 Fold the bare side of the baking parchment over the salmon, and roll the edges of the parchment over to seal each parcel very tightly.

5 Place the salmon parcels on a baking sheet and cook for 10–12 minutes, depending on the thickness of the fillets. Put the parcels on plates and serve with rice.

ROAST COD WITH PANCETTA AND LIMA BEANS

THICK COD STEAKS WRAPPED IN PANCETTA AND ROASTED MAKE A SUPERB SUPPER DISH WHEN SERVED ON A BED OF LIMA BEANS, WITH SWEET AND JUICY CHERRY TOMATOES ON THE SIDE.

SERVES FOUR

INGREDIENTS
    1 cup lima beans, soaked overnight
       in cold water to cover
    2 leeks, thinly sliced
    2 garlic cloves, chopped
    8 fresh sage leaves
    6 tablespoons fruity olive oil
    8 thin slices of pancetta
    4 thick cod steaks, skinned
    12 cherry tomatoes
    salt and ground black pepper

1 Drain the beans, transfer into a pan and cover with cold water. Bring to a boil and skim off the foam on the surface. Lower the heat, then stir in the leeks, garlic, 4 sage leaves and 2 tablespoons of the olive oil. Simmer for 1–1½ hours, until the beans are tender, adding more water if necessary. Drain, return to the pan, season, stir in 2 tablespoons olive oil and keep warm.

2 Preheat the oven to 400°F. Wrap two slices of pancetta around the edge of each cod steak, tying it on with kitchen string or securing it with a wooden toothpick. Insert a sage leaf between the pancetta and the cod. Season the fish with salt and pepper.

VARIATION
You can use cannellini beans for this recipe, and bacon instead of pancetta. It is also good made with halibut, hake, haddock or salmon.

3 Heat a heavy frying pan, add 1 tablespoon of the remaining oil and seal the cod steaks two at a time for 1 minute on each side. Transfer them to an ovenproof dish and roast for 5 minutes.

4 Add the tomatoes to the dish and drizzle on the remaining olive oil. Roast for 5 more minutes, until the cod steaks are cooked but still juicy. Serve them on a bed of lima beans with the roasted tomatoes. Garnish with parsley.

HERBED GRILLED SHARK STEAKS

SHARK IS VERY LOW IN FAT, WITH DENSE, WELL-FLAVORED FLESH. OTHER CLOSE-TEXTURED FISH LIKE TUNA, BONITO AND MARLIN WORK EQUALLY WELL IN THIS RECIPE, WHICH IS IDEAL FOR A BARBECUE. SERVE THE FISH WITH A TANGY TOMATO SALAD.

SERVES FOUR

INGREDIENTS
3 tablespoons olive oil
2 fresh bay leaves, chopped
1 tablespoon chopped fresh basil
1 tablespoon chopped fresh oregano
2 tablespoons chopped fresh parsley
1 teaspoon finely chopped
   fresh rosemary
1 teaspoon fresh thyme leaves
2 garlic cloves, crushed
4 pieces drained sun-dried tomatoes
   in oil, chopped
4 shark steaks, about 7 ounces each
juice of 1 lemon
1 tablespoon drained small
   capers in vinegar (optional)
salt and ground black pepper

1 Whisk the oil, herbs, garlic and sun-dried tomatoes in a bowl, then pour the mixture into a shallow dish that is large enough to hold the shark steaks in a single layer. Season the shark steaks with salt and pepper and brush the lemon juice on both sides. Lay the fish in the dish, turning the steaks to coat them all over. Cover and marinate in the refrigerator for 1–2 hours.

2 Heat a ridged pan or grill until very hot. Lift the shark steaks out of the marinade, pat dry with paper towels and cook for about 5 minutes on each side, until they are cooked through. Pour the marinade into a small saucepan and bring to a boil. Stir in the capers, if you are using them. Spoon onto the grilled shark steaks and serve immediately.

CHINESE-STYLE SCALLOPS <u>AND</u> SHRIMP

SERVE THIS LIGHT, DELICATE DISH FOR LUNCH OR SUPPER ACCOMPANIED BY AROMATIC STEAMED RICE OR FINE RICE NOODLES AND STIR-FRIED BOK CHOY.

SERVES FOUR

INGREDIENTS
1 tablespoon stir-fry or sunflower oil
1¼ pounds jumbo shrimp, peeled
1 star anise
8 ounces scallops, halved horizontally
   if large
1-inch piece fresh ginger root, peeled
   and grated
2 garlic cloves, thinly sliced
1 red bell pepper, seeded and cut
   into thin strips
1¾ cups shiitake or button
   mushrooms, thinly sliced
juice of 1 lemon
1 teaspoon cornstarch, mixed to a
   paste with 2 tablespoons cold water
2 tablespoons light soy sauce
snipped fresh chives, to garnish
salt and ground black pepper

1 Heat the oil in a wok until very hot. Put in the shrimp and star anise and stir-fry over high heat for 2 minutes. Add the scallops, ginger and garlic and stir-fry for 1 more minute, by which time the shrimp should have turned pink and the scallops opaque. Season with a little salt and plenty of pepper and then remove from the wok using a slotted spoon. Discard the star anise.

2 Add the red pepper and mushrooms to the wok and stir-fry for 1–2 minutes. Pour in the lemon juice, cornstarch paste and soy sauce, bring to a boil and bubble for 1–2 minutes, stirring constantly, until the sauce is smooth and slightly thickened.

3 Stir the shrimp and scallops into the sauce, cook for a few seconds until heated through, then season with salt and ground black pepper and serve garnished with chives.

VARIATIONS
Use other prepared shellfish in this dish; try thinly sliced rings or squid, or mussels or clams, or substitute chunks of firm white fish, such as monkfish fillet, for the scallops.

PHYLLO FISH PIES

THIS LIGHT PHYLLO-WRAPPED FISH PIES CAN BE MADE WITH ANY FIRM WHITE FISH FILLETS, SUCH AS ORANGE ROUGHY, COD, HALIBUT OR HOKI. SERVE WITH SALAD AND MAYONNAISE ON THE SIDE.

2 Brush the inside of six 5-inch tart pans with a little of the melted butter. Fit a piece of phyllo pastry into the pans, draping it so that it hangs over the sides. Brush with butter, then add another sheet at right angles to the first. Brush with butter. Continue to line the pans in this way.

3 Spread the spinach evenly on the pastry. Add the diced fish and season well. Stir the chives into the crème fraîche and spread the mixture on the top of the fish. Sprinkle on the dill.

SERVES SIX

INGREDIENTS
14 ounces spinach, trimmed
1 egg, lightly beaten
2 garlic cloves, crushed
1 pound orange roughy or other white
   fish fillet
juice of 1 lemon
¼ cup butter, melted
8–12 phyllo pastry sheets, thawed
   if frozen, quartered
1 tablespoon finely snipped
   fresh chives
scant 1 cup low-fat crème fraîche
1 tablespoon chopped fresh dill
salt and ground black pepper

VARIATION
If you prefer to make one large pie, use
an 8-inch pan and cook for 45 minutes.

1 Preheat the oven to 375°F. Wash the spinach, then cook it in a lidded heavy pan with just the water that clings to the leaves. As soon as the leaves are tender, drain, squeeze as dry as possible and chop. Put the spinach in a bowl, add the egg and garlic, season with salt and pepper and set aside. Dice the fish and place it in a bowl. Stir in the lemon juice. Season with salt and pepper and toss lightly.

4 Draw the overhanging pieces of pastry together and scrunch lightly to make a lid. Brush with butter. Bake for 15–20 minutes, until golden brown.

HOKI STIR-FRY

ANY FIRM WHITE FISH, SUCH AS MONKFISH, HAKE OR COD, CAN BE USED FOR THIS ATTRACTIVE STIR-FRY. VARY THE VEGETABLES ACCORDING TO WHAT IS AVAILABLE, BUT TRY TO INCLUDE AT LEAST THREE DIFFERENT COLORS. SHRIMP-FRIED RICE WOULD BE THE PERFECT ACCOMPANIMENT.

SERVES FOUR TO SIX

INGREDIENTS

1½ pounds hoki fillet, skinned
pinch of five-spice powder
2 carrots
1 cup small snowpeas
4 ounces asparagus spears
4 scallions
3 tablespoons peanut or stir-fry oil
1-inch piece fresh ginger root, peeled
    and cut into thin slivers
2 garlic cloves, finely chopped
11 ounces bean sprouts
8–12 small baby corn
1–2 tablespoons light soy sauce
salt and ground black pepper

3 Heat a wok, then pour in the oil. As soon as it is hot, add the ginger and garlic. Stir-fry for 1 minute, then add the white parts of the scallions and cook for 1 more minute.

COOK'S TIP
When adding the oil to the hot wok, drizzle it around the inner rim like a necklace. The oil will run down to coat the entire surface of the wok. Swirl the wok to make sure the coating is even.

4 Add the hoki strips and stir-fry for 2–3 minutes, until all the pieces of fish are opaque. Add the bean sprouts. Toss them around to coat them in the oil, then put in the carrots, snowpeas, asparagus and corn. Continue to stir-fry for 3–4 minutes, by which time the fish should be cooked, but all the vegetables will still be crunchy. Add soy sauce to taste, toss everything quickly together, then stir in the green parts of the scallions. Serve immediately.

1 Cut the hoki into finger-size strips and season with salt, pepper and five-spice powder. Cut the carrots diagonally into slices as thin as the snowpeas.

2 Trim the snowpeas. Trim the asparagus spears and cut in half crosswise. Trim the scallions and cut them diagonally into ¾-inch pieces, keeping the white and green parts separate. Set aside.

BRAISED PORGY WITH SEAFOOD

THIS VERSATILE DISH IS EXTREMELY LOW IN CALORIES, BUT FULL OF FLAVOR. USE ANY MIXTURE OF FRESH OR FROZEN SEAFOOD YOU LIKE (A FEW MUSSELS OR CLAMS IN THE SHELL ARE PARTICULARLY ATTRACTIVE). SERVE WITH NOODLES OR PASTA SHELLS.

SERVES FOUR

INGREDIENTS
2 tablespoons olive oil
1 onion, thinly sliced
1 yellow or orange bell pepper, or
   ½ of each, seeded and cut into strips
1⅔ cups well-reduced tomato sauce
3 tablespoons dry white wine or
   fish stock
2 zucchini, sliced
12 ounces porgy fillets, skinned and
   cut into 2-inch chunks
1 pound ready-prepared mixed
   shellfish, thawed if frozen
juice of ½ lemon
1 tablespoon shredded fresh
   marjoram or basil leaves
salt and ground black pepper
basil leaves, to garnish
cooked pasta or noodles, to serve

1 Heat the olive oil in a large frying pan. Add the onion slices and yellow and/or orange pepper strips and stir-fry the vegetables for about 2 minutes, until the onion is transparent.

COOK'S TIP
If you are short on time, use a 14-ounce jar of good quality, ready-prepared tomato sauce.

2 Stir in the tomato sauce, with the white wine or fish stock and bring to a boil. Lower the heat and then simmer for about 2 minutes.

3 Add the zucchini and the chunks of porgy; cover and cook gently for about 5 minutes, stirring once or twice during this time. Add the shellfish and stir well to coat it with the sauce.

4 Season to taste with salt, pepper and lemon juice, cover the pan and simmer for 2–3 minutes, until heated through. Stir in the shredded marjoram or basil, and garnish with basil leaves. Serve with noodles or pasta.

VARIATIONS
Fillets of snapper, bass or red mullet could be used in place of the porgy in this recipe.

MALAYSIAN STEAMED TROUT FILLETS

THIS SIMPLE DISH CAN BE PREPARED EXTREMELY QUICKLY, AND IS SUITABLE FOR ANY FISH FILLETS. SERVE IT ON A BED OF NOODLES ACCOMPANIED BY RIBBONS OF COLORFUL VEGETABLES.

SERVES FOUR

INGREDIENTS
8 pink trout fillets of even thickness,
   about 4 ounces each, skinned
3 tablespoons coconut milk
grated zest and juice of 2 limes
3 tablespoons chopped cilantro
1 tablespoon sunflower or
   peanut oil
½–1 teaspoon chili oil
salt and ground black pepper
lime slices and cilantro sprigs,
   to garnish

1 Cut four rectangles of waxed paper or baking parchment, about twice the size of the trout fillets. Place a fillet on each piece and season lightly.

2 Combine the coconut milk, lime zest and chopped cilantro and spread a quarter of the mixture on each trout fillet. Sandwich another trout fillet on top. Mix the lime juice with the oils, adjusting the amount of chili oil to your own taste, and drizzle the mixture on the trout "sandwiches."

3 Prepare a steamer. Fold up the edges of the paper and pleat them over the trout to make parcels, making sure they are well sealed. Place in the steamer insert and steam over the simmering water for 10–15 minutes, depending on the thickness of the trout fillets. Serve immediately.

ELEGANT DISHES FOR ENTERTAINING

For sheer elegance, fish and shellfish are hard to beat and so quick to prepare that they make light work of entertaining. A whole fish baked in a salt crust looks intriguing and tastes superb. For breathtaking elegance and taste, treat your guests to Lobster Thermidor, Vegetable-stuffed Squid or Fillets of Turbot with Oysters. Whatever the occasion, delight your guests with these superb party dishes.

HAKE AU POIVRE WITH RED BELL PEPPER RELISH

THIS PISCINE VERSION OF THE CLASSIC STEAK AU POIVRE CAN BE MADE WITH MONKFISH OR COD INSTEAD OF HAKE. VARY THE AMOUNT OF PEPPERCORNS ACCORDING TO YOUR PERSONAL TASTE.

SERVES FOUR

INGREDIENTS
   2–3 tablespoons mixed peppercorns
     (black, white, pink and green)
   4 hake steaks, about 6 ounces each
   2 tablespoons olive oil
For the red bell pepper relish
   2 red bell peppers
   1 tablespoon olive oil
   2 garlic cloves, chopped
   4 ripe tomatoes, peeled, seeded
     and quartered
   4 drained canned anchovy
     fillets, chopped
   1 teaspoon capers
   1 tablespoon balsamic vinegar
   12 fresh basil leaves, shredded, plus
     a few extra to garnish
   salt and ground black pepper

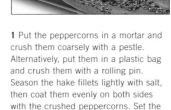

1 Put the peppercorns in a mortar and crush them coarsely with a pestle. Alternatively, put them in a plastic bag and crush them with a rolling pin. Season the hake fillets lightly with salt, then coat them evenly on both sides with the crushed peppercorns. Set the coated fish steaks aside while you make the red pepper relish.

2 Make the relish. Cut the red peppers in half lengthwise, remove the core and seeds from each and cut the flesh into ½-inch wide strips. Heat the olive oil in a wok or a shallow pan that has a lid. Add the peppers and stir them for about 5 minutes, until they are slightly softened. Stir in the chopped garlic, tomatoes and the anchovies, then cover the pan and simmer the mixture very gently for about 20 minutes, until the peppers are very soft.

3 Transfer the contents of the pan to a food processor and process into a coarse purée. Transfer to a bowl and season to taste. Stir in the capers, balsamic vinegar and basil. Keep the relish hot.

4 Heat the olive oil in a shallow pan, add the hake steaks and fry them, in batches if necessary, for 5 minutes on each side, turning them once or twice, until they are just cooked through.

5 Place the fish on individual plates and spoon a little red pepper relish onto each plate. Garnish with basil leaves and a little extra balsamic vinegar. Pass the rest of the relish separately.

MOROCCAN FISH TAGINE

THIS SPICY, AROMATIC DISH PROVES JUST HOW EXCITING AN INGREDIENT FISH CAN BE. SERVE IT WITH COUSCOUS FLAVORED WITH CHOPPED MINT.

SERVES EIGHT

INGREDIENTS

3 pounds firm fish fillets, skinned
   and cut into 2-inch chunks
¼ cup olive oil
4 onions, chopped
1 large eggplant, cut into
   ½-inch cubes
2 zucchini, cut into ½-inch cubes
14-ounce can chopped tomatoes
1⅔ cups passata
scant 1 cup fish stock
1 preserved lemon, chopped
scant 1 cup olives
¼ cup chopped cilantro
salt and ground black pepper
cilantro sprigs, to garnish
For the harissa
3 large fresh red chiles, seeded
   and chopped
3 garlic cloves, peeled
1 tablespoon ground coriander
2 tablespoons ground cumin
1 teaspoon ground cinnamon
grated zest of 1 lemon
2 tablespoons sunflower oil

1 Make the harissa. Process everything in a blender into a smooth paste.

2 Put the chunks of fish in a wide bowl and add 2 tablespoons of the harissa. Toss to coat, cover and chill for at least 1 hour or overnight.

3 Heat half the oil in a shallow, heavy pan. Cook the onions gently for 10 minutes, until golden brown. Stir in the remaining harissa; cook for 5 minutes, stirring occasionally.

4 Heat the remaining olive oil in a separate shallow saucepan. Add the eggplant cubes and cook for about 10 minutes, until they are golden brown. Add the cubed zucchini and cook for another 2 minutes.

5 Transfer the mixture to the shallow pan and combine with the onions, then stir in the chopped tomatoes, the passata and fish stock. Bring to a boil, then lower the heat and simmer the mixture for about 20 minutes.

6 Stir the fish chunks and preserved lemon into the pan. Add the olives and stir gently. Cover and simmer over low heat for 15–20 minutes, until the fish is just cooked through. Season to taste. Stir in the chopped cilantro. Serve with couscous, if desired, and garnish with cilantro sprigs.

COOK'S TIP
To make the fish go further, you could add 1¼ cups cooked chickpeas to the tagine.

SQUID WITH CHORIZO

THE BEST WAY TO COOK THIS DISH IS IN A RIDGED PAN. IF YOU CAN ONLY FIND MEDIUM-SIZE SQUID, ALLOW TWO PER SERVING AND HALVE THEM LENGTHWISE FROM THE TAIL END TO THE CAVITY.

SERVES SIX

INGREDIENTS

24 small squid, cleaned
²/₃ cup extra virgin olive oil
11 ounces cooking chorizo, cut into
    12 slices
3 tomatoes, halved and seasoned
    with salt and pepper
juice of 1 lemon
24 cooked new potatoes, halved
a handful of fresh arugula leaves
salt and ground black pepper
lemon slices, to garnish

1 Separate the body and tentacles of the squid and cut the bodies in half lengthwise if they are large.

2 Pour half the oil into a bowl, season with salt and pepper, then toss all the squid in the oil. Heat a ridged pan to very hot.

3 Cook the prepared squid bodies for about 45 seconds on each side until the flesh is opaque and tender. Then transfer to a plate and keep hot. Cook the tentacles for about 1 minute on each side, then place them on the plate. Cook the chorizo slices for about 30 seconds on each side, until golden brown, then set them aside with the squid. Cook the tomato halves for 1–2 minutes on each side, until they are softened and browned.

4 Place the potatoes and arugula in a large bowl.

5 Pour the lemon juice into a bowl and whisk in the remaining oil. Season. Reserve 2 tablespoons of this dressing in a pitcher. Pour the dressing onto the potatoes and arugula, toss lightly and divide among 6 plates. Pile a portion of the squid, tomatoes and chorizo on each salad, and drizzle on the reserved dressing. Garnish with lemon slices and serve immediately.

SOLE WITH WILD MUSHROOMS

IF POSSIBLE, USE CHANTERELLES FOR THIS DISH; THEIR GLOWING ORANGE COLOR COMBINES REALLY WONDERFULLY WITH THE INTENSELY GOLDEN SAUCE. OTHERWISE, USE ANY PALE-COLORED OR OYSTER MUSHROOMS THAT YOU CAN FIND INSTEAD.

SERVES FOUR

INGREDIENTS

4 Dover sole fillets, about 4 ounces
    each, skinned
¼ cup butter
generous 2 cups fish stock
2 cups chanterelles
a large pinch of saffron threads
²/₃ cup heavy cream
1 egg yolk
salt and ground white pepper
finely chopped fresh parsley, and
    parsley sprigs to garnish
boiled new potatoes, to serve

1 Preheat the oven to 400°F. Cut the sole fillets in half lengthwise and place them on a board with the skinned-side facing up. Season them with salt and white pepper, then roll them up. Use a little of the butter to grease a baking dish just large enough to hold all the sole fillets in a single layer, arrange the sole rolls in it, then pour in the fish stock. Cover tightly with aluminum foil and bake for 12–15 minutes, until cooked through.

2 Meanwhile, pick off any bits of fern or twig from the chanterelles and wipe the mushrooms with a damp cloth. Halve or quarter any large ones. Heat the remaining butter in a frying pan until foaming, and sauté the mushrooms for 3–4 minutes, until just tender. Season with salt and pepper and keep hot.

3 Lift the cooked sole fillets out of the cooking liquid and place them on a heated serving dish. Keep hot. Strain the liquid into a small saucepan, add the saffron, set over very high heat and boil down until reduced to about 1 cup. Stir in the cream and then let the sauce bubble gently once or twice.

4 Lightly beat the egg yolk in a small bowl, pour on a little of the hot sauce and stir well. Stir the mixture into the remaining sauce in the pan and cook over very low heat for 1–2 minutes, until slightly thickened. Season to taste. Stir the chanterelles into the sauce and pour it onto the sole fillets. Garnish with parsley sprigs and serve immediately. Boiled new potatoes make the perfect accompaniment.

LOBSTER THERMIDOR

*ONE OF THE CLASSIC FRENCH DISHES, LOBSTER THERMIDOR MAKES A LITTLE LOBSTER GO A LONG WAY.
IT IS BEST TO USE ONE BIG RATHER THAN TWO SMALL LOBSTERS, AS A LARGER LOBSTER WILL CONTAIN
A HIGHER PROPORTION OF FLESH AND THE MEAT WILL BE SWEETER. IDEALLY, USE A LIVE CRUSTACEAN
AND COOK IT YOURSELF, BUT A BOILED LOBSTER FROM THE FISHMONGER WILL DO.*

SERVES TWO

INGREDIENTS
    1 large lobster, about
      1¾–2¼ pounds, boiled
    3 tablespoons brandy
    2 tablespoons butter
    2 shallots, finely chopped
    1½ cups white button mushrooms,
      thinly sliced
    1 tablespoon all-purpose flour
    7 tablespoons fish or shellfish stock
    ½ cup heavy cream
    1 teaspoon Dijon mustard
    2 egg yolks, beaten
    3 tablespoons dry white wine
    3 tablespoons freshly grated
      Parmesan cheese
salt, ground black pepper and
    cayenne pepper

1 Split the lobster in half lengthwise;
crack the claws. Discard the stomach
sac; keep the coral for another dish.
Keeping each half-shell intact, extract
the meat from the tail and claws, then
cut into large dice. Place in a shallow
dish; sprinkle on the brandy. Cover and
set aside. Wipe and dry the half-shells
and set them aside.

2 Melt the butter in a saucepan and
cook the shallots over low heat until
soft. Add the mushrooms and cook until
just tender, stirring constantly. Stir in
the flour and a pinch of cayenne; cook,
stirring, for 2 minutes. Gradually add
the stock, stirring until the sauce boils
and thickens.

3 Stir in the cream and mustard and
continue to cook until the sauce is
smooth and thick. Season to taste with
salt, black pepper and cayenne. Pour
half the sauce on to the egg yolks, stir
well and return the mixture to the pan.
Stir in the wine; adjust the seasoning,
being generous with the cayenne.

4 Preheat the broiler to medium-high.
Stir the diced lobster and the brandy
into the sauce. Arrange the lobster half-
shells in a broiler pan and divide the
mixture among them. Sprinkle with
Parmesan and place under the broiler
until browned. Serve with steamed
rice and salad.

RED SNAPPER SALTIMBOCCA

THE RICH RED COLOR OF THE SNAPPER IS INTENSIFIED BY RUBBING SAFFRON INTO THE SKIN, COMPLEMENTING THE PROSCUITTO BEAUTIFULLY. SERVE WITH BRIGHTLY COLORED ROASTED MEDITERRANEAN VEGETABLES AND CRISPLY COOKED BEANS, IF DESIRED.

SERVES FOUR

INGREDIENTS
8 red snapper fillets, scaled but
  not skinned
a pinch of saffron threads or
  powdered saffron
1 tablespoon olive oil
8 fresh sage leaves
8 thin slices of prosciutto
2 tablespoons butter
⅔ cup mixed olives
salt and ground black pepper
For the dressing
1 tablespoon sugar
7 tablespoons balsamic vinegar
1¼ cups extra virgin olive oil
2-inch slice red bell pepper, diced
1 small zucchini, very finely diced
1 ripe tomato, peeled, seeded and
  very finely diced

1 Score the red snapper skin lightly in three or four places. Season both sides of each fillet with salt and ground black pepper. If you are using saffron threads, crumble them onto the skin-side of each red snapper fillet, or sprinkle the powdered saffron onto the skin. Drizzle on a little olive oil and then rub the saffron in well with your fingertips. This will enhance the color of the fish skin dramatically.

2 Heat a nonstick frying pan until very hot, then put in the fillets, skin-side down, and cook over high heat for 2 minutes. Turn the fillets over and cook them for 2 more minutes. Drain on paper towels and set aside until cool enough to handle.

3 Place a sage leaf on each cooked fillet, then wrap the fillets in a slice of prosciutto to cover them completely. Melt the butter in the frying pan and continue to heat until it foams. Fry the prosciutto and red snapper parcels over high heat for 1–2 minutes on each side, until pale golden. Transfer to warmed serving plates and keep hot while you make the dressing.

4 Mix the sugar and vinegar in a small saucepan, set over high heat and boil until syrupy.

5 Meanwhile, pour the olive oil into a bowl, stir in the diced vegetables and season. Stir the hot vinegar syrup into the dressing. Drizzle it over and around the fish. Place the olives on the plates and serve immediately.

ROAST MONKFISH WITH GARLIC

MONKFISH TIED UP AND COOKED IN THIS WAY IS KNOWN IN FRENCH AS A "GIGOT," BECAUSE IT
RESEMBLES A LEG OF LAMB. THE COMBINATION OF MONKFISH AND GARLIC IS SUPERB. FOR A CONTRAST
IN COLOR, SERVE IT WITH VIBRANT GREEN BEANS.

SERVES FOUR TO SIX

INGREDIENTS
  2¼ pounds monkfish tail, skinned
  14 fat garlic cloves
  1 teaspoon fresh thyme leaves
  2 tablespoons olive oil
  juice of 1 lemon
  2 bay leaves
  salt and ground black pepper

1 Preheat the oven to 425°F. Remove
any membrane from the monkfish tail
and cut out the central bone. Peel
2 garlic cloves and cut them into thin
slivers. Sprinkle a quarter of these and
half the thyme leaves on the cut-side of
the fish, then close it up and use fine
kitchen string to tie it into a neat shape,
like a boned piece of meat. Pat dry with
paper towels.

2 Make incisions on both sides of the
fish and push in the remaining garlic
slivers. Heat half the olive oil in a frying
pan that can safely be used in the
oven. When the oil is hot, put in the
monkfish and brown it all over for about
5 minutes, until evenly colored. Season
with salt and pepper, sprinkle with
lemon juice and the remaining thyme.

3 Tuck the bay leaves under the
monkfish, arrange the remaining
(unpeeled) garlic cloves around it and
drizzle the remaining olive oil on the
fish and the garlic. Transfer the frying
pan to the oven and roast the monkfish
for 20–25 minutes, until the flesh is
cooked through.

4 Place on a warmed serving dish with
the garlic and some green beans. To
serve, remove the string and cut the
monkfish into ¾-inch thick slices.

COOK'S TIPS
• The garlic heads can be used whole.
• When serving the monkfish, invite
each guest to pop out the soft garlic
pulp with a fork and spread it on
the monkfish.

SEA BASS WITH GINGER AND LEEKS

YOU CAN USE WHOLE FISH OR THICK FILLETS FOR THIS RECIPE, WHICH IS ALSO EXCELLENT MADE WITH SNAPPER. SERVE THE FISH WITH FRIED RICE AND STIR-FRIED CHINESE GREENS SUCH AS BOK CHOY, IF DESIRED.

SERVES FOUR

INGREDIENTS

1 sea bass, about 3–3½ pounds,
  scaled and cleaned
8 scallions
¼ cup teriyaki marinade or
  dark soy sauce
2 tablespoons cornstarch
juice of 1 lemon
2 tablespoons rice wine vinegar
1 teaspoon ground ginger
¼ cup oil
2 leeks, shredded
1-inch piece fresh ginger root, peeled
  and grated
7 tablespoons chicken or fish stock
2 tablespoons rice wine or dry sherry
1 teaspoon sugar
salt and ground black pepper

1 Make several diagonal slashes using a sharp knife on either side of the sea bass so it can absorb the flavors, then season the fish inside and out with salt and ground black pepper. Trim the scallions, cut them in half lengthwise, then slice them diagonally into ¾-inch lengths. Put half of the scallions in the cavity of the fish and reserve the rest for later use.

2 In a shallow dish, combine the teriyaki marinade or dark soy sauce, the cornstarch, lemon juice, rice wine vinegar and ground ginger to make a smooth, runny paste. Turn the fish in the marinade to coat it thoroughly, working it into the slashes, then let it marinate for 20–30 minutes, turning it several times.

3 Heat a wok or frying pan that is large enough to hold the sea bass comfortably. Add the oil, then the leeks and grated ginger. Sauté gently for about 5 minutes, until the leeks are tender. Remove the leeks and ginger with a slotted spoon, and drain on paper towels, leaving the oil in the wok or pan.

4 Lift the sea bass out of the marinade and lower it carefully into the hot oil. Fry over medium heat for 2–3 minutes on each side. Stir the stock, rice wine or sherry and sugar into the marinade, with salt and pepper to taste. Pour the mixture onto the fish. Return the leeks and ginger to the wok, together with the reserved scallions. Cover and simmer for about 15 minutes, until the fish is cooked through. Serve immediately.

GRILLED LANGOUSTINES WITH HERBS

THIS SIMPLE COOKING METHOD ENHANCES BOTH THE DELICATE COLOR AND FLAVOR OF THE LANGOUSTINES. TRY TO FIND LIVE LANGOUSTINES FOR THIS RECIPE. CHOOSE THE LARGEST YOU CAN FIND (OR AFFORD) FOR THIS DISH, AND ALLOW 5–6 PER SERVING. LOBSTER AND CRAYFISH ARE ALSO DELICIOUS COOKED THIS WAY

SERVES FOUR AS A MAIN COURSE,
SIX AS AN APPETIZER

INGREDIENTS
¼ cup extra virgin olive oil
¼ cup hazelnut oil
1 tablespoon each finely chopped
  fresh basil, chives, chervil, parsley
  and tarragon
pinch of ground ginger
20–24 large langoustines or large
  shrimp, preferably live
lemon wedges and arugula leaves,
  to garnish
salt and ground black pepper

COOK'S TIPS
• Don't forget to provide your guests with fingerbowls of warm water and plenty of paper napkins.
• If you use cooked langoustines, then broil them for just 2–3 minutes to warm them through.

1 Preheat the broiler to very hot. Combine the olive and hazelnut oils in a small bowl. Add the herbs, a pinch of ground ginger and salt and pepper to taste. Whisk thoroughly until slightly thickened and emulsified.

2 If you are using live langoustines immerse them in a pan of boiling water for 1–2 minutes, then drain and let them cool.

3 Split the langoustines lengthwise using a large sharp knife and arrange them on an aluminum foil-lined broiler pan. Spoon on the herb-flavored oil.

4 Broil for 8–10 minutes, basting the langoustines two or three times, until they are cooked and lightly browned.

5 Arrange the langoustines on a warmed serving dish, pour the juices from the broiler pan over and serve immediately garnished with lemon wedges and arugula leaves.

SEA BASS IN A SALT CRUST

BAKING FISH IN A CRUST OF SEA SALT ENHANCES THE FLAVOR AND BRINGS OUT THE TASTE OF THE SEA. ANY FIRM FISH CAN BE COOKED IN THIS WAY. BREAK OPEN THE CRUST AT THE TABLE TO RELEASE THE GLORIOUS AROMA.

SERVES FOUR

INGREDIENTS
1 sea bass, about 2¼ pounds,
  cleaned and scaled
1 sprig each of fresh fennel,
  rosemary and thyme
4½ pounds coarse sea salt
mixed peppercorns
seaweed or samphire, blanched, and
  lemon slices, to garnish

1 Preheat the oven to 475°F. Fill the cavity of the sea bass with all the herbs and grind on some of the mixed peppercorns.

2 Spread half the salt on a shallow baking sheet (ideally oval) and lay the sea bass on it. Cover the fish all over with a ½-inch layer of salt, pressing the salt down firmly. Moisten the salt lightly by spraying with water from an atomizer. Bake the fish for 30–40 minutes, until the salt crust is just beginning to color.

3 Garnish the baking sheet with seaweed or samphire and bring the fish to the table in its salt crust. Use a sharp knife to break open the crust. Serve the fish, adding lemon slices to each plate.

FILLETS OF BRILL IN RED WINE SAUCE

FORGET THE OLD MAXIM THAT RED WINE AND FISH DO NOT GO WELL TOGETHER. THE ROBUST SAUCE ADDS COLOR AND RICHNESS TO THIS EXCELLENT DISH. TURBOT, HALIBUT AND JOHN DORY ARE ALSO GOOD COOKED THIS WAY.

SERVES FOUR

INGREDIENTS

4 fillets of brill, about 6–7 ounces
  each, skinned
⅔ cup chilled butter, diced, plus
  extra for greasing
4 ounces shallots, thinly sliced
scant 1 cup robust red wine
scant 1 cup fish stock
salt and ground white pepper
fresh chervil or flat-leaf parsley
  leaves, to garnish

3 Using a spatula, carefully lift the fish and shallots onto a serving dish, cover with aluminum foil and keep hot.

4 Transfer the casserole to the stove and bring the cooking liquid to a boil over high heat. Cook it until it has reduced by half. Lower the heat and whisk in the chilled butter, one piece at a time, to make a smooth, shiny sauce. Season with salt and ground white pepper, set aside and keep hot.

5 Divide the shallots among four warmed plates and lay the brill fillets on top. Pour the sauce onto and around the fish and garnish with the chervil or flat-leaf parsley.

1 Preheat the oven to 350°F. Season the fish on both sides with salt and pepper. Generously butter a flameproof dish, which is large enough to hold all the brill fillets in a single layer without overlapping. Spread the shallots on the bottom and lay the fish fillets on top. Season.

2 Pour in the red wine and fish stock, cover the dish and bring the liquid to just below the boiling point. Transfer the dish to the oven and bake for 6–8 minutes, until the brill is just cooked.

BAKED PORGY <u>WITH</u> TOMATOES

JOHN DORY, TURBOT OR SEA BASS CAN ALL BE COOKED THIS WAY. IF YOU PREFER TO USE FILLETED FISH, CHOOSE COD, AND ROAST IT SKIN-SIDE UP. ROASTING THE TOMATOES BRINGS OUT THEIR SWEETNESS, WHICH CONTRASTS BEAUTIFULLY WITH THE FLAVOR OF THE FISH.

2 Meanwhile, cut the potatoes into ½-inch slices. Parboil for 5 minutes. Drain and set aside.

3 Grease a baking dish with oil. Arrange the potatoes in a single layer with the lemon slices; sprinkle on the bay leaf, thyme and basil. Season and drizzle with half the remaining olive oil. Lay the fish on top, season; pour on the wine and the rest of the oil. Arrange the tomatoes around the fish.

SERVES FOUR TO SIX

INGREDIENTS
   8 ripe tomatoes
   2 teaspoons sugar
   scant 1 cup olive oil
   1 pound new potatoes
   1 lemon, sliced
   1 bay leaf
   1 fresh thyme sprig
   8 fresh basil leaves
   1 porgy, about 2–2¼ pounds,
     cleaned and scaled
   ⅔ cup dry white wine
   2 tablespoons fresh white
     bread crumbs
   2 garlic cloves, crushed
   1 tablespoon finely chopped parsley
   salt and ground black pepper
   fresh parsley or basil leaves,
     chopped, to garnish

1 Preheat the oven to 475°F. Cut the tomatoes in half lengthwise and arrange them in a single layer in a baking dish, cut-side facing up. Sprinkle with sugar, salt and pepper and drizzle on a little of the olive oil. Roast for 30–40 minutes, until soft and lightly browned.

4 Combine the bread crumbs, garlic and parsley; sprinkle on the fish. Bake for 30 minutes, until the flesh comes away easily from the bone. Garnish with chopped parsley or basil.

FILLETS OF PORGY IN PHYLLO PASTRY

ANY FIRM FISH FILLETS CAN BE USED FOR THIS DISH—BASS, GROUPER AND RED SNAPPER ARE PARTICULARLY GOOD. EACH LITTLE PARCEL IS A MEAL IN ITSELF AND CAN BE PREPARED SEVERAL HOURS IN ADVANCE, WHICH MAKES THIS AN IDEAL RECIPE FOR ENTERTAINING. IF DESIRED, SERVE THE PASTRIES WITH FENNEL BRAISED WITH ORANGE JUICE OR A MIXED SALAD.

2 Thinly slice the potatoes lengthwise. Brush a baking sheet with a little of the oil. Lay a sheet of phyllo pastry on the sheet, brush it with oil, then lay a second sheet crosswise over the first. Repeat with two more sheets. Arrange a quarter of the sliced potatoes in the center, season and add a quarter of the shredded sorrel. Lay a porgy fillet on top, skin-side up. Season.

3 Loosely fold the phyllo pastry up and over to make a neat parcel. Make three more parcels; place on the baking sheet. Brush with half the butter. Bake for about 20 minutes, until the phyllo is puffed up and golden brown.

SERVES FOUR

INGREDIENTS
  8 small waxy salad potatoes,
    preferably red-skinned
  7 ounces sorrel, stems removed
  2 tablespoons olive oil
  16 phyllo pastry sheets, thawed
    if frozen
  4 porgy fillets, about 6 ounces each,
    scaled but not skinned
  ¼ cup butter, melted
  ½ cup fish stock
  1 cup whipping cream
  salt and ground black pepper
  finely diced red bell pepper, to garnish

VARIATION
Use small spinach leaves instead of
the sorrel.

1 Preheat the oven to 400°F. Cook the potatoes in a saucepan of lightly salted boiling water for 15–20 minutes, until just tender. Drain and let cool. Set about half the sorrel leaves aside. Shred the remaining leaves by piling up 6 or 8 at a time, rolling them up like a fat cigar and slicing them with a sharp knife.

4 Meanwhile, make the sorrel sauce. Heat the remaining butter in a pan, add the reserved sorrel and cook gently for 3 minutes, stirring, until it wilts. Stir in the stock and cream. Heat almost to the boiling point, stirring so that the sorrel breaks down. Season to taste and keep hot until the fish parcels are ready. Serve garnished with red pepper. Pass the sauce separately.

OCTOPUS STEW

THIS RUSTIC STEW IS A PERFECT DISH FOR ENTERTAINING, AS IT TASTES EVEN BETTER IF MADE A DAY IN ADVANCE. SERVE WITH A COLORFUL SALAD OF ARUGULA AND RADICCHIO.

SERVES FOUR TO SIX

INGREDIENTS

2¼ pounds octopus, cleaned
3 tablespoons olive oil
1 large red onion, chopped
3 garlic cloves, finely chopped
2 tablespoons brandy
1¼ cups dry white wine
1¾ pounds ripe plum tomatoes,
  peeled and chopped or two
  14-ounce cans chopped tomatoes
1 fresh red chile, seeded and
  chopped (optional)
1 pound small new potatoes
1 tablespoon chopped fresh rosemary
1 tablespoon fresh thyme leaves
5 cups fish stock
2 tablespoons fresh flat-leaf
  parsley leaves
salt and ground black pepper
rosemary sprigs, to garnish
For the garlic croûtes
1 fat garlic clove, peeled
8 thick slices of baguette or ciabatta
2 tablespoons olive oil

3 Pour the brandy over the octopus and light it on fire. When the flames have died down, add the wine, bring to a boil and bubble gently for about 5 minutes. Stir in the tomatoes, with the chile, if using, then add the potatoes, rosemary and thyme. Simmer for 5 minutes.

4 Pour in the fish stock and season well. Cover the pan and simmer for 20–30 minutes, stirring occasionally. The octopus and potatoes should be very tender and the sauce should have thickened slightly. At this stage, you can let the stew cool, then put it in the refrigerator overnight.

5 Preheat a medium-hot broiler. To make the garlic croûtes, cut the garlic clove in half and rub both sides of the slices of baguette or ciabatta with the cut-side. Crush the garlic, stir it into the oil and brush the mixture on both sides of the bread. Broil on both sides until the croûtes are golden brown and crisp.

6 To serve the stew, reheat it gently if it has been in the refrigerator overnight, check the seasoning and stir in the parsley leaves. Serve piping hot in individual warmed bowls, garnished with rosemary sprigs and accompanied by the warm garlic croûtes.

1 Cut the octopus into large pieces, put these in a saucepan and pour in cold water to cover. Season with salt, bring to a boil, then lower the heat and simmer for 30 minutes to tenderize. Drain and cut into bite-size pieces.

2 Heat the oil in a large shallow pan. Sauté the onion for 2–3 minutes, until lightly colored, then add the garlic and cook for 1 more minute. Add the octopus and cook for 2–3 minutes, stirring and tossing to color it lightly on all sides.

FISH PLAKI

EVERY MEDITERRANEAN COUNTRY HAS A SLIGHTLY DIFFERENT VERSION OF THIS SIMPLE BUT VERY DELICIOUS DISH, WHICH MAKES THE MOST OF THE LOCAL FRESH FISH. A WHOLE FISH CAN BE USED INSTEAD OF A LARGE FILLET, IF YOU PREFER. THIS DISH ALSO WORKS WELL WITH SEA BASS OR BREAM, JOHN DORY, TURBOT, HALIBUT OR BRILL.

SERVES FOUR

INGREDIENTS
⅔ cup olive oil
2 large Spanish onions, chopped
2 celery stalks, chopped
4 fat garlic cloves, chopped
4 potatoes, peeled and diced
4 carrots, cut into small dice
1 tablespoon sugar
2 bay leaves
1 thick middle-cut fillet of grouper or cod, about 2¼ pounds
16–20 large black olives (optional)
4 large ripe tomatoes, peeled, seeded and chopped
⅔ cup dry white wine or vermouth
salt and ground black pepper
herbs, to garnish
saffron rice, to serve

1 Preheat the oven to 375°F. Heat the olive oil in a large frying pan, add the chopped onions and celery and sauté until they are transparent. Add the garlic and cook for 2 more minutes.

2 Stir in the potatoes and carrots and cook for 5 minutes, stirring occasionally. Sprinkle with the sugar and season to taste with salt and ground black pepper.

3 Spoon the vegetable mixture into an oval or rectangular baking dish slightly larger than the fish and tuck in the bay leaves. Season the fish and lay it on the bed of vegetables, skin-side up. Sprinkle the olives around the edge, if using. Spread the chopped tomatoes on the fish, pour in the wine or vermouth and season.

4 Bake for 30–40 minutes, until the fish is cooked through. Serve straight from the dish. Garnish with herb leaves. Saffron rice would be the ideal accompaniment.

COOK'S TIP
If you use a whole fish, be sure to season it inside as well as outside.

SALMON WITH WHISKEY AND CREAM

THIS DISH COMBINES TWO OF THE FINEST FLAVORS OF SCOTLAND—SALMON AND WHISKEY. IT TAKES VERY LITTLE TIME TO MAKE, SO COOK IT AT THE LAST MOMENT WHEN YOU ARE READY TO SERVE. YOUR GUESTS WILL DEEM IT WORTH THE WAIT. SERVE WITH NEW POTATOES AND GREEN BEANS.

SERVES FOUR

INGREDIENTS
4 salmon fillets, about 6 ounces each
1 teaspoon chopped fresh thyme leaves
¼ cup butter
5 tablespoons whiskey
⅔ cup heavy cream
juice of ½ lemon (optional)
salt and ground black pepper
dill sprigs, to garnish

1 Season the salmon with salt, pepper and thyme. Melt half the butter in a frying pan large enough to hold two fillets side by side. When the butter is foaming, fry the first two fillets for about 1 minute on each side, until they are golden on the outside and just cooked through.

2 Pour in 2 tablespoons of the whiskey and light it on fire. When the flames have died down, carefully transfer the salmon to a plate and keep hot. Heat the remaining butter and cook the other two fillets the same way. Keep them hot.

3 Pour the cream into the pan and bring to a boil, stirring constantly and scraping up the cooking juices from the bottom of the pan. Let bubble until reduced and slightly thickened, then season and add the last of the whiskey and a squeeze of lemon, if desired.

4 Place the salmon on individual warmed plates, pour on the sauce and serve garnished with dill.

FILLETS OF TURBOT WITH OYSTERS

THIS LUXURIOUS DISH IS PERFECT FOR SPECIAL OCCASIONS. IT IS WORTH BUYING A WHOLE TURBOT AND ASKING THE FISHMONGER TO FILLET AND SKIN IT FOR YOU. KEEP THE HEAD, BONES AND TRIMMINGS FOR STOCK. SOLE, BRILL AND HALIBUT CAN ALL BE SUBSTITUTED FOR THE TURBOT.

SERVES FOUR

INGREDIENTS

12 Pacific (rock) oysters
½ cup butter
2 carrots, cut into julienne strips
7 ounces celeriac, cut into
  julienne strips
the white parts of 2 leeks, cut into
  julienne strips
generous 1½ cups Champagne
  or dry white sparkling wine
  (about ½ bottle)
7 tablespoons whipping cream
1 turbot, about 4–4½ pounds,
  filleted and skinned
salt and ground white pepper

1 Using an oyster knife, open the oysters over a bowl to catch the juices, then carefully remove them from their shells, discarding the shells, and place them in a separate bowl. Set aside until needed.

2 Melt 2 tablespoons of the butter in a shallow pan, add the vegetable julienne and cook over low heat until tender but not colored. Pour in half the Champagne or sparkling wine and cook very gently until all the liquid has evaporated. Keep the heat low so that the vegetables do not color.

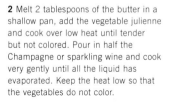

3 Strain the oyster juices into a small saucepan and add the cream and the remaining Champagne or sparkling wine. Place over medium heat until the mixture has reduced to the consistency of thin cream. Dice half the remaining butter and whisk it into the sauce, one piece at a time, until smooth. Season to taste, then pour the sauce into a blender and process until velvety smooth.

4 Return the sauce to the pan, bring it to just below the boiling point, then drop in the oysters. Poach for about 1 minute, to warm but barely cook. Keep warm, but do not let the sauce boil.

5 Season the turbot fillets with salt and pepper. Heat the remaining butter in a large frying pan until foaming, then fry the fillets over medium heat for 2–3 minutes on each side, until cooked through and golden.

6 Cut each turbot fillet into three pieces and arrange on individual warmed plates. Pile the vegetable julienne on top, place three oysters around the turbot fillets on each plate and pour the sauce around the edge.

JOHN DORY <u>WITH</u> LIGHT CURRY SAUCE

THIS EXCELLENT COMBINATION OF FLAVORS ALSO WORKS WELL WITH OTHER FLAT FISH LIKE TURBOT, HALIBUT AND BRILL, OR MORE EXOTIC SPECIES LIKE MAHI-MAHI OR ORANGE ROUGHY. THE CURRY TASTE SHOULD BE VERY SUBTLE, SO USE A MILD CURRY POWDER. SERVE THE FISH WITH RICE PILAF AND MANGO CHUTNEY. IT LOOKS WONDERFUL ARRANGED ON BANANA LEAVES, IF YOU CAN FIND SOME.

<u>SERVES FOUR</u>

INGREDIENTS
    4 John Dory fillets, each about
        6 ounces, skinned
    1 tablespoon sunflower oil
    2 tablespoons butter
    salt and ground black pepper
    1 tablespoon cilantro leaves,
        4 banana leaves (optional), and
        1 small mango, peeled and diced,
        to garnish
For the curry sauce
    2 tablespoons sunflower oil
    1 carrot, chopped
    1 onion, chopped
    1 celery stalk, chopped
    white of 1 leek, chopped
    2 garlic cloves, crushed
    ¼ cup coconut milk
    2 tomatoes, peeled, seeded
        and diced
    1-inch piece fresh
        ginger root, grated
    1 tablespoon tomato paste
    1–2 teaspoons mild curry powder
    generous 2 cups chicken
        or fish stock

1 Make the sauce. Heat the oil in a pan; add the vegetables and garlic. Cook gently until soft but not brown.

COOK'S TIP
The coconut sauce must be cooked over very low heat, so use a heat diffuser if you have one.

2 Add the coconut, tomatoes and ginger. Cook for 1–2 minutes; stir in the tomato paste and curry powder to taste. Add the stock, stir and season.

3 Bring to a boil, then lower the heat, cover the pan and cook the sauce over the lowest heat for about 50 minutes. Stir once or twice to prevent burning. Let the sauce cool; pour into a food processor or blender and process until smooth. Return to a clean pan and reheat very gently, adding a little water if too thick.

4 Season the fish fillets with salt and pepper. Heat the oil in a large frying pan, add the butter and heat until sizzling. Put in the fish and fry for 2–3 minutes on each side, until pale golden and cooked through. Drain on paper towels.

5 If you have banana leaves, place them on individual warmed plates and arrange the fillets on top. Pour the sauce around the fish and sprinkle on the finely diced mango. Decorate with cilantro leaves and serve immediately.

GRILLED HALIBUT WITH SAUCE VIERGE

ANY THICK WHITE FISH FILLETS CAN BE COOKED IN THIS VERSATILE DISH; TURBOT, BRILL AND JOHN DORY ARE ESPECIALLY DELICIOUS, BUT THE FLAVORFUL SAUCE ALSO GIVES HUMBLER FISH LIKE COD, HADDOCK OR HAKE A REAL LIFT.

SERVES FOUR

INGREDIENTS
  7 tablespoons olive oil
  $1/2$ teaspoon fennel seeds
  $1/2$ teaspoon celery seeds
  1 teaspoon mixed peppercorns
  $1^1/2$–$1^3/4$ pounds middle cut of
    halibut, about $1^1/4$-inck thick, cut
    into 4 pieces
  coarse sea salt
  1 teaspoon fresh thyme
    leaves, chopped
  1 teaspoon fresh rosemary
    leaves, chopped
  1 teaspoon fresh oregano or marjoram
    leaves, chopped
For the sauce
  7 tablespoons extra virgin olive oil
  juice of 1 lemon
  1 garlic clove, finely chopped
  2 tomatoes, peeled, seeded
    and diced
  1 teaspoon small capers
  2 drained canned anchovy
    fillets, chopped
  1 teaspoon snipped fresh chives
  1 tablespoon shredded fresh
    basil leaves
  1 tablespoon chopped fresh chervil

1 Heat a ridged pan or preheat the broiler to high. Brush the pan or broiler pan with a little of the olive oil. Mix the fennel and celery seeds with the peppercorns in a mortar. Crush with a pestle, and then stir in the coarse sea salt to taste. Spoon the mixture into a shallow dish and stir in the herbs and the remaining olive oil.

2 Add the halibut pieces to the olive oil mixture, turning them to coat them thoroughly, then arrange them with the dark skin facing up in the oiled pan or broiler pan. Cook for 6–8 minutes, until the fish is cooked all the way through and the skin has browned.

3 Combine all the sauce ingredients except the fresh herbs in a saucepan and heat gently until warm but not hot. Stir in the chives, basil and chervil.

4 Place the halibut on four warmed plates. Spoon the sauce around and onto the fish and serve immediately, with lightly-cooked green cabbage.

VEGETABLE-STUFFED SQUID

SHIRLEY CONRAN FAMOUSLY SAID THAT LIFE IS TOO SHORT TO STUFF A MUSHROOM. THE SAME MIGHT BE SAID OF SQUID, EXCEPT THAT THE RESULTS ARE SO DELICIOUS THAT IT MAKES THE EFFORT SEEM WORTHWHILE. SMALL CUTTLEFISH CAN BE PREPARED IN THE SAME WAY. SERVE WITH SAFFRON RICE.

SERVES FOUR

INGREDIENTS

4 medium squid, or 12 small squid,
   skinned and cleaned
6 tablespoons butter
1 cup fresh white bread crumbs
2 shallots, chopped
4 garlic cloves, chopped
1 leek, finely diced
2 carrots, finely diced
⅔ cup fish stock
2 tablespoons olive oil
2 tablespoons chopped fresh parsley
salt and ground black pepper
rosemary sprigs, to garnish
saffron rice, to serve

1 Preheat the oven to 425°F. Cut off the tentacles and side flaps from the squid and chop finely. Set the squid aside. Melt half the butter in a large frying pan that can safely be used in the oven. Add the fresh white bread crumbs and fry until they are golden brown, stirring to prevent them from burning. Using a slotted spoon, transfer the bread crumbs to a bowl and set aside until needed.

2 Heat the remaining butter in the frying pan and add the chopped and diced vegetables. Cook until softened but not browned, then stir in the fish stock and cook until the stock has reduced and the vegetables are very soft. Season to taste with salt and ground black pepper and transfer to the bowl with the bread crumbs. Mix lightly.

3 Heat half the olive oil in the frying pan, add the chopped squid and fry over high heat for 1 minute. Remove the squid with a slotted spoon; stir into the vegetable mixture. Stir in the parsley.

4 Put the stuffing mixture into a piping bag, or use a teaspoon to stuff the squid tubes with the mixture. Do not overfill them, as the stuffing will swell lightly during cooking. Secure the openings with wooden toothpicks, or sew up with fine kitchen thread.

5 Heat the remaining olive oil in the frying pan, place the stuffed squid in the pan and fry until they are sealed on all sides and golden brown. Transfer the frying pan to the oven and roast the squid for 20 minutes.

6 Unless the squid are very small, carefully cut them into 3 or 4 slices and arrange on a bed of saffron rice. Spoon the cooking juices onto and around the squid and serve immediately, with each serving garnished with sprigs of rosemary.

SAUCES FOR FISH AND SHELLFISH

MANY TYPES OF FISH ARE SO DELICIOUS THAT THEY DO NOT NEED TO BE COOKED IN A SAUCE, BUT A GOOD ACCOMPANYING SAUCE WILL CERTAINLY ENHANCE PLAINLY COOKED FISH.

NEVER-FAIL MAYONNAISE

Some people find classic mayonnaise difficult to make, but this simple version takes away the mystery. The essential thing is to have all the ingredients at room temperature before you start. Be aware that this recipe contains raw eggs. If this is a concern, use bought mayonnaise instead.

SERVES FOUR TO SIX

INGREDIENTS
  1 egg, plus 1 egg yolk
  1 tablespoon Dijon mustard
  juice of 1 large lemon
  ³/₄ cup olive oil
  ³/₄ cup grapeseed, sunflower
    or corn oil
  salt and ground white pepper

1 Put the whole egg and yolk in a food processor and process for 20 seconds. Add the mustard, half the lemon juice, and a generous pinch of salt and pepper. Process for about 30 seconds, until thoroughly mixed.

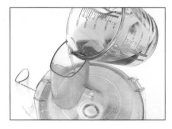

2 With the motor running, pour in the oils through the feeder tube in a thin, steady stream. Process until the oils are incorporated and the mayonnaise is pale and thick. Taste and add more lemon juice and seasoning if necessary.

VARIATIONS

Vary the oil according to the fish the mayonnaise is to accompany. Use all olive oil for robust fish such as salmon or tuna, a mixture of olive and light vegetable oil for more delicate fish.

BEURRE BLANC

Legend has it that this exquisite sauce was invented by a cook who forgot to put egg yolks into a béarnaise sauce. Whether or not this is true doesn't matter: this light sauce goes perfectly with poached or grilled fish.

SERVES FOUR

INGREDIENTS
  3 shallots, very finely chopped
  3 tablespoons dry white wine or
    court-bouillon
  3 tablespoons white wine or
    tarragon vinegar
  ½ cup chilled unsalted butter, diced
  lemon juice (optional)
  salt and ground white pepper

1 Put the shallots in a small saucepan with the wine or court bouillon and vinegar. Bring to a boil and cook over high heat until only about 2 tablespoons liquid remains. Remove the pan from heat and let cool until the liquid is just lukewarm.

2 Whisk in the chilled butter, one piece at a time, to make a pale, creamy sauce. Taste the sauce, then season with salt and pepper and add a little lemon juice to taste.

3 If you are not serving the sauce immediately, keep it warm in the top of a double boiler set over barely simmering water.

HOLLANDAISE SAUCE

This rich sauce goes well with any poached fish. Serve it warm. As the egg yolks are barely cooked, do not serve to children, the elderly or anyone with a compromised immune system.

SERVES FOUR

INGREDIENTS
  ½ cup unsalted butter
  2 egg yolks
  1–2 tablespoons lemon juice or white
    wine or tarragon vinegar
  salt and ground white pepper

1 Melt the butter in a small saucepan Put the egg yolks and lemon juice or vinegar in a bowl. Add salt and pepper and whisk until completely smooth.

2 Pour the melted butter in a steady stream onto the egg yolk mixture, beating vigorously with a wooden spoon to make a smooth, creamy sauce. Alternatively, put the mixture in a food processor and add the butter through the feeder tube, with the motor running. Taste the sauce and add more lemon juice or vinegar if necessary.

PARSLEY SAUCE

Forget the pallid, lumpy parsley sauce of your youth; when this classic sauce is well made it is delicious. Serve it with poached cod, haddock or any white fish. If possible, use the poaching liquid to enhance the flavor of the sauce.

SERVES FOUR

INGREDIENTS

¼ cup butter
3 tablespoons all-purpose flour
1¼ cups milk
1¼ cups poaching liquid from the fish (or an extra 1¼ cups milk)
¼ cup heavy cream
lemon juice (see method)
6 tablespoons chopped fresh parsley
salt and ground black pepper

1 Melt half the butter in a small saucepan, add the flour and stir for 2–3 minutes to make a smooth roux. Take the pan off the heat, add a couple of spoonfuls of milk and stir in until completely absorbed. Continue to add small amounts of milk and poaching liquid, if available, stirring until the sauce has the consistency of heavy cream. Add the rest of the milk and poaching liquid and whisk to break down any lumps.

2 Return the pan to the heat and bring the sauce to a boil. Lower the heat and simmer gently for about 5 minutes, stirring frequently. Stir in the cream and lemon juice to taste, and season with salt and pepper. If the sauce is at all lumpy at this stage, whisk it thoroughly with a hand-held blender or a balloon whisk.

3 Stir in the parsley, then whisk in the remaining butter and serve hot.

MUSTARD AND DILL SAUCE

Serve this fresh-tasting sauce with any cold, smoked or raw marinated fish. Note that it contains raw egg yolk.

SERVES FOUR

INGREDIENTS

1 egg yolk
2 tablespoons brown French mustard
½–1 teaspoon dark brown sugar
1 tablespoon white wine vinegar
6 tablespoons sunflower or vegetable oil
2 tablespoons finely chopped fresh dill
salt and ground black pepper

1 Put the egg yolk in a small bowl and add the mustard with a little brown sugar to taste. Beat with a wooden spoon until smooth. Stir in the white wine vinegar, then gradually whisk in the oil, a little at a time, mixing well after each addition.

2 When the oil has been completely amalgamated, season the sauce with salt and pepper, then stir in the finely chopped dill. Chill for an hour or more before serving.

CRAWFISH SAUCE

This sauce, also known as Nantua sauce, is perfect for using up the shells left over from seafood recipes. It can be made with other crustaceans, such as lobster or large shrimp. Use it to enhance any white fish or shellfish.

SERVES FOUR

INGREDIENTS

1 cooked crawfish (rock lobster), about 1 pound
3 tablespoons butter
1 tablespoon olive oil
3 tablespoons brandy
generous 2 cups fish or shellfish stock
1 tablespoon all-purpose flour
3 tablespoons heavy cream
2 egg yolks
salt and ground white pepper

1 Remove the tail meat from the crawfish and keep for another recipe. Break up the shells and legs and crush them coarsely in a food processor.

2 Melt 2 tablespoons of the butter in the oil in a pan, add the shells and cook for about 3 minutes, stirring frequently. Add the brandy and stock, bring to a boil, then simmer for 10 minutes.

3 Mash the remaining butter with the flour to make *beurre manié*. Whisk this into the sauce, a small piece at a time, and cook gently until thickened. Season the sauce and strain it through a fine sieve. Stir in the cream and bring back to just below the boiling point.

4 Beat the egg yolks lightly in a bowl, mix in a couple of spoonfuls of the hot sauce. Return the mixture to the pan and cook gently until smooth. Adjust the seasoning and serve immediately.

Shopping For Fish and Shellfish

UNITED STATES

Fishmongers

Katch Seafood
765 Fish Dock Road
Homer, AK 99603
Tel: (800) 368-7400
www.efish.com

Alioto-Lazio Fish Company
440 Jefferson Street
San Francisco, CA 94100
Tel: (888) 673-5868

Flanders Fish Market
22 Chesterfield Road
East Lyme, CT 06333
Tel: (800) 638-8189

Big Tom's Seafood Market
4031 Thomas Drive
Panama Beach, FL 32408
Tel: (850) 235-2926
www.bigtomseafood.com

The Fish House
102401 Overseas Highway
Key Largo, FL 33037
Tel: (305) 451-HOOK
www.fishhouse.com

Robert's Quality Seafood
7722 Merrill Road
Jacksonville, FL 32099
Tel: (904) 744-0200
www.robertsseafood.com

Big Tom's Seafood
Market
4403 17th Avenue
Columbus, GA 31904
Tel: (706) 320-9733
www.bigtomseafood.com

The Fishery
250 Center Street

Auburn, Maine 04210
Tel: (800) 515-LOBS
www.mk.net/~fishery

Middlebay Seafood Inc.
45 Ellen Way
Harpswell, Maine 04079
Tel: (207)798-5868
www.maineseafood.com

The Crab Place
P.O. Box 247
101 North Fourth
Street
Crisfield, MD 21817
Tel: (877) EAT-CRAB
Fax: (410) 968-2457
www.crabplace.com

George's Ultimate
Seafood
112 Green Street
Worcester, MA 01604
Tel: (508) 755-8331
www.ultimateseafood.com

Balducci's
424 Sixth Avenue
New York, NY 10011
Tel: (212) 673-2600
www.balducci.com

Citarella
1313 Third Avenue
New York, NY 10021
Tel: (212) 874-0383

Eli's Manhattan
1411 Third Avenue
New York, NY 10028
Tel: (212) 717-8100

Pisacane Midtown
940 1st Avenue
New York, NY 10022
Tel: (212) 355-1850

Fitts Seafoods
1175 Edgewater N.W.
Salem, OR 97304
www.fitts.net

Blue Crab Seafood, Inc.
Corporate Headquarters
3441 South Lawrence Street
Philadelphia, PA 19148
Tel: (877) SEND-FISH

Long Wharf Seafood
17 Connell Highway
Newport, RI 02840
Tel: (401) 846-6320
www3.edgenet.net/lws/

Leo's Live Seafood
4098 Legoe Bay Road
Lummi Island, WA 98262
Tel: (360) 758-7318
www.leoslive.com

Ohana Seafood Market
168 Lake Street South
Kirkland, WA 98033
Tel: (425) 576-1887
Fax: (425) 576-8417
www.fish2go.com

Pure Food Fish Market
Pike Place Market
Seattle, WA 98100
Tel: (206) 622-5765
Fax: (206) 622-2050
www.freshseafood.com

Lake Superior Fish Company
1507 North 1st Street
Superior, WI 54880
Tel: (715) 392-3101
www.lakesuperiorfish.com

Cooking Equipment

Bowery Kitchen Supply
The Chelsea Market
460 West 16th Street
New York, NY 10011
Tel: (212) 376-4982
www.bowerykitchens.com

Chef's Catalog
P.O. Box 620048
Dallas, TX 75262-0048
Tel: (800) 884-CHEF
www.chefscatalog.com

A Cook's Wares
211 37th Street
Beaver Falls, PA 15010
Tel: (800) 915-9788
www.cookswares.com

Sur La Table
Catalog Division
1765 Sixth Avenue South
Seattle, WA 98134
Tel: (800) 243-0852
www.surlatable.com

UNITED KINGDOM

Fishmongers

Ashdown plc
Fish, Poultry and Game
23 Leadenhall Market
London EC3V 1LR
Tel: 020 7621 1365

B & M Seafoods
250 Kentish Town Road
London NW5 2AA
Tel: 020 7485 0346

Chalmers and Gray
67 Nottinghill Gate
London W11 3JS
Tel: 020 7221 6177

Corney, J. A. Limited (kosher)
16 Hallswelle Parade
Finchley Road
London NW11 0DL
Tel: 020 8455 9588

Covent Garden Fishmongers
Phil Diamond
37 Turnham Green Terrace
London W4 1RG
Tel: 020 8995 9273

Cutty Catering Supplies
Unit 4
57 Sandgate Street
London SE15 1LE
Tel: 020 7277 7759

Dagon's Ltd.
16, Granvill Arcade
Brixton Market
London SW9 8PR
Tel: 020 7274 1665

Filipino Supermarket
1 Kenway Road
London SW5 0RP
Tel: 020 7244 0007

France Fresh Fish (tropical
  fish)
99 Stroud Green Road
London N4 3PX
Tel: 020 7263 9767

Good Harvest Fish and Meat
  Market
14 Newport Place
London WC2H 7PR
Tel: 020 7437 0712

Harrods Food Hall
87 Brompton Road
Knightsbridge
London SW1X 7XL
Tel: 020 7730 1234

Harvey Nichols Food Hall
109–125 Knightsbridge
London SW1X 7RJ
Tel: 020 7235 5000

Jarvis
55 Coombe Road
Kingston
Surrey KT3 4QN
Tel: 020 8546 0989

John Blagdens
65 Paddington Street
London W1M 3RR
Tel: 020 7935 8321

John Nicholson Fishmongers
108 Manor Road
Wallington
Surrey SN6 0DW
Tel: 020 8647 3922

Loaves and Fishes
52 Thoroughfare
Woodbridge
Suffolk IP12 1AL
Tel: 01394 385650

The Seafood Store
16 Downing Street
Farnham
Surrey GU9 7PB
Tel: 01252 715010

Selfridge's
400 Oxford Street
London W1A 1AB
Tel: 020 7629 1234

Steve Hatt
88–90 Essex Road
London N1 8LU
Tel: 020 7226 3963

Mail Order Companies

Atlantic Harvest Limited
Pennyburn Industrial Estate
Buncrana Road
Londonderry
Co Londonderry
BT48 0LU
Tel: 028 7126 4275
Fax: 028 7126 2955

Atlantis Smoked Fish
Fore Street
Grampound, Truro
Cornwall TR2 4SB
Tel: 01726 883201

Cornish Smoked Fish
  Company Limited
Charlestown
St Austell

Cornwall PL25 3NY
Tel: 01726 72356
Fax: 01726 72360

Cooking Equipment

Divertimenti
45–47 Wigmore Street
London W1H 9LA
Tel: 020 7935 0689

and
139 Fulham Road
London SW3 6SD
Tel: 020 7581 8065

David Mellor
4 Sloane Square
London SW1W 8EE
Tel: 020 7730 4259

Picture Acknowledgements

All photographs are by Willaim
Lingwood except those on the
following pages: p8bl Life
File/Barry Mayes, p8tr Life
file/Jeremy Hoare, p9 Tony
Stone/Joe Cornish; p51t New
Zealand Seafoods, p51b Kate
Whiteman, pp61tr and 72b
Food Features (fish supplied
by Tesco), p108 Sydney Fish
Market, p112 Cephas/Alain
Proust, 122tl and tr Janine
Hosegood.

INDEX

NOTES

NOTES

NOTES

NOTES

NOTES

NOTES

NOTES